W9-AQZ-046

DRUGS

AND THE

SPECIAL CHILD

DRUGS
AND THE
SPECIAL CHILD

Edited by Michael Jay Cohen, Ed.D.

GARDNER PRESS, INC., New York

Distributed by HALSTED PRESS
Division of JOHN WILEY & SONS, Inc.

New York • Toronto • London • Sydney

Copyright © 1979 by Gardner Press, Inc.

All rights reserved.
No part of this book may be reproduced in any form,
by photostat, microform, retrieval system,
or any means now known or later devised,
without prior written permission of the publisher.

GARDNER PRESS, INC.
19 Union Square West
New York 10003

Distributed solely by the Halsted Press Division
of John Wiley & Sons, Inc., New York

Library of Congress Cataloging in Publication Data
Main entry under title:
Drugs and the special child.

1. Psychopharmacology. 2. Child psychotherapy.
3. Problem children. I. Cohen, Michael Jay.
[DNLM: 1. Learning disorders—Drug therapy. 2. Child,
Exceptional. LC4704 C678d]
RJ504.7.D78   618.9′28′5884   77-10151
ISBN 0-470-99278-6

Printed in the United States of America

CONTENTS

Preface   *vii*

1   DRUG RESEARCH: A FOUNDATION FOR   *11*
     DECISION MAKING
     Arthur R. DeLong, Ph.D.

2   DRUG THERAPY WITH CHILDREN   *33*
     AND ADOLESCENTS
     Larry B. Silver, M.D.

3   DRUGS: CLASSROOM FACILITATORS   *63*
     Joseph N. Murray, Ph.D.

4   PERSPECTIVES ON DRUG TREATMENT   *85*
     FOR HYPERACTIVITY
     Corrine J. Weithorn, Ph.D.

5   DRUG THERAPY FOR HYPERACTIVITY: EXISTING   *99*
     PRACTICES IN PHYSICIAN–SCHOOL
     COMMUNICATION
     Roslyn P. Ross, Ph.D.

6   DRUGS AND THE FAMILY   *111*
     Bettijane Eisenpreis, M.S.

7   HYPERACTIVE CHILDREN AT RISK   *129*
     Karen Preis, M.D.
     Hans R. Huessy, M.D.

8   LONG TERM EFFECTS OF STIMULANT   *189*
     THERAPY FOR HA CHILDREN:
     RISK BENEFITS ANALYSIS
     Richard P. Allen, Ph.D.
     Daniel Safer, M.D.

9   DRUG THERAPY—CHILDREN'S RIGHTS   *203*
     Lois Weithorn, M.S.

Appendix
     Report of the Conference on the Use of Stimulant   *239*
     Drugs in the Treatment of Behaviorally Disturbed
     Young School Children

Index   *249*

CONTRIBUTORS

ALLEN, Richard P., Ph.D. Department of Psychiatry, Baltimore City Hospitals, Baltimore, Md.

COHEN, Michael J., Ed.D. Coordinator of Special Education, East Brunswick Public Schools, East Brunswick, New Jersey

DELONG, Arthur, Ph.D. Professor, Psychology Department College of Arts & Sciences, Grand Valley State Colleges, Allendale, Mich.

EISENPREIS, Bettijane, M.S. Member of Executive Board, New York Association for the Learning Disabled (NYALD), New York, N.Y. Mother of a learning disabled youngster

HUESSY, Hans Rosenstock, M.D. Professor, Child Psychiatry Section, Medical Center Hospital of Vermont, University of Vermont, Burlington, Vt.

MURRAY, Joseph N., Ph.D. Associate Professor, School Psychologist Training Program, Department of Counseling & Personnel Services, Kent State University, Kent, Oh.

PREIS, Karen, M.D. Assistant Professor, Child Psychiatry Section, Medical Center Hospital of Vermont, University of Vermont, Burlington, Vt.

ROSS, Roslyn P., Ph.D. Assistant Professor, Graduate Programs in Educational Services, Queens College–CUNY, Flushing, N.Y.

SAFER, Daniel, M.D. Baltimore County Department of Health, Rowson, Md.

SILVER, Larry B., M.D. Professor of Psychiatry, Chief Section of Child & Adolescent Psychiatry, College of Medicine & Dentistry of New Jersey, Rutgers Medical School, Piscataway, N.J.

WEITHORN, Corrine J., Ph.D. Associate Professor, Graduate Programs in Educational Services, Queens College–CUNY, Flushing, N.Y.

WEITHORN, Lois, M.S. Clinical Psychology Center, University of Pittsburgh, Pittsburgh, Pa.

PREFACE

The recent upsurge in reported cases of classroom and individual drug abuse (suspected or real) has made it necessary for those of us concerned with educational policy making to reexamine positions associated with drug therapy and the special child. An examination of the literature has failed to turn up one single volume that addresses the problem in terms of major issues. It also has become apparent that much of the available literature is too constricted in its treatment of the problem. Medical personnel look at the issues from one perspective, educators see another side of the coin, and parents seem to be caught somewhere "between heaven and hell."

There are very real considerations that need to be discussed relevant to the continued and growing use of drugs as therapeutic agents in a classroom, issues that go beyond specific professional disciplines and interests. Included among the issues that need to be discussed are: the questions of how to measure behavior change; the definitions and working parameters indicating behavior change; the short-term and long-term side effects; the responsibilities and patterns of professional staffing prior to and during drug administration; the monitoring of drugs; the use of other therapies in conjunction with or instead of drug therapy; the problems of evaluating real or imagined changes in children's learning styles and capacities; the roles of parents in the entire process; the rights of children; and the educating of new professionals as well as the reeducation of persons already involved in working with children. All of these issues need to be addressed and made available within a single reference source.

This volume is offered as a first attempt to fill the need for a reference source that presents the problems and issues of drug therapy in terms that, it is hoped, can help to clarify some of the confusion that now exists. The text is meant not to solve any problems but to encourage a comprehensive examination of the issues, both positive and negative, associated with the problem.

With the exception of the Appendix, this volume contains original contributions addressing many of the relevant problems and issues. It is intended to give professionals, parents, students, and other interested persons a first hand report on the state of the field. It presents the thinking, research, evaluation, and critical reviews of persons actively searching for a clearer understanding of the use of drugs as a therapeutic technique for use with special populations. The paper in the Appendix, a report on a conference sponsored by the Department of Health, Education, and Welfare, is included to remind us that the Federal government has a very important role to play as a prime facilitator of research and dissemination. In this case it must be added, however, that little follow-up seems to have occured since the original conference was held in 1971.

If we are to advance in our thinking and plan for the future, we need first to understand the breadth of the available material concerning drug usage as a therapeutic facilitator of classroom learning and to appreciate associated problems.

The futures of children rest on providing learning environments and growth situations conducive to each child's realizing his or her optimal performance level. If drug therapy has a proper place in providing that positive ecological system, then we must be sure that it takes its rightful position. If, on the other hand, additional research is called for before even more children and their families come to rely on this therapy, then let us get on with the task: our children are waiting.

Michael J. Cohen
New York

1

DRUG RESEARCH: A FOUNDATION FOR DECISION MAKING

ARTHUR R. DeLONG, Ph.D.

More and more children growing up in the last half of the twentieth century are becoming dependent upon professional intervention to help them grow up effectively. One such intervention that is being used increasingly is pharmacology, or drug therapy. Those responsible for making decisions about whether or not to use drugs need to know more and more to feel reasonably comfortable when the need to make such decisions arises.

This chapter is designed to assist parents, teachers, and clinicians to better understand, and therefore more effectively use, the complex area of drug research. Four objectives are used to attempt to shed light on this important type of intervention:

To provide a representative sampling of drug studies to enable one not familiar with drug research to get a feel for not only the findings but for the state of the art—that is, to see how far the research has developed as to what it can and as yet can not tell us.

To reveal through questions the issues crucial to understanding research at present, that are generated by the review.

To suggest a framework to enable thoughtful observers of research to better evaluate the quality of research.

To provide a basis for decision making in regard to using the results or findings of research.

A REPRESENTATIVE SAMPLING OF DRUG RESEARCH STUDIES

The numbers of drug research studies have been increasing at an increasing rate. Merely listing the studies that have so far been published would fill the pages of a fairly good sized book. Reading all the literature, therefore, is an impossibility for anyone who does not have almost unlimited free time and the proper resources.

Because most individuals responsible for children have many other uses for their time, it is necessary to get what one can from a small number of studies. Any attempt to select even a dozen or two drug studies can be highly misleading. It almost surely would result in a biased perspective of the findings as well as of the present state of the art of drug research.

The following studies have been selected to provide a picture of the range of research studies and their results. The central thrust of the selection of articles is related to the use of psychoactive drugs on children diagnosed as hyperactive for at least a part of their complaint.

The first studies dealing with the use of psychoactive drugs to modify behavior were published in 1937. One was authored by Bradley, who described how benzedrine had a calming effect on hyperactive children. Two others were written by Moltich and Eccles (1937) and Moltich and Sullivan (1937) who expressed enthusiasm about the possibilities for the use of amphetamines in improving the learning behavior of children. They reported significantly improved learning in 93 delinquent boys who had been administered benzedrine sulfate. Their study was placebo controlled but their data were not analyzed statistically.

Large numbers of articles dealing with the use of psychoactive drugs did not begin to appear until 1955. Between 1937 and then only seven others were located. Bradley, who has been widely quoted and appears to have had considerable influence on the widespread use of amphetamines, was involved in four of these: Bradley and Green (1940), Bradley and Bowen (1940, 1941), and Bradley (1950). The others were authored by Cutler, Little, and Strauss (1940), Bender and Cottington (1942), and Effron and Freedman (1953).

As the numbers of studies began to increase after 1955, a variety of questions or concerns arose in this reviewers mind. The selected studies will be organized chronologically by each of the concerns.

Names and Terms with Which One Must Become Familiar to Make Sure That Significant Studies Are not Overlooked

The term "hyperactive," although widely used, is but one of many. "Hyperkinetic" is often used as a substitute, as are the initials MBD. Even these initials have different meanings in various studies: minimal brain dysfunction,[1] minimal brain damage. Some investigators use "hyperkinetic impulse syndrome"; others use cerebral dysfunction, organic behavior syndrome, or hyperkinetic syndrome. Ciba, the manufacturers of Ritalin (methylphenidate), uses the term "functional behavior problem." "Hyperexcitability" has also been used.

This complexity arose not so much from the variety of terms but from the meaning users appeared to intend. Some writers using identical terms described different behaviors, whereas others using different terms described similar behaviors.

Chess (1960) defined hyperactivity as follows: "The hyperactive child is one who carries out activities at a higher rate of speed than the average child, or who is constantly in motion or both." Eisenberg (1966) states "by definition hyperkinesis refers to activity in excess of the range normal for age and sex." Werry (1968) states that "hyperactivity or hyperkinesis may be defined as a total daily motor activity (or movement of the body or any portion of it) which is significantly greater than the norm." Lesser (1970) concludes that "many hyperactive children do not move more than normal children but appear more active because of disorganization of behavior." Although Chess (1960) cautioned against subjectivity, both her definition and Eisenberg's make objectivity extremely difficult. Werry's enables objectivity to be determined arbitrarily by a choice of .05 or .01 level of significance if it can be assumed that he means statistical significance and if the mean and standard deviation of normal total daily motor activity is known.

Knobel (1962) is considerably more detailed in his description of what he terms the hyperkinetic child. He differentiates among organic factors, psychogenic factors, and a combination of both. He presents

---

[1]This is true in spite of the fact that a group of child specialists agreed that minimal brain dysfunction is a suitable medical diagnostic term for children with learning disabilities. Their symptoms, however, resemble those that others have designated by many of the other terms.

the following methods as means for "simplifying" the delineation among them.

> Psychomotor instability, lack of attention, impulsivity seem to be the main symptoms. These symptoms associated with a few others describe what is known as the "hyperkinetic impulse disorder," the "acting out boy," "character impulse disorder," "children with organic brain disease," and "choreatiform syndrome." At first glance it is possible to see conceptually how we may be oriented toward a psychological or an organic etiology of the nosologic entity we are considering.

He characterizes it by the presence of at least seven of the following "hyperkinetic-like" symptoms and no more than two of the hypokinetic symptoms: (1) hyperactivity, (2) low frustration tolerance, (3) aggressivity (including destructive bullying and cruel behavior), (4) impulsivity, (5) looking for companionship, (6) inability to postpone gratification (including making excessive demands and poor capacity to sustain an effort), (7) poor school performance, (8) poor peer relationships, and (9) hostility (including rebelliousness, resenting authority, and stubbornness). His hypokinetic or withdrawal symptoms are: (1) depression, (2) sullenness (including seclusiveness and loneliness), (3) indifference (including being apathetic or passive), (4) moodiness, and (5) withdrawal.

Laufer and Denhoff (1957) in an article entitled "Hyperkinetic Behavior Syndrome in Children" stated that they will refer to what Bradley termed the "organic behavior syndrome" as the "hyperkinetic impulse disorder." They termed the following as "essential symptoms": (1) hyperactivity, (2) short attention span and poor powers of concentration, (3) variability, (4) impulsivity and inability to delay gratification, (5) irritability, (6) explosiveness, and (7) poor school work.

Comly (1962) characterizes hyperkinetic as disrupted–overinvolved. Werry, Weiss, Douglas, and Martin (1966) in a later study define hyperactivity as "a chronic, sustained, excessive level of motor activity which is the cause of significant and continued complaint both at home and at school." This definition requires a subjective assessment be added to that of the actual physical activity that may be measured objectively. They pointed out that this "differs from that of the hyperkinetic syndrome which usually includes other symptoms such as poor emotional control, irritability, aggressivity, and specific cognitive defects."

Cruickshank and Paul (1971) consider distractibility to be the more central characteristic of brain-damaged children, that is, their inability to filter out extraneous stimuli and focus selectively on a task.

Other researchers using the same types of psychoactive drugs deal only with learning disabilities and/or school behavior (Conners, Eisenberg, & Barcai, 1967; Conners, Rothschild, Eisenberg, Schwartz, & Robinson, 1969; Knights & Hinton, 1969.

Kraft, Marcus, Wilson, Swander, Rumage, and Schulhofer (1959) and Fish (1968) have studied disturbed children and numerous authors have dealt with institutionalized children.

The variety of terms and of definitions within terms, coupled with the differences in types of subjects, would make comparisons among studies or assessment of the effectiveness of the drugs difficult, if not impossible, even if all of the studies were tightly controlled and the results were objectively measured.

Apparently, concern about etiology is at least partially responsible for this confusion. Many wish to refer to, if not identify, the source of the problem. Others are less concerned. Lesser (1970) states:

> Hyperkinesis in children may be viewed as an ego disorder of motility, control of drives and learning. Diverse methods of treatment reflect widely differing concepts of the nature of the disorder. Treatment and research formulations may be more rationally designed when based upon etiologic considerations.

The Etiology of the Disorders

Theoretically, at least, one cannot have confidence that a disease disorder has been cured until its cause has been eliminated. It therefore appears to follow logically that one must at least have a reasonable hypothesis of etiology to diagnose and treat. In practice, however, many extenuating circumstances preclude ideal action.

There are a number of reasonable etiology hypotheses cited by different researchers. Most who specify a locus or a source for hyperactivity cite the brain.

Comly (1962) states:

> children's learning or behavior disorders may be due primarily to disturbances of brain activity which interferes with perception, integration of perception. . . . Cerebral dysfunction may result from injury to, or anomalous growth of brain tissue. Similar behavioral syndromes arise from genetic, maturational, infectious, toxic, neoplastic, traumatic or other sources.

Knobel and Lytton (1959) postulate that hyperactivity results from derangement in the midbrain function, cortical function, or both. Comly, in an early mimeographed paper, (1962) states that "any factor or combinations of factors which infringe upon the functional integrity of the integrative centers must be suspect."

Millichap and Boldrey (1967) cite Strauss and Lehtinen and Prechtle and Stemmer as ascribing the etiology to "diffuse brain lesions sustained during pregnancy and delivery," or as resulting from encephalitis according to Levy. They point out that "abnormalities in the neurologic examination and the electroencephalogram are inconsistent findings in hyperactive children, and emotional disorders, constitutional factors, and delays in anatomical and biochemical maturation of the brain may be invoked as explanations in some cases."

Chess (1960) used five diagnostic categories. The first two were physiologic hyperactivity and organic brain damage. Laufer and Denhoff (1957) state: "In some, the hyperkinetic impulse disorder was associated with some other of the 'syndromes of cerebral malfunction'. . . ." Later in the same article under the heading of etiology they state, "Apparently anything which produces dysfunction of the diencephalon and the diencephalocortical interrelations before birth, during birth or during the first five years of life may result in this syndrome."

Knobel (1962) made one of the most definite statements found in the literature up to that time in regard to diagnosing etiology. "We were able to establish, empirically, criteria for differentiating whether the condition was of organic or psychogenetic etiology." His criteria for organicity were positive findings in two of the following three: a neurological examination, an electroencaphalographic record, and psychological tests.

Paine (1962) considers the following as definite evidence of neurological abnormalities: mild choreathetosis, hyperreflexia, tremor of the hands, and varying degrees of dysarthria. Menkes, Rowe, and Menkes (1967) consider poor coordination, visual motor dysfunction, or speech impairment as indications of neurologic abnormalities. Other researchers appear to be skeptical about etiology, most by ignoring references to etiology and a few by direct statements. Myers and Pless (1976) state that presumed causes are anoxia at birth, genetic influence, lead intoxication, and a disturbed family influence.

Werry et al. (1966) suggested that the etiology of hyperactivity is probably heterogeneous and much more difficult to evaluate than may be assumed from a study of the literature. In a later article Werry et al. (1968 a) point out that even though hyperactives have shown significantly more dysrhythmia, a specific EEG abnormality, this does not necessarily reflect structural brain damage.

Eisenberg (1966) states "typically, hyperkinesis shows a developmental course, diminishing in later childhood and usually disappearing by adolescence." Werry (1968 b) distinguishes between organic and developmental hyperactivity even though he views the distinction as artificial. He states: "It has the merit of clearing up some of the confusion about the etiology and symptomatology of hyperactivity. . . ." Rapaport and Quinn (1975) state that the label "minimal brain dysfunction" is likely to be applied where symptoms are found, "but without known neurological disease or major psychiatric illness."

Lubechenco, Bard, Goldman, et al. (1974) reported that children who weighed more than 2500 grams at birth but whose gestations were less than 38 weeks had a higher incidence of CNS disorders at birth.

Silbergeld and Goldberg (1973) attempted to get at etiology in an indirect manner. They exposed mice to inorganic lead at regular intervals from birth. These mice exhibited hyperactive behavior. They then administered the drugs considered useful in treating hyperactivity. The lead-treated mice were calmed by the drugs, whereas those in the control group were not. The lead-treated mice were also reactive to stimulation, while those on the medication were not. It would seem logical that postmortems would discover brain damage if it was responsible for the hyperactivity. They found that "gross histiopathology was not detectable." They concluded that "M.B.D. hyperactivity or hyperkinesis is a behavioral disorder of diverse symptomology and multiple etiologies in children."

Several of the more recent publications contain similarly cautious statements regarding etiology. Klein and Gittleman-Klein (1975) use carefully couched technical language to conclude that our lack of knowledge requires a careful diagnostician to only infer etiology. Dubey (1976) recommends not making the assumption of an organic base because it can diminish pursuit of other likely avenues of treatment.

Bower and Mercer (1975) provide logical support for this concern when they conclude that not only are "etiology and terminology complex and debatable" but that "hyperactivity is often times embedded in a matrix of other debilitating behaviors." They quote the statement of the 1971 Conference on the Use of Stimulating Drugs on Etiology. It begins, "We know little about definitive causes."

Dubey (1976) in interpreting research from the United Kingdom concurs. He states that the evidence as a whole does not support the assumption that organic factors play a significant role in the behavior of hyperkinetic children. He points out, however, that it has not been proved that organicity plays no part.

Keith (1974) notes that the hyperkinetic syndrome in the United Kingdom is rare, whereas it is the commonest reason for referral to child guidance clinics in the United States. He charges that it is not a complaint by children but by parents, teachers, and doctors. Weithorn & Ross (1976) state "Few studies are related to the behavioral research on which current clinical practice is based. Thus, the correspondence between the underlying physiological actions of the drugs and their indirect behavioral components remain largely theoretical at the present time." This fact suggests we take a closer look at behavior.

The Specific Behaviors to be Modified by Psychoactive Drugs

An early question that comes to mind when considering research relating to human behavior involves the basis for selecting a control group. This question appears especially frustrating in this area because of the wide varieties of behaviors involved. They might be classified under three headings: (a) symptoms of hyperactivity, (b) learning, and (c) disturbances, including mental retardation and delinquency.

Symptoms of hyperactivity.

Werry, Weiss, Douglas & Martin (1966) listed motor activity; Eisenberg (1966) irritability, boundless energy, poor judgment, overstimulation, and overactivity in presence of siblings; Knobel (1962) psychomotor instability, lack of attention, impulsivity, classroom discipline, poor peer relationships, aggressivity, distorted perception, destructive behavior, low frustration tolerance, inability to postpone gratification, poor capacity to sustain effort, bullying, cruel behavior, poor school performance, hostility, stubbornness, choreoathetosic movement, abnormality in drawing figures, and erratic, senseless, directionless behavior. Chess (1960) lists short attention span, teasing, restlessness, negativism, perseverative tendencies, symptoms of school phobia, lack of maturational basis for hyperactivity, demands for excessive personal servicing, exploitation of sympathy, and sleep disturbances. Laufer and Denhoff (1957) cite poor powers of concentration, shifting from one activity to another, variability, explosiveness, volcanic reactions, reading reversals, crabbed, irregular or otherwise poor handwriting, emotional disturbances, great discomfort from tension, hyperactivity, and demanding. Millichap and Boldrey (1967) add marked distractibility and hyperexcitability. Comly (1962) includes disruptive, overinvolved, inattentive, forgetful, easily overstimulated, often used as a scapegoat. Knights and Hinton (1969) cite laziness, restlessness, and disobedience. Menkes, Rowe & Menkes, et al. (1967) add emotional lability and low frustration tolerance. Several of the above authors cited behaviors previously listed by another.

Learning

Behaviors termed as learning ranged widely. Knights and Hinton (1969) used the WISC along with four other psychological tests and behavior ratings by parents and teachers to assess "the effects of methylphenidate on the motor skills and behavior of children with learning problems." Conners et al. (1967), in a similarly entitled study utilizing dextroamphetamines, reported improvement in teacher ratings and assertiveness. They reported that intellectual ability was unchanged. Conners et al. (1969) actually used two reading measures as well as one in arithmetic and another in spelling. They also used the WISC, the Porteus maze, the Frostig Test of Developmental Perception, Paired Associative Learning, and parent ratings.

Freeman (1966), whose "Review of Thirty Years of Research On the Effect of Drugs on Children's Learning" is an outstanding contribution to drug research, devotes considerable discussion to definitions of learning. He concludes that "the types of agents and activities that favor the learning process are so varied that a precise definition of learning reinforcers is at present impossible."

Douglas (1975) quotes Sroufe's then in-press article that "to date there is no compelling evidence that stimulant drugs have a beneficial effect on problem solving, reasoning, non-rote learning or actual school achievement." She further points out that research has so far failed to show long-term gains on some measures that looked encouraging in the short-term studies. Freedman (1971) and makes a point of even stronger concern: "More attention should be directed to learning deficits which result from the medication."

Disturbances

Drug studies are most easily controlled when children are in institutions so that many studies are naturally conducted under institutional conditions.

Bradley's subjects were all residents of the Emma Pendleton Bradley Home. Millichap and Boldrey (1967) studied children admitted for investigation for seizures and involuntary movements. Chess's (1960) subjects included mental retardates without previous brain damage, reactives, and neurotics, as well as childhood schizophrenics. Fish (1968) reported effects of drugs on disturbed children. Mentally retarded subjects in institutions were studied by McConnel and Cromwell (1964), Badham, Bardon, Reeves, and Young (1963), Blair and Harold (1955), Bell and Zubek (1961), Black, Kato, and Walker (1966), Bowman and Blumberg (1958), and many others. Moltich and Eccles

(1937) and Moltich and Sullivan (1937) studied delinquent children.

The wide variety of behaviors and types of subjects from both institutionalized and home settings makes comparison of studies impossible and evaluation of results most difficult. No report was found in which even a majority of the listed behaviors were studied. Then too, no two studies were found that studied the same pattern of specific behaviors. The problem involved in attempting to match groups is considerably compounded by the variety of instruments used to measure the behaviors studied.

The Measurement of Specific Behaviors

It is axiomatic in psychological measurement that different ways of measuring a specific behavior produce different results. It therefore follows that even after the behaviors to be modified are agreed upon, measuring instruments and techniques must be standardized. For example, Herring (1924) developed an "intelligence test" that correlated .991 with the Stanford Binet. Because his data have been gathered scrupulously it is difficult not to conclude that these tests would produce similar measurements. Carroll and Hollingsworth (1930) demonstrated that in spite of the practically perfect correlation there was an average difference of -17.2 IQ points in Herring Binet results as compared with Stanford Binet scores of the same children. DeLong (1961) in analyzing the individual measures discovered that the scores differed by a range of $+10$ to -39.

In two studies utilizing the WISC, Conners et al. (1969) reported full-scale, verbal, and performance IQ's plus all subscores; whereas Werry et al. (1966) reported only the arithmetic score, Conners reported pre- and posttreatment scores for both placebo and active drug. The change in each was less than one point. Werry noted that the drug produced no change but the placebo showed improvement. Keogh, Wetter, and McGinty (1973) report that summarizing the subtest values of the WISC masks functional differences in problem solving skills. Miller, Palkes, and Stewart (1973) report significant differences betwen hyperactive girls and normals as well as between hyperactive boys and normals on full-scale as well as verbal and nonverbal IQ scores.

Two studies that reported motor activity measurement used different instruments for different periods of time. Millichap and Boldrey (1967) used an actometer and reported their measurements for 24-hour periods, while McConnel and Cromwell (1964) used a ballistograph and reported their measurements for 4-minute periods after a 2-minute acclimation time. Millichap and Boldrey reported only posttreatment scores along with control scores. The results were interpreted on the basis of percentage of change.

Conners et al. (1967) was one of the few studies to report achievement test scores as a measure of learning. They used the reading, arithmetic, and spelling score from the Wide Range Achievement Test (WRAT) and the Gray Oral Reading Test Scores. The two reading scores produced different results.

The following studies used behavioral rating scales as part of or all of the reported measurements: Conners et al. (1967, 1969), Eisenberg (1966), McConnel and Cromwell (1964), Werry (1968), and Werry et al. (1966). Other than the Werry–Weiss–Peters rating scale reported in two of the studies no two scales could be reported as similar.

Clinical judgments provided the basis for arriving at differences in studies by Chess (1960), Knobel (1962), and Kraft et al. (1959). Zrull et al. (1966) report both rating scales and clinical judgment.

Canter (1963) introduced his background interference procedure (BIP) as a means for diagnosing brain damage. A number of research studies provided evidence confirming its usefulness: Canter (1970), Canter and Straumanis (1969), and Masini (1969). Canter reported a scoring system for his procedure in 1970. A later study, however, casts doubt on the usefulness of the preceeding work. Adams, Hayden, and Canter (1974) studied the relationship between scores on the BIP and hyperkinetic behavior symptoms and reported that although their results were consistent with those of previous studies their results were too small to reliably classify an individual child.

Standardization of measurement instruments and techniques would appear to be a *sine qua non* for a comparison of the results of different studies; however, even comparable measurements have different meanings when they are used under different conditions or with differing drugs and dosages.

The Drug and Dosage To Be Used

There is a wide variety of drugs that have been studied for a variety of reasons. Although the range of drugs intended to deal with hyperactivity is smaller than the total range, it is still quite broad. Millichap and Fowler (1967) listed 18 under eight categories. The percent termed "improved" varied from a low of 21 to a high of 100. The table listed six in order of their recommended choice. The percentage designated as "improved" in this total ranged from 83 to 34 with an average of 62. These were methylphenidate, 83%; amphetamine, 69%; chlordiazepoxide, 60%; chlorpromazine, 55%; Deanol, 47%; and reserpine, 34%. To the degree that this summary table represents valid measures of the total population of hyperactives, it implies that no single drug can be useful in all cases and that even the least useful effect can be effective with as many as one child in three.

Although methylphenidate appears to be the most favored drug, specific documentation for it as most favored is hard to find. Other than the Millichap and Fowler (1967) article, all reviewed through 1971 which favored methylphenidate give another researcher credit for the documentation. Experience with the documentation of drug studies indicated that one may not with impunity accept such at face value.

The amphetamines were the first drugs used to treat hyperactivity and most studies in the literature through the 1960's are those dealing with the amphetamines. The two most widely cited amphetamines are benzedrine and dexedrine. They were considered sufficiently closely related that many writers failed to distinguish between them. There were, however, three forms of amphetamines used. The dextro *(d)* and levo *(l)* forms, which are mirror images of each other chemically, and a racemic or *(dl)* form, which is composed of equal mixtures of the other two. Bergersen and Krug (1966) state "The levo component has more effect on the cardiovascular system and the dextro component is more active as a stimulant of the central nervous system." Perhaps the overlooking of this information has been at least in part responsible for R. Freeman's (1966) disappointment with amphetamine research. He states "while the usefulness of this class of drugs has become almost axiomatic in child psychiatry, it should be clearly recognized that most studies employing the amphetamines leave a great deal to be desired and the final word is not yet available."

Caffeine as a means for calming hyperactive behavior began to be suggested in the early 1970's. Conners (1975) conducted a well-designed study to appraise its efficacy. He concluded that "on the basis of the present study, it is not recommended that caffeine be employed as a treatment for hyperkinetics until further research is undertaken."

Safer and Allen (1975) suggested that the size of the dose is responsible for side effects. Werry and Sprague (1974) in a cross-cultural study in which data from New Zealand and the United States replicated each other almost perfectly concluded that .3 mg/kg of weight was as effective as higher doses. This dosage is considerably lower than that recommended in several standard texts (2 mg/kg) or in the dosages that have resulted in side effects. Studies on Ritalin range to as high as 200 mg/day.

Considerable concern is expressed not only how hyperactivity can be calmed by a stimulant but by how another child with a similar diagnosis can be calmed by a tranquilizer.

The Courageousness of the Recommendations

New directions as well as the methods and techniques to achieve them are obtained more often and more rapidly when courageous individuals are willing to try operating with less sophisticated procedures and fewer objective data than are desirable. Their enthusiastic recommendations, which are often necessarily based upon clinical judgments, encourage others to follow. As a result of the data collected by such pioneers we tend to progress more rapidly than we otherwise might.

There comes a point, however, where objective research must replace clinical reports. The conclusions of the skeptical, hard-nosed researcher must corroborate the enthusiasm and the judgment of the clinician if we are to insure that unnoticed effects neither accompany nor follow the central treatment as well as to insure that the reported results are caused by the treatment rather than by the circumstances accompanying it. DeLong (1972) is one of a number of reviewers who points out "that the research raises more questions for the critical reviewer and the physician than it answers."

Bradley can be credited as the pioneer in the use of stimulants to treat hyperactive children. His work is widely cited by researchers as a basis for their own work.

Bradley's first article, published in 1937, reported 15 out of 30 children improved as a result of the administration of from 10 to 20 mg of an amphetamine for 1 week. He reported one child as being less well off. There were no objective measures reported nor was use of a placebo. His second, (Bradley & Green, 1940), referred to 21 children, 14 boys and 7 girls, who were resident patients in the Emma Pendleton Bradley Home. They were referred to the home for a variety of neuropsychiatric complaints. Each child was given the M form of the Stanford Binet from 1 to 3 hours after having received a single oral dose of amphetamine sulfate. Those who had previously tolerated it were administered 20 mg/day; those who had not were given 10 mg. On a subsequent day the children were administered form L of the Standford Binet without medication. Psychomotor tests were also administered but were not reported because the results were inconclusive. The Binet scores were reported and an average improvement of .4 IQ points was noted.

In their discussion they state,

> In spite of the lack of consistent demonstrable changes or correlations in the material of this study, its results are by no means insignificant. Other workers have observed that amphetamine sulfate has been effective in improving performance on similar tests. Many of the children in the present study had shown some striking change in school

performance following the same doses of amphetamine sulfate which failed to alter their psychological test results.

The last sentence of their summary reads: "It is suggested that amphetamine sulfate may result in apparent intellectual improvement in certain situations by its effect on the emotional attitude of the individual toward his task."

In a 1941 publication Bradley and Bowen reported reactions of 100 children also in the Emma Pendelton Bradley Home who were being treated for various disorders. They were given from 10 to 40 mg of amphetamine sulfate administered in varying doses which were increased or decreased on the basis of response. The children were observed for from 1 to 4 weeks, during which time they participated in a full program of activities suited to their age and abilities. Although the writers report that placebos were administered in a few cases no other controls were reported nor were the results of those receiving placebos differentiated from the gross results.

The following three sentences from their summary represent the essence of their report.

> The drug produced a subdued type of behavior in 54 children, failed to alter the activities of 21 and stimulated psychomotor activity in 19 patients. Six children responded by improved scholastic performance without other behavior changes. Only 7 patients became clinically worse while receiving amphetamine sulfate. And these were all children in whom problems of hyperactive, irritable behavior appeared to be accentuated by the drug.

There is an interesting statement in their discussion:

> There is considerable confirmatory evidence that amphetamine sulfate influences children's behavior indirectly through its effect upon emotional state. Bradley and Green (1940) in a controlled study of psychometric test results, and Bradley and Bowen (1940) in an analysis of the academic progress of elementary school children, concluded that amphetamine sulfate induces better performance in these two spheres only insofar as the drug alters the emotional attitude of individuals toward their intellectual tasks.

It appears amazing how strong enthusiasm for one's work can affect the interpretation of the results of that work.

When the data upon which enthusiastic conclusions are reached are reported in a study, the careful reader can confirm or refute the conclusion. Stevens, Boydstun, Dykman, Peters, and Sinton (1967) state, "In this study we have shown that MBD children cannot respond as rapidly or as accurately as normal children on standard laboratory tasks." Although there may be a difference of opinion about the meaning of "cannot," it suggests stronger meaning than "almost all means favor the normal group." Their table indicates no differences as large as one standard deviation of either pre- or post-test results.

A study that may well be a classic in the courageousness of its conclusions was reported by Millichap and Fowler (1967). The stated purpose of their study was to select drugs to treat children with hyperactivity. They began with a detailed description of their interpretation of minimal brain dysfunction (MBD). They indicated etiology and its locus and presented a theory that might also explain MBD.

They state that "the requisites for an optimal design for such a study are that it be double blind and include 1) a uniform group of patients of sufficient size to permit statistical analysis and 2) matched controls and random assignment of patients to drug treatment or placebo." Eighteen different drugs grouped into one of eight categories were described. Summaries of 48 different studies involving these drugs were then cited and the efficiency of the drugs were evaluated by ranking them in the order of the authors' recommendations.

The authors state that "the majority of investigations are of limited significance because of unsatisfactory design but the recommendations are the closest approximations possible with the evidence available."

Their recommendation is that methylphenidate (Ritalin) is the most efficacious of the drugs listed as useful in the treatment of minimal brain dysfunction syndromes and learning disabilities. They present a table which indicates that 83% of 337 patients treated with Ritalin showed improvement, whereas 14% experienced side effects on dosages of 5–60 mg/day.

A study of the data that formed the basis for their recommendation indicates that six Ritalin studies were used, the first three of which indicated that 75%, 87%, and 90% showed improvement when treated on daily doses of 15–200, 60–80, and 40–80 mg/day. These studies involved 20, 31, and 150 patients for from 8 to 20, ——,[2] and 32 weeks. None of these studies utilized a double blind procedure, or a placebo, or objective measurements. The fourth study utilized all three design requisites. In this study no patients were judged improved and 70% were listed as experiencing side effects. The fifth study, as the first three, utilized no design controls. Seventy out of 100 were indicated to have improved on a dosage of 5–10 mg/day. The sixth study cited utilized placebo control and objective tests; however, none of the four patients who were given .2–.5 mg of Ritalin for one day showed improvement. The 83% showing improvement—279 of 337—was the largest of the eight categories tested and therefore was recommended as their first choice for the treatment of hyperactivity. How they arrived at the reccommendations of 5–60 mg daily dosage from the data is a mystery, although they happen to be the dosage limits that the manufacturer recommends. Their courage would be noteworthy if they merely failed to discourage the use of Ritalin on the basis of their data, because the only study that conforms to their stated requirements resulted in no improvements and 70% experiencing side effects. Their recommending Ritalin as first choice implies clinical confidence of an outstanding degree.

Highly developed clinical judgment is essential to effective medical practice. It is also responsible for many of the recommendations that lead to early generation research.

Early generation research, although essential to understanding the effect of drugs, can be highly misleading and must be evaluated cautiously. Not all its findings are validated by later generation research.

It may be helpful to note that research that occurs at a later date may not be of a later generation, that is, built upon the findings of previous research. Some clinicians and researchers see promise in clues they find without having had knowledge about segments of the literature in which previous similar research has been reported. Each segment of the literature does not contain the previous foundations of all other segments.

Another caution regarding "courageous" recommendations is in order. Not only do they appear earlier in the time sequence of the research process than do those of cautious recommendations, they also tend to get more attention. It is, therefore, incumbent upon decision makers to have a systematic basis for evaluating the results of research as well as one for using research results in their decision making regarding the nature of treatment they wish their children to have.

Research Design: A Framework for Evaluating Its Effectiveness

It is clear that the design of a drug research study is one of the most significant factors influencing the trustworthiness of its outcome. It matters little what was intended to be achieved or how strongly, or weakly, the conclusions were worded. The outcomes of research are determined by the specific provisions of its design.

A sophisticated research study provides for dealing with each of the variables that has an effect on its outcome. Each variable in the study may be likened to a gate; the function of the research design is to close and lock each gate. When all gates have been closed and locked, a study is said to be tightly designed and the results may be considered trustworthy. Each variable unaccounted for by the design renders the study results proportionately less useful.

Although some studies dealing with the use of psychoactive drugs to modify behavior were less loosely controlled than others, no study was found that dealt rigorously with all the variables known to be involved in determining the effects of such drug therapy. A very few dealt rigorously with many of the variables for which concern was expressed.

The following characteristics are considered minimal in an effectively designed drug study.

Placebo control.

The administration of medication often has a profound psychological effect on those involved. "The placebo effect has long been recognized" (R. Freeman, 1966). Freed (1962) pointed out that about one-third of a population of children experiences placebo effect. Beecher (1955) reported it to be between 30 and 35%. Some investigators have attributed as much as 70% of improvement to placebo effect. R. Freeman (1966) has pointed out that placebo effect can sometimes exceed drug responses. Davis's (1965) data verify this conclusion.

Blind procedures.

Although the use of a placebo is essential to effective drug research, it is not sufficient. It is obvious that if the patient knows a placebo is being used, it cannot have the same effect as it can if he or she believes it to be the active drug. It is less obvious that when the dispenser of the drug believes a placebo is being administered it will result in lower improvement in the patient. Heaton-Ward (1962) changed the numbers identifying placebo and active drug and the behavioral ratings changed even though there was no exchange of drug and placebo. Studies in which neither patient nor dispenser can distinguish between active drug and placebo are termed double blind.

Cole (1962) has pointed out that "patients receiving the active agent in a setting of drug-positive physician behavior remain in treatment to a much greater extent than patients on placebo or patients receiving the active drug in a neutral setting." To be completely certain that what the researcher does does not contaminate the results, a triple blind procedure can be used. In this procedure even the researcher cannot distinguish between placebo and active drug until all the data are in and analyzed. McConnell and Cromwell (1964) noted that of the three subjects who were removed from their triple blind study because the attendants noted an extreme increase in activity, two were later discovered to have been on placebo.

Random assignment of patients to placebo and active drug.

This procedure assures that experimenter bias will not affect the assignment of patients to one group or the other. Even the researcher who intends to be highly objective can be influenced by clues of which he or she is unaware. Kraft et al. (1959) explained that the results of their study could not be generalized as broadly as the data would otherwise warrant because the psychiatrist was reluctant to assign children with severe difficulties to a placebo group.

A uniform group of patients of sufficient size to permit statistical analysis.

Cole (1962) states that the question most often asked in clinical psychiatric drug use is, "Does Drug A in patients of Type B at dosage C as administered by Therapist D in Setting E produce changes in Measure F as noted by Observer G?" A careful analysis of this question indicates much about design considerations. When a design does not specify a uniform group of patients it implies that the drug being tested is expected to operate, as do claims for patent medicines, on all types of patients with a variety of complaints. A study with only four subjects, for example, should not be considered meaningful. In like manner a study with as many as 100 subjects should be considered equally meaningless if the subjects represent 25 different types. Obviously the statistical procedure should be adapted to the data and the problem.

A detailed description and measurement of the children to be studied.

A statement that the children to be studied have all been referred because of behavior problems is not sufficiently detailed, nor is the statement that all the children have been diagnosed as hyperkinetic. There is a score or more behaviors associated with hyperactivity and each of them with which the study elects to deal should therefore not only be specified but measured objectively.

McConnell and Cromwell (1964), in an otherwise well-designed study, used 57 retarded children with no restrictions on IQ and representing the entire range of retardation. There is no way one can confidently compare their results with other studies because one cannot identify the specific characteristics that have been present either before or after treatment.

A precise description of the measurements and the criteria by which they are to be evaluated.

Motor activity, for example, is usually considered a specific behavior. How change in motor activity is specified, however, can have a variety of meanings. McConnell and Cromwell (1964) used a ballistograph to measure motor activity. They specified 2 minutes in the chair before 4 minutes of measurement were recorded. Their conclusions, therefore, can be confidently compared with all other studies that measure motor activity in the same way. Their results, however, almost surely will have different meaning from the results of Millichap and Boldrey (1967), who report a significant increase in motor activity as measured with an actometer. There may even be some question whether measurements with an actometer on the preferred wrist read once a day measures the same motor activity as do actometers on both the preferred wrist and preferred leg which are read six times per day.

The criterion of significance is also basic to understanding the meaning of measurement. Some studies specify statistical significance at the .05 level of confidence or greater, whereas others appear to mean a change that appears large. To say that those on an active drug changed more than did those on a placebo should be taken to actually mean that there was no difference unless, of course, one wishes to speculate. The size of the difference in and of itself has meaning only in relation to the mean and dispersion of that difference. One study translated differences into percentages. The numbers, thereby, appeared considerably larger than before the transformation. The criterion for change must be specified in the design.

A detailed description of the social setting in which the children live.

It is clear that the setting in which a child lives influences not only his or her behavior but his or her reaction to drugs. It should be obvious that a hospitalized patient will react differently to drugs than an outpatient, yet many studies appear not to take this into consideration. Cole (1962) pointed out that even two types of hospitals can produce differing results. He described how a smaller hospital with more intensive treatment showed a higher patient discharge rate than did a larger hospital with a less active social treatment program. He also cautions that the importance of social factors not be underestimated. He cited Uhlenhuth, Canter, Neustadt, & Payson's 1959 study in which both patients and experimental subjects were shown to have responded differently to identical drugs given in different social situations with different treatment styles. In like manner Zrull, Westman, Arthur, and Rice (1966) warned that "judgments about the child in one setting, taken out of context, can give a misleading view of the drug's efficiency."

Knights and Hinton (1969) provide an example of one of the more tightly designed studies. Their design includes a double blind procedure, placebo control, and objective measures of several specifically described behaviors. They provide for random assignment to control and treatment groups and include a sophisticated statistical analysis procedure. In addition, their interpretations and conclusions with one exception, possibly a misprint, are well within the limits of their design. They report that there was a significant change in diastolic blood pressure, while their data indicated a P of $<.10$.

Their cautious concluding sentence was typical of the more tightly designed studies: "In general the results indicate that the predictions of drug effectiveness for an individual child will require a more detailed study of both etiology and family attitude."

The chief weaknesses in their design were the small numbers of patients of even a relatively homogeneous type, i.e., 17 referred for hyperactivity, 12 for learning problems, 7 for slow progress, failure, and 4 for clumsiness and poor coordination; and their failure to cross-check and specify the validity of the referral complaint.

The quality of the question.

No research can be more effective than the quality of the question to be answered or the problem to be solved. A low-quality question results in low-quality conclusions, no matter how effective the subsequent research happens to be. Although it is also true that a high-quality question followed by less than adequate research does not produce useful research, at least the asking of a high-quality question provides the possibility that profitable results can be produced. Apparently large numbers of drug researchers and larger numbers of interpreters of such research fail to understand this basic principle.

A question such as, "What changes will occur if I give x mg of Y drug to this group of n children?" is an interesting question and should be asked. It can be highly useful in generating hypotheses for future research. It should not, however, be considered as quality research for at least the following reasons: (1) it does not describe the type of children studied; (2) it does not indicate even the target symptoms, let alone the characteristics of the behaviors to be studied; (3) it does not account for the setting in which the children live; (4) nor does it account for how the children have been treated. Therefore, for such a question to be considered research, at least in the sense that any conclusions could be useful beyond the children so treated, the following assumptions would have to be made:

1. Any group of comparable numbers of children selected at random would have the same characteristics as does this group of n children.
2. Any such group would exhibit the same symptoms.
3. The environment in which this group of children lived during treatment was no different than any other environment would be.
4. The treatment setting permitted no factor other than the drug to be responsible for all changes in the children.

A question of the quality of the one verbalized by Cole therefore must either be asked specifically or implied in order for it to produce results that can be trusted by others.

Asking a quality question verbally does not necessarily mean that the research will be of that quality. There are at least two additional ways in which the quality of the question is operationalized.

The study design can be considered as an operationalized question. Therefore, if even one of the conditions implied by the above question is omitted from the design, the quality of the results or, if one prefers, the quality of the question is commensurately reduced. For example, if the use of a placebo were omitted from the design, one could be fairly sure that at least one-third of the results would be attributed to a pill. One cannot be sure that no more than a third has been due to expectation because many studies have shown that the use of a placebo produces equal or better results than has the active drug (Davis, 1965).

The conclusions can also be considered as an operationalized question. When statements in the conclusion go beyond the design limitations of the study they have in effect reduced the quality of the question asked. For example, a conclusion such as "The use of drug A produced spectacular improvement in behavior B," when behavior B has been neither measured nor specified in the design, must be attributed to the enthusiasm of an unsophisticated researcher rather than to the results of treatment even though the possibility exists that they have been achieved by the treatment.

A knowledgeable interpreter of research is one who is aware that no research can be more useful than the quality of the question that the researcher operationally asks. He or she will, therefore, accept no conclusions regarding the success of treatment, except to generate hypotheses, without checking to determine whether the quality of the design is sufficiently tight to warrant the conclusions that are attributed to the treatment. Most studies do not take into consideration all of these variables.

Framework for Decision Making

Knowledge of the research results are useful only when supplemented by mature judgment. The following is recommended as a foundation for effective decision-making judgment by parents and teachers, as well as by clinicians. These four questions can provide a sound base from which to begin responsible decision making:

1. What goals are to be achieved?
2. What options are available that are likely to achieve the stated goal?
3. Are the long-range consequences of the option of consideration likely to be in harmony with its short-range consequences?
4. What are the probabilities of likely negative effects interferring in the process?

Goals of intervention.

What is expected to be achieved by drug treatment seems so obvious that it too often is not put into words. Failure to make treatment goals explicit often results in the achievement of lower than desirable priority goals and even in the primary goal being subverted.

A principle that may not be obvious is that all intervention achieves a goal. Responsible decision making requires that high-priority goals should not be sacrificed for the sake of those of lower priority. This requires the results to be interpreted on the basis of the implicit goals they achieve.

Results such as the following are examples for application of the above principle.

"The children exhibited significantly fewer behavior problems when treated with the active drug."

"The attention span of the children treated with the active drug was longer than that of those receiving the placebo."

"The children received higher grades during the period in which the drug was administered."

Less behavior that is a problem for adults, longer periods of paying attention to the task at hand, and higher grades are all worthwhile goals. Only the decision maker can judge their priority value. Such value may change when compared with other goals. To help a child develop in harmony with his or her natural endowments may or may not be achieved along with those stated above. Katz, Saraf, Gittleman-Klein, & Klein, (1975) state that "the purpose of medication is to free the child from disabling effects of hyperactivity and permit him to function in a more autonomous manner." Being well behaved, working longer at a task, and getting higher grades in many instances requires a child to surrender some or even all of his or her autonomy. The point is not that being well behaved is not desirable, but that it should be seen in relation to one's treatment goals.

The following are among the wide variety of treatment goals available to decision makers:

To help the child understand her- or himself and his or her behavior more fully so as to increase his or her chances of becoming a fully responsible adult.

To reduce the child's discomfort.

To buy time to study causes and treatment options more carefully.

To relieve the stress of parents, siblings, and teachers so that they can function normally; his or her behavior may trouble others sufficiently that they may take their discomfort out on him or her.

To protect the child from secondary effects.

To assist researchers to better understand the condition so as to develop more effective treatment.

To relieve one of the responsibility of selecting other options for fear they may not be ideal.

The range of available options.

When individuals are distraught, busy, or both, the natural tendency is to select the first option that presents itself. Most goals can be achieved by a variety of means, some of which are better or more efficient than are others. The greater the variety of options considered, the higher are the chances of selecting the most efficient as well as the most effective treatment alternative.

Simpson (1974) reports, "While drug therapy has grown considerably, it is not regarded as the ideal method of treatment. For the present drug medication represents a convenient but imperfect alternative that is frequently selected as a treatment modality." He warns that the child may learn to inhibit motor behavior and still fail to attend to appropriate stimuli. He recommends attention training through breathing control to treat hyperactivity.

Walker (1976) is both worried and dismayed about the widespread use of drug therapy. He not only states that "stimulants merely mask the symptoms without curing the disease," he demonstrates with specific cases how he discovered causes the removal of which cured the disease. He found a heart problem, a low level of glucose, subtle seizures, pinworms, and even tight underwear responsible for symptoms of hyperactivity.

Zaro (1973) tested 24 4-year-olds, defined as hyperactive by a physician experienced in diagnosis and evaluation of the syndrome, under three stimulant drug therapy conditions: (1) on drugs, (2) off drugs after having been on, and (3) never on drugs. She reported that the never-on-drug group developed verbal control of nonverbal behavior, while the other two groups failed to do so. These two groups developed cognitive inflexibility that the never-on-drug children did not.

More and more researchers are recommending that nondrug treatment options be considered as viable options.

Dubey (1976) states, "The assumption of an organic basis and the frequently dramatic effects of medication can lead to diminished emphasis on preventive efforts and to ignoring important psychological and educational aspects of the therapy process." He recommends biological, educational, and sociofamilial options.

Katz et al. (1975) list environmental manipulation, counseling, and behavior modification, while Krippner (1975) reports the results of focusing on neurological organization procedures (NO), orthomolecular medicine (OM), and open classrooms. He reports significant results on a wide variety of measures on children from 9 to 13 years of age.

Munro (1974) found a work box first described by Patterson to be a viable option. Punishment was studied by Worland (1974); Douglas (1975) indicated that drugs were not enough; Richardson (1973) found that speech pathology was highly effective.

The duration of the effects of treatment.

The National Institute of Mental Health recently brought together a group of professionals to discuss the long-term effects of drug treatment on hyperactive children. They discovered no satisfactory solutions (Douglas, 1975). She also reports that because virtually all well-designed drug studies with hyperactive children have been short term, most of no more than 2 months duration, therefore, longitudinal studies are needed. She believes that most of the group would agree that the concern of a child therapist is the development of the child over a longer period of time. Satterfield and Cantwell (1975) report that, although they judge the use of stimulant treatment effective in the short run and promising for the prevention of juvenile delinquent and adult criminal behavior, there are no data to substantiate the latter. They note that "follow up studies of hyperactive children in their early and mid teens have reported serious delinquent behavior of the type that often predicts adult criminal behavior."

Huessy, Metoyer, and Townsend (1974) located all but 9 of 84 rural Vermont children who had been treated 8–10 years previously. They report mixed findings. Most were found to be progressing from fair to satisfactory in several areas. Eighteen, however, were found to have been institutionalized. This rate is 20 times greater than is typical. Huessy and Cohen (1976) report another follow-up study in which 500 children in the second, fourth, and fifth grades were rated for behavior problems and rerated after 7 years. They report only the children with the highest scores (greatest disabilities) as having a greater proportion of later behavior problems. Those in the lowest 30% of the scores did not have a single person functioning poorly in the ninth grade. Of the middle group (thirtieth to seventieth percentile), only 5% were functioning poorly.

Treating of a low-priority, short-range goal could exacerbate long-range adjustment.

Side effects.

Werry and Sprague (1974) report that methylphenidate, although a valuable drug, results in side effects that are more common than usually stated. They also report that many children are receiving higher doses than necessary.

Weithorn and Ross (1976) suggest that one must be aware of the negative while benefiting from the positive in their conclusions.

> A further concern relates to the ideo-syncratic effects of the drugs which vary from one child to the next also in relation to dosage and length of time on medication. Thus while certain stimulant drugs are effective in producing more focused attention and improved behavior in some hyperactive children, they may either produce no improvement or exacerbation of symptoms or even lethargy in others and they are speci-

fically contraindicated for certain disorders such as anxiety reactions in which the overt symptomology may be similar to hyperactivity.

Summary and Conclusions

The state of the art of drug research on hyperactive children has demonstrated consistently greater sophistication during the four decades in which it has been undertaken. It has contributed considerably to the data background necessary to more complete understanding of the effects of drug therapy on children.

Drug research has not yet advanced to the point where we can be assured that final answers are available.

One can make most effective use of what is now known about drugs by careful analysis of the crucial aspects of the specific situation. Lambert, Windmiller, Sandaval, (1976) predict that the more research that is available, the more focus will center on individual differences.

Among the crucial aspects of the individual situations are: the physical and environmental factors affecting the child; the quality of the research dealing specifically with such factors; the goals to be achieved by treatment, long range as well as immediate; the range of options available to achieve those goals; and the awareness of possible side effects.

Functioning in this manner should assure decision makers that they have acted as responsibly as is possible for human beings at this stage of our knowledge.

In addition, the child can know that despite the problems involved, he or she is special in the eyes of those who care for him or her.

REFERENCES

Adams, J., Hayden, B., & Canter, A. The relationship between the Canter background interference procedure and the hyperkinetic behavior syndrome. *Journal of Learning Disabilities*, Feb. 1974, *7*, 54–59.

Badham, J., Bardon, L., Reeves, P., & Young, A. A trial of Thioridazine in mental deficiency. *British Journal of Psychiatry*, 1963, *109*, 408–410.

Beecher, H. The powerful placebo. *Journal of the American Medical Association*, 1955, *149*, 1602–1606.

Bell, A., & Zubek, J. Effects of Deanol on the intellectual performance of mental defectives. *Canadian Journal of Psychology*, 1961, *15*, 172–175.

Bender, L., & Cottington, F. The use of amphetamine sulfate (Benzedrine) in child psychiatry. *American Journal of Psychiatry*, 1942, *99*, 116–121.

Bergerson, B. & Krug, E. *Pharmacology in nursing.* New York: C.V. Mosby, 1966.

Black, D., Kato, J., & Walker, G. A study of improvement in mentally retarded children occurring from Siccacell therapy. *American Journal of Mental Deficiency,* 1966, *70,* 449–508.

Blair, H., & Harold, W. Efficiency of Chlorpromazine in hyperactive mentally retarded children. *American Medical Association Archives of Neurology and Psychiatry,* 1955, *74,* 365.

Bower, K., & Mercer, C. Hyperactivity: Etiology and intervention techniques. *The Journal of School Health,* April 1975, *45,* 195–202.

Bowman, P., & Blumberg, E. Ataractic therapy of hyperactive, mentally retarded patients. *Journal of the Maine Medical Association,* July 1958, *49,* 272–273.

Bradley, C. The behavior of children receiving Benzedrine. *American Journal of Psychiatry,* 1937, *94,* 577–585.

Bradley, C., & Bowen, M. School performance of children receiving amphetamine (Benzedrine) sulfate. *American Journal of Orthopsychiatry,* 1940, *10,* 782–788.

Bradley, C., & Bowen, M. Amphetamine (Benzedrine) therapy of children's behavior disorders. *American Journal of Orthopsychiatry,* 1941, *11,* 92–103.

Bradley, C., & Green, E. Psychometric performance of children receiving amphetamine (Benzedrine) sulfate. *American Journal of Psychiatry,* 1940, *97,* 388–394.

Bradley, C. Benzedrine and Dexedrine in the treatment of children's behavior disorders. *Pediatrics,* 1950, *5,* 24.

Canter, A. A background interference procedure for graphomotor tests in the study of deficit. *Perceptual and Motor Skills,* 1963, *16,* 914.

Canter, A. *The Canter background interference procedure for the detection of organic brain disorder: Modified scoring method and replication.* Iowa Psychopathic Hospital, 1970.

Canter, A., & Straumanis, J. Performance of senile and healthy aged persons on the B.I.P. Bender test. *Perceptual and Motor Skills,* 1969, *28,* 695–698.

Carrol, H., & Hollingworth, L. The systematic error of Herring Binet in rating gifted children. *Journal of Educational Psychology,* 1930, *21,* 1–11.

Chess, S. Diagnosis and treatment of the hyperactive child. *New York Journal of Medicine,* August 1960, 2379–2385.

Ciba Pharmaceutical Company. The therapeutic challenge of F.B.P. (functional behavior problem) in children. Brochure, Summit, New Jersey 07901

Clements, S. Minimal brain dysfunction in children—A task force. NINDB Monog. No. 3, U.S. Public Health Service, Washington, D.C., 1966.

Cole, J. Evaluation of drug treatments in psychiatry. *Journal of New Drugs,* September 1962, 264–275.

Comly, H. *The recognition and treatment of cerebral dysfunction in children.* Unpublished monograph, March 1962.

Conners, K. A teacher rating scale for use in drug studies with children. *American Psychiatry Association,* December 1969, *126,* 152–156.

Conners, K. A placebo-crossover study of caffeine treatment of hyperkinetic children. *International Journal of Mental Health,* 1975, *4,* 132–143.

Conners, K., Eisenberg, L., & Barcai, A. Effect of Dextroamphetamine on children. *Archives of General Psychiatry,* 1967, *17,* 478–485.

Conners, K., Rothschild, G., Eisenberg, L., Schwartz, L., & Robinson, E. Dextroamphetamine sulfate in children with learning disorders. *Archives of General Psychiatry*, 1969, *21*, 182–190.

Cruickshank, W., & Paul, J. The Psychological characteristics of brain injured children. In *The Psychology of Exceptional Children and Youth*, Englewood Cliffs, N.J.: 1971.

Cutler, M., Little, J., & Strauss, A. Effects of Benzedrine on Mentally deficient children. *American Journal of Mental Deficiency*, 1940, *45*, 59–65.

Davis, J. Efficacy of tranquilizing and antidepressant drugs. *Archives of General Psychiatry*, 1965, *13*, 552–572.

DeLong, A. Toward improved accuracy in test interpretation. *Merrill-Palmer Quarterly*, 1961, *7*, 273–285.

DeLong, A. What we have learned from psychoactive drug research on hyperactives. *American Journal of Diseases of Childhood*, 1972, *123*, 17-7–180.

Douglas, J. Are drugs enough?—to treat or train the hyperactive child. *International Journal of Mental Health*, 1975, *84*, 199–212.

Dubey, D. Organic factors in hyperkineses: A critical evaluation. *American Journal of Orthopsychiatry*, 1976, *46*, 353–366.

Effron, A., & Freedman, A. The treatment of behavior disorders in children with Benadryl. *Journal of Pediatrics*, 1953, *42*, 261–266.

Eisenberg, J. The management of the hyperkinetic child. *Developmental Medicine Child and Neurology*, 1966, *8*, 593–598.

Fish, B. Methodology in child psychopharmacology. In D. Efron (Ed.) *Psychopharmacology: A Review of Progress 1957–1967*. (Proceeding of the Sixth Annual Meeting of the American College of Neuropsychopharmacology, San Juan, December 1967). Washington, D.C.: U.S. Public Health Service Publication No. 1836, 1968. (a)

Fish, B. Drug use in psychiatric disorders of children. *American Journal of Psychiatry*, 1968, *124*, 31–36.

Freed, H. *The chemistry and therapy of behavior disorders in children*. Springfield, Ill.: Charles C. Thomas, 1962.

Freeman, D. *Report on the conference on the use of stimulant drugs in the treatment of behaviorally disturbed young school children*. Washington, D.C.: U.S. Department of Health, Education and Welfare, 1971.

Freeman, R. Drug effects on learning in children: A selective review of the past thirty years. *Journal of Special Education*, 1966, *1*, 17–44.

Heaton-Ward, W. Inference and suggestion in a clinical trial (Niamid in mongolism). *Journal of Mental Science*, 1962, *108*, 865–870.

Herring, V. *Herring, revision of the Binet-Simon test on verbal and abstract elements in intelligence examinations*. Yonkers: World Book Co., 1924.

Huessy, H., & Cohen, B. Hyperkinetic behaviors and learning disabilities followed over seven years. *Pediatrics*, 1976, *57*, 4–10.

Huessy, H., Metoyer, M., & Townsend, M. 8–10 year follow up of 84 children treated for behavior disorder in rural Vermont. *ACTA Paedopsychiatrica*, 1974, *40*, 230–235.

Katz, S., Saraf, K., Gittleman-Klein, R., & Klein, D. Clinical pharmacological management of hyperkinetic children. *International Journal of Mental Health*, 1975, *4*, 157–181.

Keogh, B. Hyperactivity and learning disorders: Review and speculation. *The Exceptional Child*, 1971, *38*, 101–109.

Keogh, B., Wetter, J., & McGinty, A. Functional analysis of WISC performance of learning-disordered and mentally retarded boys. *Psychology in the Schools*, 1973, *10*, 178–181.

Keith, R. High activity and hyperactivity. *Developmental Medicine and Child Neurology*, 1974, *16*, 543–544.

Klein, D., & Gittleman-Klein, R. Problems in the diagnosis of minimal brain dysfunction and the hyperkinetic syndrome. *International Journal of Mental Health*, 1975, *4*, 45–60.

Knights, R., & Hinton, G. The effects of methylphenidate (Ritalin) on the motor skills and behavior of children with learning problems. *Journal of Nervous and Mental Disorders*, 1969, *148*, 643–653.

Knobel, M. Psychopharmacology for the hyperkinetic child. *Archives of General Psychiatry*, 1962, *6*, 30–34.

Kraft, I., Marcus, I., Wilson, W., Swander, D., Rumage, N., & Schulhofer, E. Methodological problems in studying the effect of tranquilizers in chidlren with specific reference to meprobamate. *Southern Medical Journal*, 1959, *52*, 179–185.

Krippner, S. An alternative to drug treatment for hyperactive children. *Academic Therapy*, 1975, *10*, 433–439.

Lambert, N., Windmiller, M., Sandaval, J. Hyperactive children and the efficacy of psychoactive drugs as a treatment intervention. *American Journal of Orthopsychiatry*, 1976, *46*, 335–352.

Laufer, M., & Denhoff, E. Hyperkinetic behavior syndrome in children. *Journal of Pediatrics*, 1957, *50*, 463–474.

Laufer, M., Denhoff, E., & Rubin, E. Photo-metrazol activation in children. *Electroencephalography and Clinical Neurophysiology*, 1954, *6*, 1–8.

Lesser, L. Hyperkinesis in children. *Clinical Pediatrics*, 1970, *9*, 548–552.

Lubechenco, L., Bard, H., Goldman, A. New born intensive care and long-term prognosis. *Developmental Medicine and Child Neurology*. 1974, *16*, 421–431,

Masini, A. The background interference procedure and the Bender-Gestalt test in the discrimination of brain damage. Paper presented to the Southeastern Psychological Association Annual Convention, New Orleans, La., 1969.

McConnell, T., & Cromwell, R. Studies in activity level: VII effects of amphetamine drug administration on the activity level of retarded children. *American Journal of Mental Deficiency*, 1964, *68*, 647–651.

Menkes, M., Rowe, J., & Menkes, J. A twenty-five year follow-up study on the hyperkinetic child with minimal brain dysfunction. *Pediatrics*, 1967, *39*, 393–399.

Miller, R., Palkes, H., & Stewart, M. Hyperactive children in suburban elementary schools. *Child Psychiatry and Human Development*, 1973, *4*, 121–127.

Millichap, J., & Boldrey, E. Studies in hyperkinetic behavior II. Laboratory and clinical evaluations of drug treatments. *Neurology*, 1967, *17*, 467–471.

Millichap, J., & Fowler, G. Treatment of minimal brain dysfunction syndrome. *Pediatric Clinics of North America*, 1967, *14*, 167–777.

Molitch, M., & Eccles, A. Effects of Benzedrine sulfate on the intelligence scores of children. *American Journal of Psychiatry*, 1937, *94*, 587–590.

Molitch, M., & Sullivan, J. The effect of Benzadrine sulfate on children taking the New Stanford Achievement Test. *American Journal of Ortho-psychiatry,* 1937, *7,* 519.

Munro, B. Control of disruptive behavior in an elementary classroom: Two base studies. *Conseiller Canadien,* 1974, *8,* 257–271.

Myers, G., & Pless, I. Where's the hyperactive child going? *Pediatrics,* 1976, *57,* 1–3.

Paine, R. Minimal chronic brain syndromes in children. *Developmental Medicine and Child Neurology,* 1962, *4,* 21.

Rapaport, J., & Quinn, P. Minor physical abnormalities (stigmata) and early developmental deviation: A major biological sub group of hyperactive children. *International Journal of Mental Health,* 1975, *4,* 29–44.

Richardson, S. Neglect of children with language and learning disabilities. *Hearing and Speech,* 1973, *41,* 8–13.

Safer, D., & Allen R. Side effects from long-term use of stimulants on children. *International Journal of Mental Health,* 1975, *4,* 105–118.

Satterfield, I., & Cantwell, D. Psychopharmacology in the prevention of antisocial and delinquent behavior. *International Journal of Mental Health,* 1975, *4,* 227–237.

Silbergeld, E., & Goldberg, A. Pharmocological and neurochemical investigations of lead induced hyperactivity. *Neurology,* 1973, *14,* 431–444.

Simpson, D. Attention training through breathing control to modify hyperactivity. *Journal of Learning Disabilities,* 1974, *7,* 274–283.

Stevens, D., Boydstun, J., Dykman, R., Peters, J., & Sinton, D. Presumed minimal brain dysfunction in children. *Archives of General Psychiatry,* 1967, *16,* 281–285.

Steward, M., Mendelson, W., & Johnson, E. Hyperactive children as adolescents: How they see themselves. *Child Psychiatry and Human Medicine,* 1973, *4,* 3–11.

Uhlenhuth, E., Canter, A., Neustadt, J., & Payson, H. The symptomatic relief of anxiety with Meprobamate, Phenobarbital and placebo. *American Journal of Psychiatry,* 1959, *115,* 905.

Walker, S. Drugging the American child: We're too cavalier about hyperactivity. *Journal of Learning Disabilities,* 1976, *8,* 354–358.

Weiss, G. The natural history of hyperactivity in childhood and treatment with stimulant medication at different ages—A summary of research findings. *International Journal of Mental Health,* 1975, *4,* 213–226.

Weithorn, C., & Ross, R. Stimulant drugs for hyperactivity: Some additional disturbing questions. *American Journal of Orthopsychiatry,* 1976, *46,* 168–173.

Werry, J. Studies of the hyperactive child IV: An empirical analysis of the minimal brain dysfunction syndrome. *Archives of General Psychiatry,* 1968, *19,* 9–16. (a)

Werry, J. Developmental hyperactivity. *Pediatric Clinics of North America,* 1968, *15,* 581–599. (b)

Werry, J., & Sprague, R. Methylphenidate in children. *Australian and New Zealand Journal of Psychiatry,* 1974, *8,* 9–19.

Werry, J., Weiss, G., Douglas, V., & Martin, J. Studies on the hyperactive child III: The effect of chlorpromazine upon behavior and learning ability. *Journal of the American Academy of Child Psychiatry,* 1966, *5,* 292–312.

Worland, J. Effects of reward and punishment on behavior control in hyperactive and normal boys. *Dissertation Abstracts International*, 1974, 34, 6227–6228.

Zaro, M. Effects of medication on learning in hyperactive four year old children. *Dissertation Abstracts International*, 1973, 34, 2407.

Zrull, J., Westman, J., Arthur, B., & Rice, D. An evaluation of methodology used in the study of psychoactive drugs for children. *Journal of the American Academy of Child Psychiatry*, 1966, 5, 284–291.

2

DRUG THERAPY WITH CHILDREN AND ADOLESCENTS

LARRY B. SILVER, M.D.

INTRODUCTION

There are many children and adolescents with psychiatric difficulties who may benefit from psychopharmacological drugs. In most, if not all, of these cases the medication is but part of a total treatment program. In this chapter I would like to discuss these drugs and their role in treating child and adolescent psychopathology. Basic information on each drug will be provided; more specific details are available from the specific drug manufacturer or from standard textbooks. One specific syndrome, the minimal brain dysfunction syndrome, is most commonly seen in a public school setting and is discussed in greater detail.

Most adults see a mental health professional because they are hurting and feel a need for help. An adult can understand why medication is needed, how to monitor it, and what data to report to his or her physician. Thus, establishing a dosage pattern for adults is often not difficult.

None of this is true with children and adolescents. They are developing individuals, physically and psychologically. They usually come for help because someone else has decided they need help. They may understand why medication is needed and accept responsibility for taking the medication. They may just as likely not understand or resist taking responsibility. Peer pressure may lead to covering up or avoiding taking their medication. Family dynamics may lead to a power struggle around taking medication. The physician's task in establishing a dosage pattern is complicated by other developmental issues. A drug or dosage that may be appropriate for a 2-year-old may not be for an 8-year-old; what is effective for a 12-year-old may not help a 16-year-old. The physician cannot manage the patient alone. Parents, teachers, and other professionals play an essential role in assuring that the medication is taken, in providing the feedback necessary for establishing the dosage pattern, and in recognizing side effects.

It is hoped that this chapter will assist nonmedical professionals in playing these important roles.

Drugs can be referred to by their "trade" names (i.e., the name used commercially by a drug manufacturer) or by their chemical names. In this chapter the trade name is listed first with the chemical name noted in parenthesis. Drug dosages are usually measured in milligrams; this is abbreviated as mg.

PSYCHOPHARMACOLOGY

The first two major tranquilizers, Serpasil (reserpine) and Thorazine (chlorpromazine), were introduced during the first half of the 1950s. These medications for treating the psychoses had an enormous impact on psychiatry. The population of public mental hospitals showed a reduction, reversing a trend of half a century. This reduction has continued and has had major humanistic as well as financial implications.

The introduction of tranquilizers had an even greater impact on nonhospitalized individuals. Because of the ability of the drugs to alleviate the more deviant manifestations of psychotic illness (belligerence, extreme withdrawal, delusions, hallucinations) "patients" became people, able to care for themselves and to function in society. Out-patient care and psychotherapy became possible with many who otherwise would have had to be institutionalized.

Since the mid 1950s many new drugs have been discovered. Despite the intensive experimental efforts of various disciplines most of the useful drugs have been discovered as a result of serendipitous clinical observation. For example, Thorazine was initially used for the potentiation of anesthetic agents; its psychiatric application followed the observation of its calming effect in surgical patients.

Role of Medication

Medications for psychiatric disorders are not curative; they are compensatory. Tranquilizers may relieve an individual's emotional and behavioral symptoms, but they do not change the environmental stresses or the vulnerability of constitution and personality that combine to produce those symptoms. A schizophrenic illness (involving a specific alteration of thinking, feelings, and relatedness to the environment) may respond dramatically to treatment with a specific drug, but the underlying pathological mechanisms and vulnerabilities of schizophrenia remain. The anxiety of a neurotic patient (whose neurotic behavior is conflictually and unconsciously motivated, thus relatively inflexible and often maladaptive) may disappear in response to an antianxiety medication, but the predisposition to develop neurotic anxiety persists. The child or adolescent whose psychiatric difficulties relate to dysfunctional family interactions usually, after hospitalization and drugs, returns to the same family.

Drugs have limitations and offer no magical expectations. They are best used as but one component of a broad therapeutic approach. Furthermore, some symptoms are helpful to patients. Anxiety might be useful in alerting some individuals to stressful situations. Not all symptoms should be relieved by medication.

For many individuals symptom relief is essential. Such relief allows them to function in school, with family, and with peers. This functionality often blocks a vicious cycle. The failing student not only lacks self-confidence, but, in time, lacks the skills which justify possessing such self-confidence, thus moving him or her deeper into a pattern of failure. Likewise, a person may develop anxiety in anticipation of rejection by others and thus, develop behaviors (belligerence, shyness, etc.) which cause others to reject the individual.

Characteristics of Drugs

A drug can be defined as any chemical that has a biological action. Certain drugs alter biological functions by reacting generally and nonspecifically with the chemicals of living tissues. Others react with specific cells; these cells are called receptors.

Gradually increasing doses or concentrations of drugs may produce a gradual response or an all-or-none response. With a gradual response, lower concentrations produce minimal effects. As the dose or concentration of the drug increases the effects increase until a plateau is reached; there is a ceiling effect and a ceiling or maximally effective dose. With an all-or-none response there will be no apparent effect with the drug until a specific dose or concentration is reached.

Drugs that are introduced into the body usually have a rather short history; their breakdown or metabolism takes place almost as soon as they are introduced. The body generally contains mechanisms to break down or modify the drug's chemical structure, to make it less active biologically, and/or to excrete the foreign substances by one or more routes. The major organ involved in this biological transformation of drugs is the liver, and that of excretion is the kidney. However, enzymes in the kidney, plasma, lungs, and other tissues may play a role in altering or restricting the function of drugs. The lungs may also serve as an important route of excretion.

Inherent differences among individuals that relate to qualitative and quantitative aspects of biotransformation mechanisms often account for variations in the intensity of drug effects and required dosage. With some, the amount of drug needed does not relate to the severity of illness but to the speed of metabolic breakdown of the drug. Nutritional state, as well as the functional capacity of the liver, kidney, and lungs, also influences this process. These differences make it difficult to predict in advance what dosage of a specific medication is needed; thus, the need to use clinical observation in establishing dosage levels.

The phenomenon of drug tolerance is characterized by a diminished response to the drug on repeated exposure. Thus, as tolerance develops, larger doses are required to produce the same degree of response, if the response is elicitable at all. This tolerance may develop to some drugs because of an increased rate of metabolizing or excreting the drug. At some point a different drug may have to be considered.

Drug Dependency

Some drugs produce a physical dependency. Chronic usage produces a biological (cellular) adaptation to the continued presence of the drug. When the chronic use of the drug is abruptly stopped, there is a gradual development of hyperactivity in functions that were initially depressed by the drug.

Some individuals become so psychologically dependent on the effects of the drugs or on the placebo effect that stoppage of the drug produces anxiety and possibly an increase in the symptoms initially relieved by the drug. This psychological dependency often leads to chronic usage or abuse of drugs.

Terminology of Drugs

The tranquilizers are drugs that, in appropriate dosage, alleviate states of abnormal tension, agitation, motor activity, sensory distractibility, or emotional excitation, usually without producing sleep or impairment of intellectual (cognitive) functions.

Tranquilizers are usually classified into two groups:

1. The "major tranquilizers," often referred to as the "antipsychotic" drugs or neuroleptics. (Neurolepsis is defined as a state of selectively reduced emotionality and psychomotor activity.)
2. The "minor tranquilizers," often referred to as the "antianxiety" drugs.

In addition to these two groups of tranquilizers, several other groups of drugs will be discussed:

1. The "affect-disorder" drugs. There are two types, the antidepressants and the mood-stabilizers.
2. The "psychostimulant" drugs, used for physiologically based hyperactivity and distractibility.
3. The "antiseizure" drugs, used in the epilepsies.
4. The "specific symptom-related" drugs, used for tics, enuresis, nightmares.

To summarize:

Drug Category	Target Symptom
Major tranquilizers (antipsychotic drugs)	Decrease psychotic thought processes
Minor tranquilizers (antianxiety drugs)	Decrease anxiety
Affect-disorder drugs 1. Antidepressants 2. Mood stabilizers	1. Decrease depression 2. Stabilize mood shifts

Drug Category	Target Symptom
Psychostimulant drugs	Decrease physiologically based hyperactivity or distractibility
Antiseizure drugs	Control specific seizure disorders
Specific symptom-related drugs	Minimize or control specific symptoms (tics, enuresis, nightmares)

THE MAJOR TRANQUILIZERS

The primary group of major tranquilizers or antipsychotic drugs is the phenothiazines. Thorazine (chlorpromazine), introduced in 1952, was the first phenothiazine used in psychiatric treatment and remains the one most commonly prescribed drug. After they were introduced the phenothiazines were tried on all psychiatric disorders. Claims were made stating benefit with retarded and psychotic as well as with hyperactive and impulsive individuals.

Later studies showed that these drugs had a deleterious effect on learning and cognitive functions. They are now recommended for only the most disturbed children and adolescents.

These drugs reduce psychotic anxiety and agitation and also alleviate a wide range of schizophrenic symptoms and behaviors, including thought disturbances, delusions, hallucinations, apathy, and deterioration in self-care.

As mentioned, Thorazine (chlorpromazine) is the most frequently used phenothiazine. Mellaril (thioridazine) and Stelazine (trifluroperazine) are also often used. No clear relationship is yet known between a form of psychosis and clinical benefit from a specific drug. In general, Thorazine and Mellaril are used with agitated and Stelazine with withdrawn children and adolescents.

Treatment is started with low dosages and gradually increased. Two to 4 weeks might be needed to establish benefit. Initially these drugs have a sedative as well as antipsychotic effect. Most will develop a tolerance to this sedative effect in several weeks.

These drugs come in different strengths and forms:

Drug	How Supplied
Thorazine	10, 25, 50, 100, 200 mg tablets, syrup, liquid concentrate, injectable
Mellaril	10, 15, 25, 50, 100, 150, 200 mg tablets, liquid concentrate
Stelazine	1, 2, 5, 10 mg tablets, liquid concentrate

Minor side effects are not uncommon with the phenothiazines. Drowsiness, as noted earlier, often decreases after several weeks. Low blood pressure can occur. The individual might experience light-headedness and dizziness when standing quickly (referred to as post-ural hypotension) or might experience fainting. Heart palpitations, nasal stuffiness, dry mouth, and constipation are also seen. An increase in appetite migh lead to weight gain.

Fewer than 3% of children and adolescents on the phenothiazines will show major side effects. Because there is a possibility of such side effects, all children and adolescent on these drugs must be followed by a physician. Any other professional working with the patient needs to be aware of these possible side effects so that he or she can alert the physician. These more serious side effects usually stop once the dosage is decreased or the drug is stopped. If the drug and dosage is beneficial, the medication may be continued and another drug added to minimize or control the side effects.

The major side effects can best be described by the body system affected. Extrapyramidal side effects are noted when the basal ganglia of the brain are affected, the individual developing symptoms as those found in Parkinsonism. These "parkinsonian" behaviors might include decreased muscle activity (hypokinesis), rigidity of specific muscle groups, a masklike facial expression (caused by hypokinesis of facial muscles), tremors, and a shuffling gait. Some may have a loss of speech or difficulty with swallowing. Others may show involuntary muscle movement of the lips, mouth, tongue, fingers, or trunk. Ataxia (difficulty in maintaining body balance) might result in a stumbling, drunken gait. These extrapyramidal side effects can be controlled by the use of specific drugs. Autonomic nervous system side effects are mentioned earlier and include postural hypotension, dry mouth, constipation, and urinary retention. Jaundice might be produced because of an obstruction in the liver caused by a decrease in the flow of bile. Allergic skin rashes and sensitivity to sunlight can occur. A decrease in the production of specific blood cells (agranulocytosis) can be a serious side effect.

Despite this imposing list of side effects, the phenothiazines are considered a safe group of drugs. They relieve symptoms. There is no physical or psychological dependency. The side effects usually can be reversed by stopping the drug or lowering the dose or can be controlled by the addition of another drug. The toxicity level is low; it is almost impossible to kill oneself by taking an overdose of these drugs.

Another major tranquilizer is Serpasil (reserpine). It is not used much at this time. Haldol (haloperidol) is also used; it is discussed later in the chapter.

THE MINOR TRANQUILIZERS

These antianxiety drugs are more likely to be used with out-patient children and adolescents who have symptoms suggestive of anxiety. These symptoms may include school phobia, stomachaches, anxiety attacks, and tics or may be reflected in specific neurotic symptoms such as depression, obsessive thinking, or compulsive behavior. They are of little or no value in treating the psychoses. In addition to their ability to lower anxiety, these drugs are effective as muscle relaxants and may be used to relieve muscle tension and mild spasticities.

There is concern with using antianxiety drugs throughout the day. Anxiety need not be a negative symptom. It may be a signal to the child or adolescent that something is stressful, allowing him or her to withdraw from the situation or to mobilize psychological defenses. If medication raises the anxiety threshold the child may be less motivated to work on problems or may not be aware of stress until overwhelmed. One useful approach when such medication is needed to help the individual function is to inform the child or adolescent that he or she can take one pill every 4 hours if nervous; but, once the pill is taken, he or she must write down what may have caused the tension. Such material is then discussed in psychotherapy.

Librium (chlordiazepoxide), Valium (diasepam), Miltown (meprobamate), Atarax, and Vistaril (both are hydroxyzine) are the most frequently used minor tranquilizers.

Drug	How Supplied
Librium	5, 10, 25 mg capsules, injectable
Valium	2, 5, 10 mg tablets
Miltown	200, 400 mg tablets
Atarax	10, 20, 50, 100 mg tablets, syrup
Vistaril	25, 50, 100 mg capsules, oral suspension, injectable

Side Effects

These drugs do not produce extrapyramidal side effects; autonomic nervous system symptoms are uncommon. Occasional allergic skin rashes, nausea, and blood difficulties occur. However, drowsiness, ataxia, and impairment of visual–motor performance are not uncommon and require adjustment of dosage. Mental confusion or agitation might be noted. Unlike the major tranquilizers, all in this group can produce physical and/or psychological dependency and withdrawal reactions. They are more toxic than the major tranquilizers and an overdosage can be serious.

THE AFFECT-DISORDER DRUGS

The Antidepressants

There are many reasons for depression. Depression might be a secondary symptom of another illness or the major reflection of a neurotic or psychotic depressive process. Psychotherapy is often used to treat depression. Electroconvulsive therapy (ECT) is used with adults but only rarely with adolescents and almost never with children. The antidepressive drugs are rarely used with children and seldom used with adolescents.

A common self-medication for depression with adolescents is alcohol. It initially induces an excitant or euphoric phase. This is soon followed by a more prolonged depressant phase, often associated with amnesia. For some, alcohol provides at least temporary relief during the excitation state or through forgetting or drinking into oblivion the pain of depressive affective experience. For the same reason, such narcotics as heroin, morphine, codeine, and demerol could be considered to function like an antidepressant.

The antidepressive medications include a group of tricyclic drugs such as Tofranil (imipramine) and the amphetamines, such as Dexadrine (dextroamphetamine). Each of these drugs is discussed later.

The Mood-Stabilizers

Some individuals have mood swings, moving from manic or depressive states back to normal (called unipolar illnesses) or cycle from manic to normal to depressive to normal, etc. (called bipolar illnesses). Such manic–depressive conditions are rare in children and uncommon in adolescents. Lithium carbonate might be considered for these adolescents. The serum level of lithium needed for clinical effectiveness is close to the toxic level; thus, frequent monitoring of blood serum levels is needed. Side effects might include drowsiness, muscle involvement (weakness, twitching, tremors, slurred speech), gastrointestinal involvement (nausea, vomiting, diarrhea, abdominal pain), thirst, and frequent urination.

THE ANTISEIZURE DISORDER DRUGS

Epilepsy is a collective term for a group of chronic convulsive disorders. The clinical picture usually consists of brief episodes (seizures) associated with a loss of disturbance or consciousness, usually but not always associated with characteristic body movements (convulsions) and sometimes with increased autonomic activity. There are three common forms of epilepsy seen with children and adolescents.

Grand mal epilepsy is manifested by major convulsions, usually of a tonic–clonic nature; that is, a sequence of maximal spasms of all body musculature (tonic activity) followed by a synchronous jerking of muscles (clonic activity). This tonic–clonic episode is followed by a postseizure depression of all central nervous system functions. The individual is lethargic, confused, and disoriented. During the seizure he or she might lose bladder or bowel control. Many individuals experience a brief unique sensory response, an aura, prior to the seizure.

Petit mal epilepsy is characterized by brief attacks in which there is a loss of consciousness often associated with some symmetrical clonic motor activity varying from eyelid blinking to jerking of the entire body. Often there is no motor activity component, the only observable symptom being the brief loss of consciousness. Once the episode ends the individual is alert and has no amnesia, except probably for the time of the seizure.

Psychomotor epilepsy is characterized by attacks of confused behavior which can present in a wide variety of clinical manifestations. The patient is confused and disoriented after the episode.

Thus, in *grand mal* epilepsy the patient loses consciousness and exhibits a characteristic tonic–clonic seizure; after the episode he or she is disoriented. With *petit mal* and psychomotor epilepsy there is a brief loss of awareness or consciousness with no tonic–clonic episode. After a *petit mal* seizure the individual usually will be alert and clear; after a psychomotor seizure he or she will be confused and disoriented.

Another less common form of seizure is focal cortical epilepsy characterized by convulsions confined to single limbs or muscle groups (often called Jacksonian motor epilepsy) or to specific and localized sensory disturbances (called Jacksonian sensory epilepsy).

There are several drugs used in the treatment of epilepsy. The goal of medication is suppression of seizures at a dosage level that does not cause sedation or undesirable central nervous system toxicity. With some children and adolescents the physician is continuously struggling between controlling the seizures but having a sedated or toxic patient and lowering the dosage, resulting in a more alert, available patient but one who again has seizures.

There are four groups of drugs most commonly used, the barbituric acid derivatives, the hydantoin derivatives, the succinimide derivatives, and the oxazolidine derivatives. The barbituric acid and hydantoin derivatives are used for *grand mal* and *psychomotor* seizures; the succinimide and oxazolidine derivatives are primarily used for *petit mal* seizures.

Drug Information

Drug	How Supplied
1. Barbituric acid derivatives	
Phenobarbital	16, 32, 64, 100 mg tablets
Mebaral (mephobarbital)	32, 100, 200 mg tablets
Mysolin (primidone)	50, 250 mg tablets
2. Hydantoin derivatives	
Dilantin (diphenylhydantoin)	30, 100 mg capsules chewable infant tablets, suspension, injectable
Mysantoin (mephenytoin)	100 mg tablets
3. Succinimide derivatives	
Zarontin (ethosuximide)	250 mg capsules
Milontin (phensuximide)	250, 500 mg capsules, suspension
Celontin (methsuximide)	150, 300 mg capsules
4. Oxazolidine derivatives	
Tridione (trimethadione)	300 mg capsule, 150 mg tablet
Paradione (paramethadione)	150, 300 mg capsules

Side Effects

As noted earlier side effects are not uncommon; individuals on these medications therefore need careful monitoring. It should also be remembered that the barbiturates (e.g., phenobarbital) are central nervous system sedatives and thus neutralize some of the central nervous stimulation effect of the psychostimulants. For example, a hyperactive child on a psychostimulant (to be discussed later) may need a higher dosage if also on a barbituate.

COMMON SIDE EFFECTS

Drug	Side Effects
1. Barbituric Acid Derivatives Phenobarbital	Drowsiness, irritable behavior, skin rash, possibly delirium, high fever
Melbaral	Drowsiness, skin rash
Mysoline	Nausea, vomiting, drowsiness, irritability, ataxia, dizziness, skin rash, anemia
2. Hydatoin Derivatives Dilantin	Nausea, vomiting, nervousness, skin rash, enlarged gums, nystagmus (involuntary eye movement), double vision, ataxia, increased hair growth (especially arms), plus rarely may find enlarged lymph glands, hepatitis, anemias
Mesantoin	Skin rash, drowsiness, ataxia, enlarged lymph glands, hepatitis, anemia
3. Succinonide Derivatives Zarontin	Headache, dizziness, nausea, rash, drowsiness, occasionally find leukemia-like picture, decreased kidney or liver function
Milontin	Drowsiness, nausea, vomiting, dizziness, ataxia, skin rash, dreamlike states
Celontin	Drowsiness, ataxia, vomiting, skin rash, double vision, dizziness, redness around the eye orbit, anemias, psychotic-like behavior
4. Oxazolidine Derivatives Tridione	Skin rash, sensitivity to light, nausea, drowsiness, loss of hair, anemias, decreased kidney and liver functioning
Paradione	Skin rash, sensitivity to light, nausea, drowsiness, anemia decreased kidney and liver functioning

THE SPECIAL SYMPTOM DRUGS

Tics.

The antianxiety drugs may be used with muscle tics. If this is unsuccessful, Haldol (haloperidol) may be tried. Haldol is also used in the Gilles de la Tourette syndrome, a central nervous system disorder characterized by multiple tics associated with a grunting sound in the throat or the shouting of profanity. Haldol is available in 0.5, 1, 2, 5, and 10 mg tablets and for intramuscular injections. Side effects include Parkinsonian-like symptoms, muscular restlessness, muscle spasm or weakness, eye muscle spasm (referred to as oculogyric crisis), insomnia, restlessness, agitation, drowsiness, and depression.

Enuresis.

This is usually defined as bedwetting after the age of 4 or 5. Once all medical reasons for the bedwetting have been ruled out medication may be tried. Such medication appears to increase the bladder capacity. More importantly, it controls the level of sleep so that the child does not move into deep sleep. Tofranil (impiramine) is most often tried. It is available in 10, 25, and 50 mg tablets. The medication is given at bedtime and increased in dosage until the symptom stops. Once this point is reached, the individual is maintained on the medication for 30 days or more. Often, once stopped the enuresis does not return. If it does, another 30 day trial can be used. Side effects are not common but can include hypotension, palpitation, confusion, disorientation, numbness or tingling of extremities, dry mouth, and skin rash.

Nightmares.

These are symptoms of psychological stress and need to be clinically addressed as such. At times symptomatic relief from nightmares is needed. Mellaril (thioridazine) at bedtime can block out that stage of sleep where dreaming occurs (REM sleep), thus stopping the dreams.

THE PSYCHOSTIMULANT DRUGS

Children and adolescents diagnosed as hyperactive or having minimal brain dysfunction are so common today that this syndrome and the use of these drugs will be discussed in greater detail.

The Minimal Brain Dysfunction Syndrome

Definition.

Throughout this century physicians, educators, psychologists, and other professionals have increasingly focused their attention upon those children who appear to have difficulty learning because of the way their nervous system performs. As each aspect of their problems was studied, and as each professional group viewed these children within the context of their own discipline, different descriptions and diagnostic labels were developed. Even now, the multiple approaches to viewing these children and the many diagnostic labels in use pose major problems in reviewing the literature or in understanding the data or claims about different treatment efforts or follow-up studies. Some professionals view the child with specific learning disabilities as a unique clinical entity; others focus on the child with hyperactivity as a separate clinical picture. It appears most likely that these cases do not comprise a single clinical condition but that there is a cluster of findings often found together; that is, these children fit into a common syndrome.

Because no consensus on the clinical picture and the diagnostic label has yet been reached, different professionals often use different labels. A brief review of the history of this syndrome may clarify some of the confusion.

In the 1940s Alfred Strauss, a psychiatrist, and Heinz Werner, a psychologist, studied brain-injured children, (Werner & Strauss, 1941). They sought to account for divergent patterns of functioning in a population of mentally defective children. Based on their background histories, they classified these children into two categories, those that did and those that did not have extrinsic damage to the nervous system. When they compared the cognitive and emotional behaviors of the two groups they found that there was considerable overlap. Despite this, however, the group with a history of perinatal or later childhood nervous system damage contained a larger proportion of hyperactive, emotionally labile, perceptually disordered, impulsive, distractible, and abnormally rigid and perseverative children than did the group with no such history. It was to the cases with these peculiar patternings of behavioral organization that the term "brain damaged" or "brain injured" came to be applied, and with it came the concept of "the brain-damaged child." Because most of these children showed no overt evidence of the major forms of brain damage, they were labeled "minimal brain damage." Subsequent studies gave little support to the view that these children have tissue damage; nonetheless this label remains popular.

Later, as increasing numbers of these children were recognized and evaluated, evidence was found to suggest subtle functional disturbances of the central nervous system rather than definite brain damage. The emphasis then shifted from brain damage to the possibility of some form of dysfunction (Clements, 1966) or immaturity (Abrams, 1968) of the central nervous system. Because the primary area of learning was considered to be the cerebral cortex, another diagnostic label was "minimal cerebral dysfunction." Others referred to these children as cases of "minimal brain dysfunction." Clements (1966), in his monograph on terminology, recommended the term "minimal brain dysfunction syndrome," emphasizing that these children had combinations of learning disabilities, emotional problems, and difficulty with attention and impulsivity.

Many other investigators entered the field. Each began to observe these children, to study them, and to conceptualize their observations and diagnostic formulations in terms of their specific discipline (Silver, 1975). Thus, the child with difficulty in reading had "Dyslexia"; with difficulty in math or calculations, "dyscalcula"; with written language or graphics problems, "dysgraphia." Children with language and auditory disabilities were called cases of congenital aphasia. Children who were distractible were referred to as "distractibility" or "attentional deficit syndrom"; and children who were noted to be hyperactive were called "hyperactive" or "hyperkinetic" children. In the education literature these are often referred to as children with learning disabilities or specific learning disabilities.

In the medical literature the term "minimal brain dysfunction" (or MBD for short) is most common. The term "minimal brain dysfunction syndrome" is preferred, for, this term reflects the multiplicity of the clinical picture. These children may have multiple patterns of dysfunctional behavior. However, they all present similar groups of findings and thus fit into the same syndrome. The theme common to them all is the presence of one or more types of specific learning disabilities. In addition many (about 40%) show other evidence of altered central nervous system functioning. Hyperactivity and/or distractibility with a short attention span are the commonest findings. Some of these children are perseverative. Because of the frustrations and failures they experience, many develop secondary emotional problems. Thus, the minimal brain dysfunction syndrome consists of:

Primary finding: One or more areas of specific learning disability.

Secondary finding: Hyperactivity and/or distractibility with a short attention span (approximately 40%).

Tertiary finding: Many develop secondary emotional problems.

As is true in other syndromes, the clinical picture with these children is not homogeneous. The common factor is that most if not all cases have one or more specific types of learning disabilities; each child presenting with a different profile of learning strengths and disabilities. Of this whole group, about 40% are either hyperactive, or distractible, or hyperactive and distractible; but by the same token, about 60% are not. Most are brought to the clinician with evidence of social and/or emotional difficulties; some few may not show this difficulty.

The major focus in this chapter is on the hyperactivity and distractibility. However, as is discussed later, all aspects of this syndrome must be considered in planning a treatment approach.

Hyperactivity–Distractibility.

Hyperactivity. These children's increased motor activity is physiologically based; it is not an anxiety-based motor response. This is an important differentiation to make. With the child who utilizes an increase in motor activity as a means of coping with anxiety, the behavior usually relates to a specific life-space experience. The history will suggest that the hyperactivity began during the first grade or that it happens only in school but not at home. With physiologically based hyperactivity, there is usually a history of such activity since birth. In some cases, the parent might even report that the child kicked more *in utero* prior to birth. He or she squirmed in his mother's arms, rolled in his crib, ran before he walked, was in almost constant motion since birth. This motor hyperactivity does not relate to any specific events; it certainly is not limited to school hours; it occurs all the time and any place.

Distractibility. Some children with this syndrome have difficulty filtering sensory inputs; therefore, most or all inputs reach the cortex and compete for full attention. For some children, the distractibility relates more to visual inputs; for others, auditory inputs; and for some, both. The child with this disability may try to attend and work, but other visual and/or auditory inputs continue to distract. With each distraction, there is the need to reattend; thus, they have a short attention span.

The distractibility caused by external stimuli appears to be clinically different from a type of internal distractibility in which some children have difficulty inhibiting (dysinhibiting) their thoughts. They are distracted because their internal thoughts are competing for their attention. It is helpful to distinguish between distractibility and dysinhibition as a cause for the clinical behavior. The former, as is discussed later, often improves with the use of psychostimulants; the latter may best respond to a major tranquilizer.

All children with learning disabilities are not hyperactive and/or distractible; however, most children who are hyperactive and/or distractible have learning disabilities. It is important to note that the psychostimulants improve only the hyperactivity and/or distractibility. They do not correct or improve the specific learning disabilities; they only make the child more available for learning. It is therefore important to have an educational evaluation done on children who respond positively to such medication. To make a child less active or distractible helps; but the learning disabilities still exist and the child still needs special educational therapy.

It is also important to differentiate between physiologically based hyperactivity and increased motor activity caused by anxiety. The former often responds to the pyschostimulants; the latter may respond to a minor tranquilizer but not to a psychostimulant. A child whose aggressive or agitated behavior reflects an underlying depression may also respond to the mood lifting property of a psychostimulant with an improvement in behavior. Here, too, the history and description of the behavior offer clues in the differential diagnosis. For reasons not yet understood, the physiologically based hyperactivity and/or distractibility may disappear with puberty; children who have been on medication throughout latency may no longer need such medication after age 13–14. This is not always true, though. Clinical observations suggest that as many as 20% of these individuals need this medication throughout adolescence and into young adulthood.

The Psychostimulants.

Children with physiologically based hyperactivity or distractibility usually respond to the psychostimulants with a decrease in motor activity and an increase in attention span.

Bradley (1937) first described the paradoxical effect of Benzedrine, a psychostimulant drug, on these children. Since Bradley's work numerous papers have reported on the value of such psychostimulants as Dexadrine (detroamphetamine) and Ritalin (methylphenidate). Other psychostimulants, such as caffeine, will also be effective. Cylert (pemoline) has recently begun to be used.

The reason for the paradoxical effect of such stimulants is still unclear. One theory is that the area of the brain stem responsible for regulating specific inputs and outputs of the brain (the ascending reticular activating system) is immature or dysfunctional in these children. Thus, the sensory input screening processes are not effective and all stimuli pass through to the cortex, resulting in distractibility and a short attention span. At the same time, the motor output inhibitory processes are not effective, resulting in the motor hyperactivity. The neurochemical site of function for the psychostimulants is in the ascending reticular activating system. It is felt that such medication stimulates or "strengthens" this dysfunctional area, thus improving the sensory input screening and the motor output inhibiting processes; the result is a decrease in motor behavior and in distractibility. The psychodepressants sedate this area of the brain, acting to increase its dysfunctionality, resulting in a higher level of hyperactivity and distractibility.

Another theory suggests that the neocortex is hyposensitive and thus requires increased bombardment with stimuli in order to respond. Current neurophysiological and pharmacological data support the former dysinhibition theory.

Dexadrine (dextroamphetamine) is available as an elixir, in 5 and 10 mg tablets, and in 5, 10 and 15 mg long-acting "Spansules." The elixir may be less effective than the tablets, perhaps because alcohol is used to create the solution and it acts as a central nervous system depressant, thus counteracting some of the effect of the stimulant. A combination of dextroamphetamine and amobarbital, Dexamyl, is less effective than dextroamphetamine alone; again, the barbituate (a sedative) counteracts some of the effects of the stimulant. Once a dosage for dextroamphetamine has been established, the 12 hour timed-release spansules may be considered. If a child needs 5 mg three times a day, one 15 mg timed-release capsule in the morning may be substituted. This approach eliminates the problem of supervising the noon dose for the child in school. In addition, the even discharge of medication sometimes decreases the up-and-down shifts in the effectiveness of the tablets. As with the other psychostimulants the amount of drug needed and the frequency of dosage appears to relate to the individual differences in metabolizing and excreting the drug, not to the severity of the disability. When a daily dosage of 40 mg or more is needed it is useful to rethink the diagnosis or to consider an alternative medication.

Ritalin (methylphenidate) is available in 5, 10, and 20 mg tablets. Up to 20 mg four times a day can be used. As with dextroamphetamine, the possibility of a different drug should be considered when more is needed. Over a period of years tolerance may develop and some children may need to be shifted from one drug to another.

Cylert (pemoline) is a new drug for use with these children. It is a mild central nervous system stimulant structurally different from the amphetamines and methylphenidate. Cylert has a gradual onset of action; unlike the other psychostimulants its effects may not be noted until the third or fourth week of therapy. One advantage of pemoline is that it is long acting; one morning dose covers the day. It comes in 18.75, 37.5, and 75 mg tablets. It is also available as a 37.5 mg chewable tablet. The initial dose is 37.5 mg in the morning. Increases can be at 18.5 mg per week until clinical improvement is noted. The maximum recommended daily dose is 112.5 mg.

If none of the psychostimulants has been successful, it is helpful to determine whether the medication is being given as prescribed, whether the child is truly taking the medication, whether the hyperactivity is anxiety based rather than physiologically based, or whether the family or school situation is so stressful that the medication may be improving the physiologically based hyperactivity but not lowering the anxiety level.

It must be emphasized that the hyperactivity and/or distractibility are not only educational disabilities; they are life disabilities. Such behaviors interfere with family and peer activities. If a child responds positively to such medication, therefore, he or she should be on medication all day everyday, not just during school hours. It is just as important for a child to sit calmly and attend at the dinner table or while playing with a friend as it is to function in class. This is an important point, for many physicians still feel that the child should be on medication only during school hours. This model leaves the child off of medication during afterschool and evening hours, weekends, and summers. The hyperactive and/or distractible child who responds positively to medication needs the medication to help function better during all hours; not just during school hours. It is not fair to keep him or her off of medication during times when he or she must relax, relate, and function, such as at dinner with the family, watching television with his siblings, or at a Cub Scout meeting or Sunday school.

Parents need to be educated about the effects and duration of the medication. Dextroamphetamine and Methyphenidate work for about 4 hours with minimal or no residual effects. Knowing this, a parent can add or subtract from the usual dosage pattern to fit the activity. The child may be scheduled to take his or her last pill in the middle of the afternoon; however, if company is coming or if a Scout meeting or other activity is planned, he or she may need more medication for the last dose or an extra dose at 6:00 or 7:00 p.m. Parents should understand this concept and be given permission to alter specific dosage patterns.

The most common side effects are insomnia and anorexia (loss of appetite). In addition, the psychostimulants may produce palpitations, an increase in heart rate, elevated blood pressure, or emotional lability. The insomnia and loss of appetite often disappear after 2–3 weeks. If these symptoms persist they can often be managed by altering the dosage or time of dosage. If the anorexia persists and weight loss ensues, the drug may have to be discontinued. It is the loss of weight that is the critical issue, not the loss of appetite. The medication decreases the child's appetite so that he or she may become more selective about what he or she eats. Thus, a given child may not eat his or her meals but will eat candy and other snacks. Controlling snacks might result in better meal intakes.

Some children will have difficulty falling asleep while on these drugs and may lie in bed restlessly for 3 to 4 hours. Like anorexia, this insomnia may disappear during the first month. With some children, the sleeplessness is a legitimate result of the psychostimulant and it becomes necessary to discontinue the mid- or late-afternoon dose. With other children, the sleeplessness is caused not by the medication but by the rebound effect of being off of the medication. That is, a child on a three times a day schedule is under the effect of the medication from morning until about 4 hours after the last dose. When the medication wears off, at 8:00 or 9:00 p.m., the child rebounds to his usual level of activity or higher. The result is increased hyperactivity and restlessness at bedtime. He or she is put to bed at 9:00 or 9:30 but cannot unwind. For this child, an additional dose of the stimulant at about 8:00 p.m. may eliminate his or her difficulty with sleep. Stopping the afternoon dose helps in some cases; adding a bedtime dose helps in others. The two possible causes for insomnia are difficult to differentiate and often a trial dose at bedtime is necessary to clarify the issue.

Parents may report that their child is clinically improved on the medication but that he or she now talks constantly or breaks into tears or explodes at the slightest frustration. It is not clear how much of this emotional lability is a result of the medication and how much is functional. Because the medication lessens the motor activity, the child may be better able to interact and communicate; thus, a quiet child might become more verbal. It is also possible that, because the medication allows the child to sit still and be available for learning, he or she may be forced to deal with his or her learning problems and thus becomes frustrated and more anxious. The increased anxiety could explain an increase in verbiage or in emotional lability. If reassurance to the parents and special educational help for the child do not minimize the emotional lability, the drug dosage may be decreased. If this does not help, stopping the medication or changing to another type may have to be considered.

In addition to the psychostimulants, major tranquilizers such as the phenothiazines have been used to decrease hyperactivity. They seem to work best with children whose thinking is dysinhibited or disorganized or who display psychotic features. With children having this syndrome, any decrease in their hyperactivity on such medication might be the result of drowsiness or of extrapyramidal signs rather than a true physiological shift toward normal activity levels.

Minor tranquilizers have been tried. These medications work best for the child with anxiety-based hyperactivity but do not help those with the neurologically based symptom picture. The tricyclic antidepressants, especially Imipramine, have been shown to be effective. With some children, such anticonvulsants as Dilantin, Primidone, and Mysoline have been reported to lessen the behavioral difficulties; however, no studies show in a clear way just how effective these drugs are for children with this syndrome. Lithium carbonate has been tried and found to be ineffective in handling the hyperactivity or the distractibility.

Controversial Therapies.

Many of the treatment approaches that have been advanced to help children and adolescents with this syndrome are, to say the least, controversial (Silver, 1975). One group of such efforts relates to the concept of neurophysiological retraining. The basic premise is that by stimulating specific sensory inputs or exercising specific motor patterns one can retrain, recircuit, or in some way improve the functioning of a part of the central nervous system. Three such approaches are in use today: (1) patterning, as developed by Doman and Delacato; (2) optometric therapy; and (3) the sensory-integrative therapy described by A. Jean Ayres.

Patterning. The "patterning" theory and technique was initially developed by Robert Doman and Carl Delacato (1968), following the principle that ontogeny recapitulates phylogeny. They postulated that failure to pass properly through a certain sequence of developmental stages in modality, language, and competence in the manual, visual, auditory, and tactile areas reflected poor neurological organization and may indicate brain damage ("A Summary of Concepts, Procedure and Organizations," 1968). As described by Doman and Delacato patterning reaches ". . . the brain itself by pouring into the afferent sensory system . . . all of the stimuli normally provided by his environment but with such intensity and frequency as to draw, ultimately a response from the corresponding motor systems" ("A Summary of Concepts . . . ," 1968). In the more severe cases of brain damage, patterns of passive movement are imposed with the goal of producing normal activities that would have been the product of the injured brain level had it not been injured (Doman et al., 1960). In addition to the above methods of manipulation, other techniques used include sensory stimulation, rebreathing of expired air with a plastic face mask (alleged to increase vital capacity and to stimulate cerebral blood flow), and restriction of fluid, salt, and sugar intake (alleged to decrease cerebrospinal fluid production and cortical irritability). The American Academy of Pediatrics, the American Academy of Cerebral Palsy, the United Cerebral Palsy Association of Texas, and the Canadian Association for Retarded Children have published statements expressing concern about the effectiveness of this form of therapy (Silver, 1975).

Optometric Therapy. There are two general views held by optometrists on the roles they should play with children who have learning problems. Most optometrists evaluate the child's visual abilities and may prescribe lenses or the use of conventional visual training or orthoptic techniques, if indicated. There is, however, a particular group of optometrists who use a developmental vision approach and who see a broader role for the optometrist in learning problems (Carlson & Greenspoon, 1968). This group feels that learning in general and reading in particular are primarily tasks in visual perception. They point out that visual perceptual processes are also related to the child's sensory–motor coordination and employ a wide diversity of educational and sensory–motor–perceptual training techniques in an attempt to correct educational problems in children.

It is the second group of optometrists who have been active with children with learning disabilities. The American Academy of Pediatrics, the American Academy of Ophthalmology and Otolaryngology, and the American Association of Ophthalmology issued a joint organizational statement critical of this approach (1972). This joint communique emphasizes the need for a multidisciplinary approach to such children. It cautions that there are no peripheral eye defects that can produce dyslexia and associated learning disabilities. It minimizes the effect of visual or neurological organizational training as used by optometrists. It states that glasses have no value in treating learning problems except where there is a refracting problem. It concludes that the treatment of learning disabilities is primarily for the special educator. This controversy between ophthalmologists and optometrists often catches the parents in the middle as they try to decide what is best for their child.

Sensory Integrative Therapy. A. Jean Ayres feels that the capacity of the neocortex to react to auditory and visual processes is dependent on the brain stem's ability to organize auditory and visual processes; thus, if the brain stem is inadequate to organize such sensory integrative processes the individual may have learning disabilities (Ayres, 1965, 1969). Her research data suggest that there are disorders which are consistently observed in learning disability children. These problems can be accounted for in terms of inadequate sensory integration in the brain stem. These include immature postural reactions, poor extracurricular muscle control, poorly developed visual orientation to environmental space, difficulty in the processing of sound into percepts, and a tendency toward distractibility (Ayres, 1969).

She proposes that carefully controlled sensory input can be introduced through vestibular and somatosensory systems. Such graded stimulation enhances the capacity of the brain for intersensory integration. This allows for improved interconnections between these sensory modalities and the visual and auditory inputs (Ayres, 1972a). She further hypothesizes (1972a) that the normalization of postural mechanisms organized in the midbrain would enable better cortical interhemispheral communication, upon which reading must in fact be dependent. In the models of therapy based on these concepts vestibular stimulation is seen as improving auditory processes, thus helping with the auditory–language disorders of learning disability children (Ayres, 1972b). This vestibular stimulation might also improve visual perceptual functioning via the intersensory effect of multisensory or convergent neurons and nuclei (Ayres, 1972b).

Orthomolecular Therapy. A second group of controversial approaches to helping children and adolescents with this syndrome relates to the concept of orthomolecular medicine. Linus Pauling (1968) defines orthomolecular medicine as the treatment of mental disorders by the provision of the optimum molecular environment for the mind, especially the optimum concentrations of substances normally present in the human body. The use of megavitamins, trace elements, and other molecules has been suggested.

Megavitamins. The use of massive doses of vitamins to treat emotional or cognitive disorders began with the treatment of schizophrenia. Osmond and Smythies formulated the hypothesis that schizophrenia was the result of stress-induced anxiety and a failure of metabolism resulting in highly toxic mescaline-type compounds. Hoffer, Osmond, and Smythies (1954) proposed that adrenochrome, a psychotoxic oxidation production of epinephrine, was this mescaline-like substance. Its production was thought to be the result of the increased phenolase (oxidase) activity of schizophrenic serum. Hoffer and Osmond proposed the use of nicotinic acid and nicotinamide in the treatment of schizophrenia (Hoffer & Osmond, 1960). They reasoned that nicotinic acid as a strong methyl group accepter would compete for methyl groups and prevent the conversoin of norephinephrine to epinephrine. Diminution of epinephrine would diminish the quantities of adrenochrome and adrenolutin formed. Initially they used Niacin (nicotinic acid); later they added vitamins C and B6 (pyridoxine) to the treatment regimen.

To date, no biochemical studies on schizophrenic patients have documented Hoffer and Osmond's proposed theory on schizophrenia. A 5-year study carried out by the Board of Directors of the Canadian Mental Health Association (1973) strongly suggests no therapeutic effect from nicotinic acid treatment. The American Psychiatric Association (1973) published a task force report, *Megavitamin and Orthomolecular Therapy in Psychiatry*. After reviewing the history and literature relating to this subject, the members of this Task Force concluded that there was no valid basis for the use of megavitamins in the treatment of mental disorders.

The first paper to suggest megavitamin treatment for children with learning disabilities was written in 1971 by Dr. Allan Cott. His theory is an extension of Hoffer and Osmond's concepts of schizophrenia. The 500 cases used in the study were for the most part autistic and schizophrenic children; they were not children with minimal brain dysfunction. His conclusion that megavitamins can help these children has not been confirmed by others. Despite these negative data, this approach remains popular; Dr. Cott's paper remains the primary reference.

Trace Elements. Trace elements including copper, zinc, magnesium, manganese, and chromium, along with more common elements, such as calcium, potassium, sodium, and iron, are necessary nutrients. Their presence is essential for the maintenance of normal physiologcial function. No one to date has published data supporting the theory that deficiencies in one or more of these elements are causes of this syndrome. Yet, in many parts of the United States children are treated with such replacement therapy. In the paper by Cott (1971), discussed earlier, he spoke of the possibility of such deficiencies. He presented no research data to support this view nor has any subsequent data supported this theory. In particular, there has been no report of observed clinical improvement with such treatment.

Hypoglycemia. Another orthomolecular approach to treating children with this syndrome regards the symptoms as secondary to hypoglycemia. The treatment is therefore to place the child on a hypoglycemia diet. The possible relationship of hypoglycemia to such children was reported in the same paper by Dr. Cott (1971). Again, however, no data was presented to support this view. It is indeed possible for children to suffer from hypoglycemia and to need such a special treatment program. Currently, there is no clinical evidence to show any relationship between hypoglycemia and this syndrome. Before it is concluded that the etiology is hypoglycemia, a full 5–7 hour glucose tolerance study should be done.

Allergic Reactions. Philpott, Mandell, and Von Hilsheimer (1975) suggest that some types of learning disabilities are the result of an allergic sensitivity of the central nervous system to specific foods. They discuss specific test procedures for establishing this possible etiologic factor. To date, the relationship between food allergies and this syndrome is not clear.

Food Additives and Preservatives. A recent publication by Feingold (1975) suggests that certain food additives (artificial coloring and preservatives) in foods and beverages may cause this syndrome. Children are treated by placing them on diets free of such additives. At this time there are insufficient research data to support this view. Work is now in progress to study this hypothesis. It is too early to know the results (Conners, Coyette, Southwick, et al., 1976).

The Total Child.

The child with the Minimal Brain Dysfunction Syndrome illustrates a basic concept pertaining to using medication with children and adolescents. The symptom being treated is usually but one aspect of the total clinical picture. One must see the total child as he or she functions in school, home, and other environments. Any evaluation or intervention approach that does not focus on the total child will be less than successful.

Furthermore, when children and adolescents are worked with, the family must be informed and given an active role in helping. To illustrate this concept, an approach to informing and mobilizing the family of a child diagnosed as having the minimal brain dysfunction syndrome will be described.

Once the evaluation is complete the finding must be shared with all involved. It is best to begin with the parents. They need to understand all aspects of the syndrome and how these problems explain their child's difficulties. They must understand each phase of the treatment approach and collaborate in implementing the program.

They need to understand the learning disabilities and the type of special educational programs needed. By focusing on the needs versus the realities of their specific school district, they learn who to contact, what to request, and how to negotiate with the school system. They need to understand their child's areas of weakness and strength as it relates to the home and neighborhood. They must learn how to maximize success by building on the strengths while helping their child to compensate or avoid areas of weakness. They need to learn to run interference for their child in selecting activities outside of the home.

Once they begin to understand the learning disabilities and their child's specific areas of weakness and strength, the parents need to appreciate that these problems are not just school disabilities, they are life disabilities.

It is difficult to picture any activity in which these disabilities do not interfere with normal performance. At home the child might have problems doing chores, cutting and eating food, dressing, or listening and talking with family members—in short, with all life activities. The same is true with peers. Picture any activity, whether it be baseball, basketball, football, four-square, hopscotch, tag, jump-rope, table games, or just talking with friends and one can see how the learning disabilities interfere with mastery and success. It is not surprising that these children often have social problems and relate poorly to peers.

Follow these children through any aspect of their life—religious school, Cub Scouts, Brownies, Four-H—they do not just have a school disability; they have a life disability.

Special educational programs in school can focus on maximizing the child's strengths while compensating for or correcting the disabilities. With such help the child will make academic progress. However, if help for the learning disabilities stops with school the child continues to have major learning disabilities in other aspects of his or her life.

The parents and whole family must know and understand the child's specific learning disabilities. How can parents appropriately set up experiences and tasks that maximize the possibility of success rather than focusing on weaknesses and failure if they do not know their child's areas of weakness and strength? With such understanding they can select chores that capitalize on the child's strengths instead of expecting nothing from the child or setting up a probable failure. They can improve communication by knowing whether their child receives information best through his or her eyes or ears. Furthermore, with such knowledge the parents can move out into the community and develop potentially positive experiences for their child. If the director of the local Y or youth center knows the child's areas of strength and weakness he or she can help the parents select the appropriate programs. A child with fine motor problems may do poorly in an arts and crafts program requiring fine drawing and cutting but may do well in a photography club where most of the activities require gross motor efforts.

The same approach can lead to success in sports. If a child has fine motor, visual motor, or sequencing difficulty he or she is likely to do poorly in such sports as baseball, basketball, or football. However the same child may do well in sports that require gross motor abilities—swimming, bowling, horseback riding, soccer, hockey, skiing, golf.

The same advanced planning will be useful in other areas. An informed scout leader can assign tasks to the child he or she can do rather than ones that lead to frustrations, failure, dropping out, and another social disaster. A religious school teacher who understands that a child has a demand language disability would understand that he or she should let the child volunteer to speak but not call on him to answer a question. Knowing that the child has good motor skills, he or she may feel free asking him to write something on the blackboard.

If a professional team wants to help the total child, the parents must be as knowledgeable about their child's specific learning disabilities as the special educators. They need counseling in understanding their child's weaknesses and strengths and how to apply this knowledge toward maximizing success and minimizing failures.

If medication is indicated the parents need to understand why and how the medication works. They must understand all aspects of selecting a dosage pattern, length of activity, and side effects. Only then do they become educated, available parents. If the parents are resistive one can plan to delay implementing parts of the program until they can be helped to deal with their resistance.

Next, the focus should be on the social and emotional problems as well as the family's difficulties, trying to relate these to the years of frustration and failure the child and family have experienced. Models of helping are introduced.

Once the parents have begun to comprehend the implications of this syndrome on the total life experiences of their child, the child's school system can be contacted and the collaborative efforts needed both to develop the necessary special educational programs and to establish lines of communication can be started. Such communication is essential in getting observational data on which to base adjustments to the medication pattern.

After the parents understand, the child should be seen. He or she needs help in understanding all aspects of the problems as thoroughly as do the parents. The only variation with age is in the approach and level of language. This insight to their problems is usually received with relief. They now have an answer. They are not bad or stupid or lazy. The full treatment plan is discussed in detail.

Once the child appears to have an initial understanding a family session can be scheduled. Every member of the family needs to know and understand the problems and the treatment plans. The siblings need to know and deserve to have their questions answered. With understanding the child's image and role in the family will begin to shift. The siblings can become allies in helping.

At this point in the interpretive process the parents need help in negotiating with the school and other agencies. Together, medication plans can be worked out. All of this may take three to five sessions. These "preventive family counseling" sessions are designed to help the family understand the information and to encourage them to explore alternative styles of relating and behaving. If needed, modeling or behavioral management skills can be introduced.

With this preventive family counseling approach to the total child and family, 85 to 90% of the children and families relax and make progress. Social, emotional, and family problems fade as the stresses are lessened and as opportunities for positive relationships and successes are increased. For the few children or families who do not improve, individual or family therapy may be needed.

Conclusions.

The child with the minimal brain dysfunction syndrome does not have just a school disability—he or she has a life disability. The same group of learning disabilities that interferes with the normal learning processes also impinges on self-concept, self-image, peer relationships, family relationships, and social interactions. The same hyperactivity or distractibility that affects the child's abilities in the classroom interfere with his or her adaptation to home and neighborhood.

Such a child often does not develop normally or begins to develop secondary social and/or emotional problems and is referred to a mental health clinician for evaluation. At this time it is extremely important to differentiate between emotional problems that reflect the stresses caused by this syndrome and those that are a primary cause of the presenting symptoms.

If the emotional difficulties are secondary to the learning disabilities aspect of this syndrome, psychotherapy alone does not succeed. Indeed, it may add to the child's burden by giving credence to the theme that the academic problems are emotionally based. If special educational programs and appropriate medication are not included along with the psychotherapeutic intervention, it is difficult for the child to overcome the problems.

Properly recognized, diagnosed, and treated, the child with this syndrome has the potential of a reasonably successful future. Without help, the disabilities can become incapacitating and function as a major handicap in all aspects of life.

The confusing feature of this syndrome is the multiple types of clinical pictures such children can present. All aspects of this minimal brain dysfunction syndrome must be considered in understanding the child, planning a treatment program, and advising the family and schools. Any approach that does not see this syndrome as a serious life disability which affects both the total child and his or her family is not likely to be successful.

CONCLUSIONS

Drugs should be used conservatively with children and adolescents. When psychopharmacologic drugs are used, the physician often has to practice an art rather than a science. The proper drug, dosage, and timing of dosage has to be found through knowledgable explorations.

Cooperation and feedback from other professionals working with the individual are essential. To perform this role the nonmedical professional must have basic knowledge of psychopharmacology. The material in this chapter has been prepared in an attempt to provide such knowledge.

REFERENCES

Abrams, A.L. Delayed and irregular maturation versus minimal brain injury. Recommendations for a change in current nomenclature. *Clinical Pediatrics*, 1968, 7, 344–349.

American Academy of Pediatrics. Joint Organizational Statement: The eye and learning disabilities. *Pediatrics*, 1972, 49, 454–455.

APA Task Force on Vitamin Therapy in Psychiatry. *Megavitamin and Orthomolecular Therapy in Psychiatry.* Washington, D.C.: American Psychiatric Association, 1973.

Ayres, A.J. Patterns of perceptual-motor dysfunction in children: A factor analytic study. *Perceptual and Motor Skills*, 1965, 20, 335–368.

Ayres, A.J. "Deficits in sensory integration in educationally handicapped children", *Journal of Learning Disabilities*, 1969, 2, 160–168.

Ayres, A.J. Improving academic scores through sensory integration. *Journal of Learning Disabilities*, 1972, 5, 338–343.

Ayres, A.J. "Sensory integration dysfunction." Paper read before the Ninth International Conference of the Association for Children with Learning Disabilities, Atlantic City, New Jersey, February 1972. (b)

Board of Directors of the Canadian Mental Health Association. Quoted in: Ban, T.A. The niacin controversy: The possibility of negative effects. *Psychiatric Opinion*, 1973, 10, 19–23.

Bradley, C. The behavior of children receiving benzedrine. *American Journal of Psychiatry*, 1937, 94, 577–584.

Carlson, P.V., & Greenspoon, N.K. The uses and abuses of visual training for children with perceptual-motor learning problems. *American Journal of Opthmology,* 1968, *45*, 161–169.

Clements, S. *Minimal brain dysfunction in children.* National Institute of Neurological Diseases and Blindness Monograph No. 3. Washington, D.C., Department of Health, Education, and Welfare, 1966.

Conners, C.K., Coyette, C.H., Southwick, D.A., Lees, J.M. and Andrulunis, P.A. Food Additives and hyperkinesis: A controlled double-blind experiment. *Pediatrics,* August 1976, *58*, 154–166,

Cott, A. Orthomolecular approach to the treatment of learning disabilities. *Schizophrenia,* 1971, *3*, 95–107.

Doman, G., & Delacato, C. Doman–Delacato philosophy. *Human Potential,* 1968, *1*, 113–116.

Doman, R.J. Children with severe brain injuries: Neurological organization in terms of mobility. *Journal of the American Medical Association,* 1960, *17*, 257–261.

Feingold, B.F. *Why Your Child is Hyperactive.* New York: Random House, 1975.

Hoffer, A. & Osmond, H. *The Chemical Bases of Clinical Psychiatry.* Springfield, Ill.: Charles C Thomas, 1960.

Hoffer, A., Osmond, H., & Smythies, J. Schizophrenia: A new approach: II. Results of a year's research. *Journal of Mental Science,* 1954, *100*, 29–54.

Institutes for the Achievement of Human Potential. *A Summary of Concepts, Procedures and Organizations.* Philadelphia: IAHP, 1968.

Pauling, L. Orthomolecular psychiatry. *Science,* 1968, *160*, 265–271.

Philpott, W.H., Mandell, M., & von Hilsheimer, G. Allergic toxic and chemically defective states as causes and/or facilitating factors of emotional reactions, dyslexia, hyperkinesis, and learning problems. In A. Ansara (Ed.), *Selected Papers on Learning Disabilities. Our Challenge: The Right to Know.* Pittsburgh: Association for Children with Learning Disabilities, 1975.

Silver, L.B. Acceptable and controversial approaches to treating the child with learning disabilities. *Pediatrics,* 1975, *55*, 406–415.

Werner, H., & Strauss, A.A. Pathology of figure–background relation in the child. *Journal of Abnormal Social Psychology,* 1941, *36*, 236–248.

SUGGESTED REFERENCES

Farmer, T.W. (Ed.). *Pediatric Neurology,* (2nd ed.) New York: Harper & Row, 1975.

Gittelman-Klein, R. (Ed.). *Recent Advances in Child Psychopharmacology.* Human Sciences Press, New York, 1975.

Goodman, L.S., & Ailman, A. (Eds.). *The Pharmacological Basis of Therapeutics* (4th ed.) New York: MacMillan Co., 1970.

Hollister, L.E. *Clinical Use of Psychotherapeutic Drugs.* Springfield, Ill.: Charles C. Thomas, 1973.

Physicians Desk Reference. Published annually by Medical Econimics Co., Oradell, New Jersey, 07649.

Rech, R.H. & Moore, K.E. (Eds.). *An Introduction to Psychopharmacology.* New York: Raven Press, 1971.

3

DRUGS—CLASSROOM LEARNING FACILITATORS?

JOSEPH N. MURRAY, Ph.D.

There is a definite mystique surrounding the use of pills—both tranquilizers and stimulants—in treating learning and behavior disorders related to youngsters' overactivity. Our society places great emphasis on the curative effects of a pill, perhaps generalizing from the potent effects of wonder drugs and assuming similar effaciousness of pills in treating virtually any disorder, including learning and behavior disorders.

One has to wonder about the so-called "placebo effect," the phenomenon of perceiving that the drug is working even though in actuality it may not be. Perhaps, if we would give youngsters sugar pills we would "see" the same results as we do with Dexedrine, Ritalin, or any of the other behavior management drugs. Some have suggested, with tongue in cheek, that perhaps if we gave youngsters two sugar pills we would see even more impressive results than with one. Is it possible that very large green or black pills or miniscule yellow tablets would be more effective than aspirin-sized pills? Then again, we might increase the potency of our medication by making the pill bitter or, to really have an effect, let's inject a sugar solution directly into the child's veins. This cynical description is given merely to alert the reader to what appears to be a massive, unobjective acceptance of the use of medication for controlling childhood learning and behavior disorders. Despite large-scale subscription to medication, there is little research supporting its effectiveness and, in fact, there appears to be much research suggesting why we should *not* use medication.

In 1968, while working as a school psychologist in Ohio, I learned of a parent who was so impressed with the results of Dexedrine on a neighbor boy that she called her physician, and secured a prescription for her son. The parent had the prescription filled hoping that the pill would do something that she and her husband had been unable to do, control their son's behavior. In 1971 a youngster who had been referred to me (I was working as a school psychologist at the time) was put on 45 mg of Ritalin by a physician because of excessive motor activity. Teachers felt that there was a remarkable change in his behavior following medical intervention. Whether there was or not is not important; what is important is the large number of referrals that I received from the teachers in that particular building following this child's improvement. Each referral suggested that the students were hyperactive and that possible chemotherapeutic intervention might be in order for their particular students.

I mention both of these actual occurrences to illustrate what I have observed over the past 8 or 9 years, that being the tendency to rely heavily on a medical instead of on a behavioral approach in treating children who exhibit certain characteristics of hyperkinesis or hyperactivity. (I do not use hyperkinesis and hyperactivity synonymously and I differentiate them later in the chapter.) Parents and teachers are quite naturally both prone to want to eliminate or lessen overactivity which is disruptive and bothersome and frequently are captivated by the mystique of the pill. It is estimated that over 200,000 youngsters annually in public and private schools throughout the United States are being medicated for the purpose of controlling some behavioral or cognitive disorder (*HEW News*, 1971). All of these children will not be helped by stimulant- or depressant-type pills; in fact, many could be harmed. We are told that somewhere between one-third to one-half of children taking these stimulant drugs show "some degree" of behavioral and/or academic improvement. We are also told that longterm use of dextroamphetamine (Dexedrine) depresses growth in both height and weight. There are many pros and cons to the medication issue and teachers, being more completely and directly involved in the cognitive and behavioral lives of children than any other people, need answers to many questions related to the use of medication.

THE MEDICATION CONCEPT AND THE EDUCATIONAL SYSTEM

There are a number of issues directly related to the involvement of educators in the issuance of medication to youngsters *(Southern California Law Review,* 1973).

1. The educational system is responsible for providing an optimal educational environment in which students can learn. Each child in that system has the right to an equal and adequate education. It is conceivable that medication may be necessary in order for certain children to attain that optimal educational environment and to be given an equal or adequate education. If, in fact, it is deemed necessary for the school system to be involved in the issuance of medication to insure optimal educational environment and an equal and adequate education, then educators will need to familiarize themselves with as many concepts related to medication as possible.

2. What happens if teachers, administrators, or other involved educational personnel insist that a child be medicated in order for that child to attain the so-called optimal educational environment and thus receive an adequate or equal education? Making the use of stimulant drugs a prerequisite to receiving a public education may impair a child's first amendment right to mental autonomy/mind privacy. It is suggested by some that certain stimulant and depressant drugs cause a child to act and react in a way not similar to his or her normal modus operandi and consequently, the child is not his or her real self when taking drugs to control behavior or to improve cognition. Strict interpretation of the first amendment then would suggest that school personnel have no right to make the use of stimulant drugs a prerequisite to a child's educational opportunity. It would represent the child's parents' legal retort to the educational system's insistence of medical intervention.

3. Looking again at the school system's responsibility to educate a youngster showing hyperactive or hyperkinetic characteristics, we see another somewhat unique issue presenting itself to educators. California, like many other states, has expressly provided that special consideration and assistance be given to educationally handicapped children. California Education Code 6871 provides that:

> . . . any school district having an educationally-handicapped minor for whom special education facilities and services . . . are not available or cannot be reasonably provided . . . may, in lieu of establishing and maintaining the needed special education facilities and services at an unreasonable cost to the district, pay to the parent or guardian of such minor toward the tuition of such minor, enrolled in a public or private school . . . offering the special education facilities and services made

necessary by the minor's disabilities, an amount not to exceed the sum
per unit of average daily attendance of the regular state apportionment
to the district . . .

The category of "educationally handicapped" children includes
hyperkinetic children. If a school district does not have facilities to
offer the hyperkinetic child, and if the district is financially obligated
to the parent or guardian of the minor to educate said child, what alternatives does the school sytem have? If there are educational benefits that can be offered to a hyperkinetic child through the use of
medication, is it not conceivable that a board of education may be responsible for actually paying for a minor's pills to control his or her
behavior and to consequently help him or her attain the optimal educational environment? If one chose to interpret the California code to
mean that school districts had a financial obligation to provide helpful
intervention programs or services, then it would appear reasonable to
assume that payment for a child's medication would be made by a
school board. Would this not be insuring his or her right to an equal
or adequate education?

4. A fourth issue related to educator's involvement with the issuance of medication is again related to children's and/or their parents' rights to refuse drug treatment. For example, a child might be
told to undergo chemotherapeutic treatment for his or her hypercon-
dition or to stay out of school because his or her behavior is too disruptive. What recourse do parents have in this instance and what are
the responsibilities of school officials? Using the legal standard known
as the Rational Basis Test, school officials are responsible for demonstrating a reasonable basis for the child's needing medication.
Under the rational basis test, only discrimination which does not rest
upon any reasonable basis, but is essentially arbitrary is unconstitutional and the burden of showing it to be arbitrary is on the one as-
sailing the classification. The burden of demonstrating to the courts
the need for a child taking medication is indeed heavy in that the fac-
tual evidence indicates that classifying children into categories of
hyperkinetic (condition thought to require drug treatment) and
nonhyperkinetic (no drug treatment) is an approximation at best.
There is widespread disagreement among professional child study
personnel regarding the etiology of hyperkinesis and, more importantly, there is disagreement as to how one determines with any degree of validity the existence of a condition of hyperkinesis. With this
amount of uncertainty existing, how can school administrators establish the need for medication by diagnosing specifically an organically
based condition of hyperkinesis?

These are but a few of the major global issues that parents and educators have been forced to consider as increased emphasis has been given to chemotherapy as a treatment for learning and/or behavioral disorders.

MEDICATION TO IMPROVE COGNITION

Much has been written about the use of stimulants and depressants to modify behavior, but little attention has been given to the use of medication to improve children's ability to think and to understand. It does seem to follow logically that if one is able to modify or lessen excess motor behavior in a child and to inhibit responses to a variety of extraneous stimuli, that the child has a better chance to attend to the task at hand and consequently to understand and learn. In 1937, Dr. Charles Bradley reported what he felt were positive effects of Benzedrine (a form of amphetamine) in aiding cognition (Stewart, 1971). Dr. Bradley had prescribed Benzedrine to raise the blood pressure in certain children in an effort to rid them of headache. While the headache condition did not improve, he did note an increased interest in school, an apparent improved ability to work, and a calming effect on noisy, aggressive youngsters. The children receiving the pills began calling them the "arithmetic pills" because they felt they could do their arithmetic so much better after taking them. This marked the beginning of the use of stimulant pills to modify behavior and cognition in overactive children.

Sequentially what appears to happen with successful administration of stimulant drugs such as Ritalin or Dexedrine is that (1) the child becomes more reflective and less impulsive; (2) his or her ability to attend to a visual or auditory task is enhanced; (3) the development of permanent memory traces or bits of cortically stored information is improved because of the enhanced reflective and attentive abilities; and (4) with the creation of more and more permanent memory traces, the child has a more comprehensive data bank of information—a major factor related to cognition (Murray, 1976). A primary requisite for reasoning and comprehension is the ability to draw from a large inventory of concepts, ideas, words, and other information that one has learned previously. The more material in the memory bank, the more complete the reasoning or comprehension process should be. When a child is asked the question, "In what way are a bird and a dog alike and how are they different?" all of these steps have to have been accomplished before the question can be answered. The nouns "bird" and "dog" as well as the adjectives "alike" and "different" had to be learned and stored. The child lacking reflection capability could not have attended initially long enough to learn the meanings of the primary nouns and adjectives in the comprehension question; consequently, cognition would not be possible or would be negatively effected by only partial understanding. That which happens over a long period of time when a child is unable to attend translates to a massive loss of knowledge which could be used in all facets of education. The other important component related to improved cognition lies in the child's ability or lack of ability to attend to the actual stimuli at hand. The child may know the meaning of "bird," "dog," "alike," and "different" and may be capable of answering the question, but because of distractability, he or she may not listen or attend to the entire auditory stimulus or question. Theoretically, stimulant-type pills are able to enhance these components of cognition and consequently improve thinking ability and academic performance.

While the cognition theory sounds plausible, the research which actually attempts to measure improvement academically among children who have been given stimulant drugs is limited. The types of research that have been reported related to learning have basically focused on repetitious, mechanical-type performance tasks and have largely ignored studying the beneficial effects of stimulant drugs on problem solving, reasoning, nonrote learning, or actual school achievement. One study that did attempt to compare the achievement and behavior of children treated with dextroamphetamine with those on placebo revealed that behavior was affected by medication, but "achievement" was not (Conrad, Dworkin, Shai, & Tobiesson, 1971). Conrad et al., in a study conducted over a period of 4 to 6 months with 68 kindergarten, first, and second grade children matched for intelligence and degree of hyperactivity, divided youngsters into the following groups: placebo/no tutoring; placebo/tutoring; dextroamphetamine (Dexedrine)/no tutoring; dextroamphetamine/tutoring. Double blind procedures were used in the administration of the medication, thus insuring that judges and participants would not be affected by knowing who was given placebo and who received medication. Results from the study indicate that dextroamphetamine contributed to a reduction of hyperkinetic behavioral symptoms and to improvement in performance of various measures of perceptual motor and cognitive development. Twice a week tutoring for an average of 20 weeks resulted in gains on some WISC (Wechsler Intelligence Scale for Children) subtests but was clearly not as effective as medication. Neither experimental condition significantly influenced academic achievement as measured by the Wide Range Achievement Test. Subtests used on the Wide Range Test, however, were sight word recognition (the ability to recognize and properly pronounce words) and arithmetic (computational-type problems as opposed to reasoning or comprehension). This study indicates that no significant gain was realized on certain academic subtests and it represents the type of research that has generally been conducted with children receiving medication for learning and/or behavior disorders. More research needs to be directed toward determining what effects various medications may have on the actual thought processes beginning with attending to the stimulus through the ability to retrieve and integrate permanent memory traces. Measuring gains or lack of gains in grade equivalent scores is really evaluating a certain specific aspect of the potential effects on cognition by stimulants or depressants.

Dr. Herbert Rie (1974) and his associates in their studies of the effects of dextroamphetamine (Dexedrine) and methylphenidate (Ritalin) over one-half school year, found no drug effects on achievement with the exception of word recognition. However, this increase in word recognition could possibly lend some support to the idea that eventual cognitive improvement may be possible as a result of a youngster receiving medication, because in order to improve in word recognition capability, all of the aforementioned items in the cognitive sequence need to be effectively employed. The child would have to be reflective enough to attend and would have to attend, permanent memory traces in the form of learning the words would have to be effected, and a comprehensive storage component in the form of recognizable words would have been created. Without increased attentive ability this component of cognition would not be possible.

MEDICATION AND BEHAVIOR MODIFICATION

A tremendous amount of research has been carried out focusing on the effects of stimulant and depressant-type drugs on behavior. The emphasis has usually been placed on noting a lessening in the frequency in certain behaviors after medication, on timing attention spans, or on observing changes in the degree in intensity of the behavior(s). Medication as an intervention to modify behavior has been thought to be most efficacious when given to a youngster thought to have some "organic" cause behind his or her behavior. The organicity, it has been theorized, stems directly from some central nervous system (CNS) disorder which is thought by many to be amenable to treatment with drugs, particularly stimulant-type drugs.

Knobel (1962), as well as many other researchers studying overactivity, has suggested that there are two major types of overactivity: organic and psychogenic. The organic hyperkinetic's behavior is determined by an organic dysfunction, whereas the psychogenic is showing the results of a loosely structured environment—he or she has not been subjected to any consistent child-rearing approach. The organic, on one hand, cannot control his or her behavior; the psychogenic, on the other, can physically control his or her behavior but is preconditioned not to do so.

The organic is erratic, without direction or objective. His or her behavior is almost ceaseless and without change in home, school, or any other social situation and is generally accompanied by some slight choreathetosic movement. (Choreoathetosic refers to slight, irregular, jerking movements caused by involuntary muscular contractions.) The aggressivity and impulsivity are without goal and apparently senseless. The child's inability to postpone gratification is endless and urgent whether he or she is at home, in school, or wherever.

The psychogenic, on the other hand, shows some direction and intentionality in his or her aggressivity and impulsivity. In this child it is possible to obtain certain structure and coordination in various aspects of his or her behavior that certainly may be different according to where the child finds her or himself or with whom he or she relates himself (Knobel, 1962).

Teachers can use these guidelines in attempting to differentiate between the organic hyperactive and the psychogenic hyperactive and consequently are in a better position to determine whether or not to consider medication as an intervention.

Theoretically the nonorganic hyperactive should respond to firmness and structure on the part of the teacher plus the myriad of behavior modification techniques of which most teachers are aware. The organic may want to respond but is unable to. Frequently children who can benefit from medication do not show much overt acting-out behavior but do manifest a profound inability to stay on task or to maintain average attention span (Knobel, 1962). The nonorganic can accomplish task maintenance and concentration if he or she is sufficiently motivated.

The organic child thought to have some type of central nervous system involvement is frequently referred to as "hyperkinetic." The term "hyperactivity" is often used in a general descriptive sense to cover both organic and psychogenic cases. An understanding of the difference, however, may make a difference in how a youngster is ultimately treated for his or her particular condition. If his or her etiology is organic, the intervention chosen by many physicians is quite likely to be medication. If, however, the cause of his or her overactivity is environmentally based and not organic, the intervention should be other than medication.

Earlier in this chapter the difficult problem of determining whether or not a child is hyperkinetic has been mentioned in connection with the school personnel's responsibility to prove that hyperkinesis exists and that medication is necessary. Many people claim that because of the similarity of the presenting characteristics of a nonorganic hyperactive and an organic hyperkinetic, it is often next to impossible to differentiate between the two. Many feel that medication should be given on a trial basis and should be used diagnostically. If the child improves with medication, then he or she may well be organic. Others, however, desiring to use medication as a very last recourse, want to have as much evidence as possible suggesting that a child may need a stimulant or a depressant to control his or her behavior. Is there some observation checklist that parents and teachers can use to help them in determining whether or not to choose medication as an intervention? Possibly. If a person has established a certain degree of observational expertise and has a good frame of reference (many children to observe over an extended period of time) he or she may be able to employ successfully the following criteria to help differentiate between hyperkinetic (organics) and psychogenics (nonorganics).

Organic Characteristics

1. The child may show very little goal-directed behavior. He or she begins many things and completes very few.
2. High motoric behavior levels will exist at home, in school, on the playground, everywhere.
3. The child may demonstrate an inability to inhibit his or her impulsivity. Little, if any, prethought, reflectivity, or planning will be exhibited.
4. Poor performance on tests of visual and auditory memory may exist. The child with his or her distractibility will not "attend"; therefore he or she does not grasp the stimulus and cannot remember what he or she has never learned in the first place.
5. The child's comments frequently may be unrelated to what is presently being discussed. So-called dysrhythmic statements may be exhibited. For example, the child may be asked this question: "In what way are a baseball and an orange alike, and how are they different?" His or her dysrhythmic response might be "A baseball and orange are round and my brother eats oranges." At one point in the child's thought process, before responding, he or she was thinking that his or her brother played baseball.
6. The child may have difficulty in logical reasoning or he or she may have problems when it comes to following directions.
7. The child may be easily distracted and his or her behavior may be explosive and unpredictable.

Psychogenic Characteristics

1. The psychogenic hyperactive child may show a lack of goal-directed behavior, but if he or she becomes involved with something that interests him or her, the child has the physiological capability of pursuing and completing it.

2. The psychogenic child may demonstrate a high level of motor behavior, but individual counseling, behavior modification, and other techniques can be successful. The important observation differentiating the psychogenic from the organic is that the psychogenic does not manifest high motoric behavior in all settings, whereas the high-motoric organic does.

3. The psychogenic hyperactive has the ability to inhibit his or her behavior; he or she has the ability to be reflective and to plan. He or she may consciously choose not to, but because the physiological capability is there, various modification procedures can be used to effect the desired behavior.

4. Performance on visual and auditory retention tasks should pose no problem for the psychogenic hyperactive. This, of course, assumes that developmental and intellectual factors are held constant when the psychogenic hyperactive and the organic hyperactive are compared.

5. The psychogenic hyperactive will manifest few, if any, "off the track" or dysrhythmic responses.

6. Deficient reasoning processes and ability to follow directions are seldom seen as hard signs with the psychogenic hyperactive. Once again, these capabilities exist if the child decides to use them. The organic hyperactive may want to reason and follow directions, but his or her impairment does not permit this to happen.

7. The psychogenic's behavior may be described as much more calculated and premeditated than the organic's. The psychogenic is more in control and may be viewed as the impish class clown or trouble maker. His or her behavior will flourish with loosely structured teaching and often will be a conditioned behavior carried over from a particular nonstructured home environment.

STIMULANTS AND THE CNS

> The future may teach us how to exercise direct influence, by means of particular chemical substance, upon the amounts of energy and their distribution in the apparatus of the mind. It may be that there are other undreamed of possibilities of therapy.
>
> Sigmund Freud

Sigmund Freud, during the early part of the twentieth century, before any of the present day behavior modification drugs had been discovered, was mindful of the electrochemical nature of the mind and was becoming increasingly aware of human dependence upon the exactness of the chemical release mechanisms of the brain. Today, approximately 60 years later, we find ourselves using drugs to alter the electrochemical balance of the brain without truly understanding the specific process taking place.

What purportedly happens to cause certain drugs, particularly CNS stimulants, to affect the behavioral and cognitive characteristics of a child? Although the answers to this question are likely to vary, depending upon the researchers being asked the question, there are some generally agreed-upon concepts related to the workings of drugs.

The stimulant drugs are thought to have a direct effect on that part of the brain referred to as the central nervous system (CNS). The central nervous system has been referred to as the "gatekeeper," suggesting that one of the major functions of the CNS is to select the particular stimulus that is received from all external and internal points and to determine which messages are neurally propogated or transmitted and which are not. Children having no CNS dysfunction are thought to be able to inhibit enough of the neural messages to permit concentration and attention. Children having damage to this area of the brain have nerve cell damage that does not permit the proper amount of metabolically activated hormone to be released. Because these hormones are responsible for creating necessary inhibitory effects, youngsters having the neural incapability to release such transmitters as norepinephrine and serotonin are incapable of inhibiting enough of the messages that are synaptically transported. Consequently, a true hyperkinetic child reacts to a wide variety of visual, olfactory, visceral, auditory, and tactile stimuli at once, being unable to tune into any one in order to fully react to it.

Stimulant drugs are thought to raise the level of neurotransmitters present at the sight of nerve endings and in so doing to increase the release of chemicals responsible for necessary inhibition. Stewart and Olds (1971) in their book *Raising A Hyperactive Child* make this point in relation to stimulants and inhibition.

> There is no hard evidence that a chemical imbalance in the brain causes hyperactivity, but the astonishingly specific changes brought about by the stimulants make it seem a strong possibility. We know that stress leads to the release of norepinephrine in the brains of experimental animals; we also know that the effects of stimulant drugs often mimic the effects of situations that are stressful for the child. For example, a child who has been described by his mother as a demon may be an angel when he is in a strange situation, such as a psychiatrist's office, or he may be subdued and submissive when he goes to the doc-

tor's office for an allergy shot. The explanation may be in a stress-induced release of norepinephrine in the brain cells.

The point being made here is that certain youngsters produce hormones necessary for inhibition of stimuli while others are incapable, except on particular occasions, of reacting metabolically in such a way as to inhibit their behavior.

While educators may expect to observe an improvement in the behavior and possibly in the learning potential of some youngsters, they should be mindful of and alert to the possible long- and short-term negative effects of stimulant drugs. Safer's study on the effects of stimulant medication on 63 youngsters for 2 or more years (Safer & Allen, 1973) represents one of the few longitudinal studies undertaken with stimulant drugs.

> The effect of the regular intake of stimulant medication for two or more years on growth in weight and height was evaluated for 63 hyperactive children, (possibly both organic and psychogenic) 29 of whom received dextroamphetamine, (Dexedrine) 20 of whom received methylphenidate (Ritalin) and 14 of whom received no medication because of parental objection.
>
> Major findings were: the long term use of dextroamphetamine (Dexedrine) in hyperactive children causes a highly significant suppression of growth in height and weight; the long-term use of methylphenidate (Ritalin) causes a less striking growth suppression only when daily doses over 20 mg are administered; tolerance develops to the weight suppressant effects of dextroamphetamine, but not to its inhibition of height growth; increasing the total degree of stimulant drug use over time generally increases the degree of growth suppression. (Safer & Allen, 1973)

This study is somewhat unique in that it involves a fairly large number of youngsters being observed over an impressive time span of 2 years and longer. To date it is the one major longitudinal study revealing possible long-term side effects and suggests two things: we need more comparable research and if, in fact, these findings are valid, we need to consider seriously the net cost–net gain factor when we put youngsters on long-term drug therapy.

In addition to these reported long-range effects, the manufacturers of Ritalin and Dexedrine list the following possible side effects, more short term in nature, related to the use of their stimulant drugs:

Ritalin	Dexedrine
Nervousness	Overstimutation
Insomnia	Restlessness
Hypersensitivity	Insomnia
Anorexia (loss of appetite)	Gastrointestinal Disturbance

Ritalin	Dexedrine
Nausea	Diarrhea
Dizziness	Palpitation
Palpitation	Elevated blood pressure
Headache	Tremor
Dyskinesia	Sweating
Drowsiness	Headache
Skin Rash	

While the classroom teacher may have little opportunity to evaluate the long-term effects of medication, he or she is in a splendid position to note any short-term untoward effects of stimulant drugs on his or her students. Educators should understand that while these possible untoward effects are listed on the wrappers enclosed with the medication, the frequency and intensity of the reactions are minimal.

It should be mentioned that in addition to CNS stimulants, which are by far the most popular among physicians, there are a number of other types of medications prescribed to alter youngster's behavior. Among these are tranquilizers, sedatives, anticonvulsants, and antidepressants. Each of these drugs carries with it a certain number of untoward or side effects in addition to its purported positive effects.

THE TEACHER'S ROLE IN CHEMOTHERAPY

If a teacher observes a child over an extended period of time and feels that the child may be "organic" and thus in possible need of medication, what then? Does the teacher suggest medication to the parents? The immediate reaction to this question might well be "No." Teachers, however, have the best opportunity to observe the child in a variety of demanding situations and have the best frame of reference from which to measure the intensity and frequency of certain behaviors. While it may not be their role to suggest medication to parents, they are usually responsible for initiating the psychological workup which often leads to the suggestion of trying medication. They also are an integral part of the necessary parent conferences out of which comes the recommendation to medicate the child.

On What Basis Should Medication Be Considered?

When should a teacher suggest the possibility of medication? Many believe that as a complete professional, it is the teacher's duty to create the best possible learning atmosphere for each student. Because of this it is the teacher's responsibility to at least present the possibility of medication after basic data have been obtained to demonstrate the need. If one accepts the idea of the teacher being responsible for the provision of the best possible learning environment, and if it is felt that he or she should be responsible for cooperating in the implementation of medication, then come the questions, "On what basis should medication be recommended?" "How do we know when to begin to consider medication as a possibility?"

A RECOMMENDED PLAN

If a teacher has allowed for the normal adjustment period in his or her class at the beginning of the year and if she or he has evaluated the youngster in question and has tried the usual things, such as behavior modification, individual counseling, or perhaps moving the child's seat, all to little or no avail, then what? At this point it would seem wise to enlist the help of a professional person, such as a school psychologist or mental health worker—someone trained in behavior disorders. The teacher should have accumulated by now, as objectively as possible, notes describing the student's problem. These notes can be of help to the psychologist or mental health worker as he or she observes the youngster in a variety of settings, including the classroom. The intent of the note-taking process should be to provide a basis for attempting to differentiate between hyperkinesis and hyperactivity and should aid in the formulation of an individualized plan to help not only the youngster, but also the teacher, the class, and possibly the parents.

The prescriptive program selected may well be contingent upon whether the child's overactivity is thought to be organic or psychogenic. The organic probably will respond favorably to medication, the psychogenic to individual counseling or some form of behavior modification. Before the final diagnosis, however, educators should measure specific behaviors that handicap the child academically and socially in a systematic fashion. An accurate behavioral measurement to accompany the anecdotal record will (1) objectify the description of the behavior, and (2) make possible the opportunity to remeasure behavior after the introduction of the prescriptive program, be it medication or some form of behavior modification.

Teachers are in the best position to maintain good anecdotal records, whereas school psychologists or trained mental health workers often are best able to collect baseline data for pre and postmeasurement. There are many different plans that may be used in collecting baseline data. The important thing, however, is to obtain a representative measure of the frequency and intensity of the behavior(s). Allowance should be made for observing the child at different times of the day and on different days of the week.

The next step following the observation and recording processes of the teacher and the psychologist is one of meeting with both parents. The teacher's role, as well as that of the psychologist, is not one of recommending that the parents ask the physician to medicate their youngster. It is rather to give an objective description of the child's behavior and to modify that behavior. All the interventions tried to date should be described to the parents, and if none has been effective, it should be suggested that the parents may want to consider seeing their physician regarding medication. Educators and psychologists must be careful not to assume the role of a physician in discussing medication and its effects with the parents, although a carefully worded presentation of pros and cons of medication may be helpful to and appreciated by parents. Frequently physicians may be too busy to spend time enough with parents to answer all their questions. If the parents decide to seek the advice of their physician, all of the teacher's findings as well as the school psychologist's report should be given to the physician prior to the parents' appointment with him.

If a weak point exists in the procedure of medicating a child for some type of cognitive or behavioral disorder, it appears once the child has begun to take the medication. Far too often the teacher and the psychologist lose communication with the parents. To guard against this, the psychologist should assume the responsibility for keeping informed as to what decision has been made by the parents and the physician and should know when the youngster should start on medication. The teacher should also know this. Once the child begins to take pills to control behavior, the teacher's involvement continues in an important way. Because most children on medication take at least one dosage during the school day, the teacher must be mindful of the child's schedule to insure that he or she takes the medicine and thus gives it optimal opportunity to work. Obviously the teacher plays an integral role in observing major positive and negative behavior changes in the child. The teacher's awareness of possible side effects of medication will enable him or her to spot difficulties if they arise. The teacher's knowledge of the child's normal premedication behavior, aided by the anecdotal and the more objective data, becomes important at this point. Many physicians instruct parents to bring their youngster back after a 2 week trial period or before if necessary. Ideally, the teacher would have a brief subjective report to share with the physician along with any objective data pertinent to the child's behavior before and after the medical intervention.

MEDICATION GUIDELINES FOR EDUCATORS

In 1971 a student in a learning disabilities class in Franklin County, Ohio, fell into a deep sleep following lunch. The teacher awakened him on several occasions; each time he would quickly return to a deep sleep. The teacher, suspecting something to be abnormal, pursued the matter, eventually contacting the parents. Upon describing the behavior of the child to the parents, it was revealed that the child's medication had been changed by his physician. His parents had given him the new medication in the morning, the teacher, not knowing of the change in medication, gave him his previously prescribed medication at noon, and the mixture of the two drugs caused the sleep problem. This situation was relatively harmless; however, it points out the potential seriousness of drug ingestion among children and strongly suggests that school officials need to address themselves to the task of designing policies covering the dispensing of medication in school.

Answers to the following questions should be given in guidelines developed by school officials for issuance of medication in the schools (McIntosh, 1974):

1. Who should supervise the storing and dispensing of medications?

2. Should the student carry medication with him or her or administer it to her- or himself?

3. Do school personnel have written permission to dispense drugs to a student from his or her parents and physician?

4. Are drugs kept in a locked place or are they easily accessible to students or others in the building?

5. Does each student's medication have affixed a prescription label including his or her name, the name of the drug, and directions concerning dosage? Are there instructions regarding the duration of the medication period included?

6. Who among the school personnel should be informed of children who are on medication? Should there be a list disseminated to all school personnel?

In addition to the need for establishing guidelines and procedures for the dispensing of medication, school officials may want to consider utilization of certain forms to protect themselves legally and to insure maximum safety and efficiency in the dispensing process. What constitutes a good representative set of forms to be used in establishing medication guidelines and procedures? Although the answer to this question is situation specific and dependent upon a myriad of factors, it is felt that the following forms serve to cover all bases in the establishment of tight medication guidelines and procedures (McIntosh, 1974):

1. A form entitled "Medication List" which has the teacher's name, grade, and room number and has the names of all children taking medication in that room along with the dosage and time to be administered should be considered.

2. A parent release form giving written permission to school personnel to dispense medication to their child should be considered. The following sample represents a possible format to be used in a parent release form.

(SAMPLE)

__Anytown__ SCHOOL DISTRICT

PUPIL PERSONNEL DEPARTMENT

PARENT RELEASE FOR THE ADMINISTRATION OF

ORAL MEDICATION* AT SCHOOL

TO:_____ _____School

     (Principal's Name)   (School Name)

FOR:_____

     (Student's Name)

We (I) the undersigned who are the parent(s), foster parent(s), guardian(s), (cross out those not applicable) of_____

                                          (student's name)

request that oral medication be administered to our child in accordance with the instructions of our physician, Dr.

(see instructions other side this form). We (I) understand that the administration of said medication is to be done under the supervision of a member of the school staff.

Further, we (I) understand that the school personnel are not legally obligated to administer oral medication to any child and, therefore, we (I) agree to hold the school district and its employees free from any and all responsibility for the results of such medication or the manner in which it is administered and to indemnify each of them against loss by reason of any civil judgment arising out of these arrangements which may be rendered against them.

Further, we (I) will notify the school immediately, if we change physicians or medication or terminate the use of this medication for any reason.

**Signature of Father _____

**Signature of Mother _____

    Address of parents_____

    Home telephone No._____Business telephone No._____

Date of signature(s)

*   Oral medication, for release, refers to medication in pill form only. Liquid medication that must be measured cannot be administered. Also, the schools will not assume the responsibility for administering injections, applying ointments, or changing dressings.

**   Both parents must sign this release if they are living with or have custody of child. If parents are separated and both still retain legal custody, *both* parents must sign. If children are in foster home and placement is by agency that holds custody, agency must sign.

(Other side, top section, to be completed by family physician)

3. A physician's request for the administration of oral medication at School represents a third type of form. This form gives added protection to school officials and also helps to foster communication between the physician and the school.

(SAMPLE)

_____SCHOOL DISTRICT

PUPIL PERSONNEL DEPARTMENT

PHYSICIAN'S REQUEST FOR THE ADMINISTRATION OF

ORAL MEDICATION* AT SCHOOL

TO:_____School Personnel

Since medication for the student listed below cannot be scheduled for other than school hours and the administration of such medication may be supervised by medically untrained personnel, it is requested that the oral medication as indicated below be administered by school personnel.

(1) Name of student_____

(2) Address of student_____

(3) Medication to be administered (Name, quantity, and time of day)_____

(4) Possible reactions that, if they occur, should be reported
     to the physician_____

(5) Medication to be continued as above until_____(Date)

(6) Date of this request_____

(7) Physician's signature_____

(8) Physician's address_____

(9) Physician's Telephone No._____

*The school will supervise administration of oral medication in pill form only. It will not assume responsibility for administering liquid medication that must be measured, application of ointments, change of dressings, or injections.

To be completed by school—
 (1) Person(s) authorized to administer medication for this student:
    —Principal should list name(s)

_____   _____

_____   _____

 (2) Nurse's signature_____Date_____
 (3) Principal's signature_____Date_____

4. A behavior observation room. Some school systems may want to attempt to add a degree of objectivity to the medication process without setting up an elaborate behavior counting system. The following form suggests some of the behavioral characteristics of premedicated, medicated, and postmedicated children that teachers might want to include in their observational checklist.

Name_____ Date_____
Please check appropriate behaviors. Any additional comments you would care to add would be appreciated.
This student: COMMENTS:

Shows consistent behavior during the day	___More	___Less	No ___Change
Gets drowsy in class (Specify time block)	___More	___Less	No ___Change
Gets restless in class (Specify time block)	___More	___Less	No ___Change
Loses control of emotions	___More	___Less	No ___Change
Loses control of temper	___More	___Less	No ___Change
Is frustrated easily	___More	___Less	No ___Change
Seems depressed	___More	___Less	No ___Change
Seems quieter	___More	___Less	No ___Change
Seems noisier	___More	___Less	No ___Change

| Has trouble getting along with others | ___More | ___Less | No ___Change |

| Attention span shows | Increase | Decrease | No Change |

| Academic performance | Improving | Deterior- ating | No Change |

OVERALL IMPRESSION:
This child is   Adjusting   Succeeding   Working better
This child is not   Adjusting   Succeeding   Working better
COMMENTS:

Signed
School   Grade

Educators today, more than at any time in our history, are compelled to be knowledgeable of concepts and issues related to many disciplines and aspects of society. Legal and ethical issues in all facets of education including drug dispensing will continue to be as important as they have become during the past 5 years. Social issues posed by parents, more aware and sophisticated than before, will cause educators to look more deeply into educational policy making and into the need for establishing guidelines, medication guidelines as well as others. Research related to medication, stimulants and others, needs to be conducted to determine efficaciousness in improving learning and behavior in children. Presently much research needs to be directed specifically toward medication and its effect on the cognitive process. Educators in cooperation with parents and the medical community can play a major role in this research.

REFERENCES

Conrad, W.G., Dworkin, E.S.; Shai, A., & Tobiessen, J.E. Effects of Amphetamine Therapy and Prescriptive Tutoring on the Behavior and Achievement of Lower Class Hyperactive Children. *Journal of Learning Disabilities,* November 1971, 4, 509–517.
HEW News. March 19, 1971. Washington, D.C.: U.S. Dept. of Health, Education and Welfare.
Knobel, M. Psychopharmacology for the Hyperkinetic Child. *Archives of General Psychiatry,* 1962, 6, 30–35.
McIntosh, P. et al. *Medication in the Schools.* Guidelines for Medication developed for Portage County Public Schools, Ohio, November, 1974.
Murray, J.N. Is There a Role for the Teacher in the Use of Medication for Hyperkinetics? *Journal of Learning Disabilities,* January 1976, 9, 41–46.

Rie, H.E. Paper presented as part of a symposium on The Hyperactive Child at the Annual Convention of the American Medical Association on June 25, 1974 in Chicago.

Safer, D.J., & Allen, R.P. Factors Influencing the Suppressant Effects of Two Stimulant Drugs on the Growth of Hyperactive Children. *Pediatrics,* April 1973, *51,* 660–667.

Stewart, M.A., & Olds, S. *Raising a Hyperactive Child.* Chicago: Aldine, 1971.

Southern California Law Review. Drug Control of School Children: The Child's Right to Choose. 1973, *46,* 585–615.

4

PERSPECTIVES ON DRUG TREATMENT FOR HYPERACTIVITY

CORINNE J. WEITHORN, Ph.D.

There is little question that for some hyperactive children stimulant drug treatment is a panacea, enabling them to function satisfactorily in school and at home, where they have been unable to do so before. However, there also are some problems associated with drug treatment.[1] These problems, which exist in the use of psychotropic drugs for all populations, require thoughtful consideration. They derive from the fact that very little is known about the biochemical etiology of deviant behavior and about the action of the drugs on the CNS. As a result, criteria for both "illness" and improvement must be based on qualitative judgments of the appropriateness of behavior. Thus, there is a dilemma: on the one hand there are the medical and scientific imperatives which require that we utilize advances in psychopharmacology to alleviate suffering and to enable individuals to utilize

[1]While the question of undesirable side effects is a very important problem in this area, it is one which should be considered in connection with all forms of medication. Thus, presumably, it receives the same concern and attention in the case of drug treatment for hyperactivity as in all other areas of pharmacology.

their potential, while, on the other hand, there are the sociological, psychological, legal, and humanitarian imperatives which require us to examine, most carefully, any and all methods used by one group of individuals to control or alter the behavior of other individuals.

That dilemma is even more difficult to resolve in connection with the treatment of children. This is so because (a) the child is dependent on adults for fulfillment of biological and psychological needs and (b) the child is a constantly changing, developing organism whose behavior in particular areas may be considered appropriate at one age and inappropriate at another. With specific reference to hyperactivity in children this latter point was illustrated by Paine (1963) in the following statement:

> The two year old never walks, he runs; his span of attention and concentration is practically zero; certainly 1 or 2 seconds at the most; he is immediately distracted from whatever he is doing and turns quickly to something else; he is quite at the mercy of his stimuli, absolutely stimulus bound, to borrow a phrase from the psychologist. Hyperactivity refers to the above type of behavior in a child who ought to have outgrown it. (p. 240)

In the pages that follow, some of the problems relating specifically to stimulant drug treatment for hyperactivity are discussed, not in an effort to advocate that the treatment be abandoned but to heighten awareness of the limitations of our knowledge in order that treatment be sought judiciously and implemented carefully.

THE HYPERACTIVE CHILD SYNDROME

Hyperactivity is a subjectively defined behavioral disorder of complex, unknown, and probably diverse etiology. It can exist as a single functional disturbance in an otherwise normal child, but more often than not it is accompanied by varying combinations of other symptoms, such as distractibility, impulsivity, limited attention span, poor concentration, low frustration tolerance, neurological "soft" signs, visuoperceptive difficulties, and specific learning disabilities. Although some children with the syndrome are retarded, a significant number are of at least normal intelligence. While it is quite likely that CNS dysfunction underlies many cases of hyperactivity, the basis for such a diagnosis can only be inferential and nonspecific at the present time. This is particularly true in those cases where even neurological "soft" signs are absent.

Historically, two factors were responsible for the assumption that CNS dysfunction caused hyperactivity and the other symptoms noted above. One was the existence of the symptoms as sequalae to en-cephalitis (Ebaugh, 1923; Kahn & Cohen, 1934). The other was a series of observations by Strauss (Strauss and Lehtinen, 1947) that hyperactivity was a distinctive behavior of brain-injured children.

Most current theories of CNS dysfunction are based on a model of reciprocal excitation and inhibition within the CNS. As originally ex-pounded by Pavlov (1927) the model is of cerebral excitation as a result of stimulation, with excitation followed by (a) inhibition in the same area and (b) the induction of inhibition in surrounding areas. Thus, there is an excitation–inhibition cycle temporally for a given re-gion and spatially for a broader region. Subsequently, research on the arousal function of the reticular activating system and cortico-inhibition of arousal (Magoun, 1963) added a significant dimension to this theoretical framework in that defects in cortico-reticular relations were suggested as possible etiological factors in hyperactivity (Dykman, Ackerman, Clements & Peters, 1971; Laufer & Denhoff, 1957; Luria, 1966; Satterfield, Cantwell & Satterfield, 1974). Thus, there is a logi-cal theoretical model of the specific nature of the CNS dysfunction in-volved in hyperactivity. In addition, our limited knowledge of the ef-fects of stimulants on CNS functioning is theoretically consonant with this model. However, for the most part, neither the theoretical model of CNS dysfunction nor the biochemical research on the effect of the drugs on the CNS is directly related to the vast body of behavioral research on which the current clinical practice of prescribing stimulant drugs is based. Any correspondence between the underlying physiological action of the drugs and their indirect behavioral effects remains largely inferential at this time.

The picture is further complicated by a number of factors: (a) Hyperactive children are a heterogeneous group in that individual dif-ferences within that group frequently are greater than the differences between hyperactive children and nonhyperactive children. As a re-sult, behavioral studies differ widely with respect to populations tested and techniques used for behavioral assessment. (b) The effects of the drugs are idiosyncratic, varying not only from one child to another, but also in relation to dosage and length of time on medica-tion. Although some stimulant drugs are effective in producing more focused attention and improved behavior in some hyperactive chil-dren, they may produce no improvement, exacerbation of symptoms, or even lethargy in others, and they are specifically contraindicated for certain disorders, such as anxiety reactions, in which overt symptomatology may be similar to hyperactivity (Eisenberg, 1972; Fish, 1971). The Report of the Conference on Stimulant Drugs (1971) places the number of children for whom stimulant drugs potentially can be effective at about one-half to two-thirds of those for whom a trial of medication may be warranted. While data relating to the distinguishing characteristics of drug responsive children are quite limited, one series of studies has focused on this problem. Satterfield et al. (1974), studying a group of 24 hyperactive children, distinguished 12 (50%) who had abnormally low arousal levels as measured by galvanic skin response, EEG, and evoked cortical response. It was found that the six best responders to methylphenidate treatment (as based on teachers' evaluations) were from among those with low arousal level. These six children also showed a significant increase in CNS arousal level as a result of the treatment. Although this research is not conclusive, it does provide direction for further studies on clinical ways of determining some physiological correlates of behavioral hyperactivity as well as for determining individual potential for drug responsiveness.

BEHAVIORAL RESEARCH

Research on the effects of stimulants on hyperactivity dates back to the 1930s, when Bradley (1937) reported positive changes and a "calming" effect following the use of Benzedrine on a group of 30 children who had been institutionalized for a variety of neurological and behavioral disorders. Much of the research in the immediately ensuing years involved a "mixed bag" of behavioral disorders that in most cases occurred in institutionalized patients. In the next 30 years, many drugs were researched, some of which were discarded either because they did not produce the desired effects or because they produced undesirable side effects. In an excellent review of some of the drug research, Freeman (1966) highlights some of the deficiencies in the research up to that time. Among those were: (a) inadequate operational definitions of such variables as "learning" and "behavior"; (b) poor reliability of judgments of behavioral change; (c) omission of baseline data on which to estimate improvement; (d) selectivity of samples; (e) interaction of drug and diet, particularly in institutionalized populations; (f) dosage levels; (g) the presence of placebo effects; and (h) heterogeneity of symptoms found among hyperactive children. By 1970, in testimony before the Committee on Government Operations (1970) it was estimated that 200,000 children in the United States were receiving stimulant drugs for treatment of hyperactivity. Since that time, most studies generally have improved in scientific rigor, particularly with respect to the use of double blind techniques and in the refinement of behavioral assessment (Freeman, 1970; Sprague & Werry, 1971). However, ethical and practical considerations have prevented research on two important aspects of the drug treatment. The absence of information in these areas has not been dealt with adequately. The first of these relates to the way in which stimulant drugs may affect normal children. There really is no evidence that these drugs act differently on the central nervous systems of hyperactive children than on the central nervous systems of anyone else. Studies conducted with normal adults have indicated that amphetamines enhance attention, prolong concentration, and counteract the effects of fatigue (Weiss & Laties, 1962). It has been suggested that the "calming" effect reported by Bradley (1937) is merely an artifact and that the action of the stimulants on CNS functioning is the same for hyperactive children as it is for adults (Connors, 1966; Fish, 1975). One study in which volunteer medical students were given methylphenidate indicated improved motor and verbal performance but not improved learning (Frolich & Heckel, 1962). (One might assume that medical students, representing a select population to begin with, would be learning fairly close to their maximum potential.)

The second major omission in the behavioral research relates to the specific effect of stimulants on classroom learning. While there have been some studies on specific learning tasks, such as Continuous Performance Test, maze learning, and short-term memory (Conners, Eisenberg & Sharpe, 1964; Satterfield et al., 1974), these have been done in a laboratory setting. There still are little or no data available on the specific effects of stimulant drugs on learning in the school setting. Thus, clinical use of stimulant drugs still is based on extrapolation of conclusions from a few laboratory studies and on behavioral rating scales.

While most of the recent behavioral research has indicated that some stimulant drugs, notably methylphenidate, are more effective than both other drugs and placebos in enhancing the focus of attention and in decreasing excessive motor activity, it must be remembered that most of these studies have involved subjects in whom behavioral disturbance has been severe enough to warrant referral (Conners, Rothschild, Eisenberg, Schwartz & Robinson, 1969; Sykes, Douglas, Weiss & Minde, 1971; Weiss, Werry, Minde, Douglas & Sykes, 1968) and, in some cases, hospitalization (Bender & Cottington, 1942; Bradley, 1937; Bradley & Bowen, 1941). There has been a marked increase in the number of children considered to be hyperactive. Although it is possible that the number of hyperactive children actually has risen, there are other more probable reasons for this increase. One such reason is that we now may be diagnosing children as hyperactive who in earlier years would have been placed in other diagnostic categories, such as emotionally disturbed or antisocial. However, it is entirely possible that the expectation that medication will be prescribed and will alter undesirable behavior may be influencing the referral process so that it now includes children far less disturbed and far less in need of medical treatment than those about whom the original successes were reported.

HYPERACTIVITY—A MEDICAL PROBLEM OR AN EDUCATIONAL PROBLEM?

The rapid proliferation of psychopharmacological agents has resulted in the medical treatment of a wide variety of psychological and behavioral problems. In a searching discussion of drug treatment for hyperactivity, Conrad (1975) refers to the "medicalization" of behavior problems. This point also is made by Lennard, Epstein, Bernstein and Ransom (1970), who state:

> The question that must now bear the most exhaustive scrutiny is the applicability of the medical model of drug action as a rationale for the use of chemical agents to accomplish psychological (as opposed to physiological) alteration. In other words what is the conceptual justification for the belief that specific chemical agents can be found and utilized for the control and alteration of specific cognitive and emotional states. (p. 249)

Throughout their article, those authors provide dramatic examples of drug manufacturers' advertisements in medical journals advocating the use of psychotropic drugs for a wide range of rather common human problems. Unquestionably, drug manufacturers are, in large measure, responsible for what may be referred to as legitimatized "pushing." Several writers have addressed themselves to this disturbing phenomenon (Conrad, 1975; Grinspoon & Singer, 1973; Ladd, 1970). Greenberg and Lipman (1971) found that pediatricians, in contrast to child psychiatrists, showed a predilection for prescribing mild tranquilizers rather than stimulants for hyperactivity. The authors, in discussing these findings, report that drug companies tend to promote mild tranquilizers to pediatricians as effective in the treatment of hyperactivity, while promoting these minor tranquilizers to child psychiatrists as being effective in the treatment of anxiety states, but not in the treatment of hyperactivity.

The dearth of educational treatment programs for hyperactivity is another factor contributing to the medicalization of behavior problems. Most responsible professionals agree that medication for hyperactivity should be considered only as an adjunct to other remedial and therapeutic measures, yet the field of special education, which abounds in good techniques and services for speech problems, reading retardation, etc., does not seem to be deploying its resources for training children's attention or for training them in self-regulatory techniques for dealing with the target symptoms of the medication— the distractibility and poorly focused attention. In discussing the effectiveness of stimulants to help in the focus of attention, Cohen (1974) has stated:

> Thus, medication may alter constitution to allow a child to make use of environmental provision; if the reconstituted child is then provided for environmentally, he may learn to sustain his attentional skills without the assistance of medication. When such a shift occurs, might one speak of enduring constitutional shifts catalyzed, or facilitated by medication.

The question that professionals must ask themselves, then, is whether or not environmental provisions are made for enabling the "reconstituted" medicated child to develop control mechanisms which could replace medication.

The need for more involvement by educators is further heightened by the remoteness of the private practitioner from the school milieu. The behaviors associated with hyperactivity usually come to professional notice when the child begins school, where his distractibility, poor concentration, impulsivity, and aggressive behavior not only make learning difficult but create enormous problems in classroom management. Referral usually involves a succession of nonpedagogical professionals removed from the day-to-day problems posed by that classroom management. Generally, it is not the physician's medical examination, nor even the child's complaints that constitute the primary basis for the diagnosis, but the reported failure of the child to cope with the complex demands of his or her life situation. This life situation may include a number of variables intervening between observed hyperactivity and possible dysfunctioning of the central nervous system. Among these are the child–teacher ratio in the classroom, the frustration tolerance of the teacher or parent, the type and appropriateness of instructional materials, the degree of disorganization of the child's home life, emotional stress, inadequacy of nutrition and diet, boredom, and even, possibly, the existence of extraneous agents, such as excessive lead in the atmosphere (Needleman, 1973) or additives in packaged foods (Feingold, 1974). In the often-encountered absence of neurological signs, medical diagnosis and treatment are based largely on a combination of reports of the child's behavior and the physician's office observation.

Once medication is prescribed, its effect takes place outside the doctor's office. Moreover, this effect is not a simple one but involves a complex pattern of behavioral, cognitive, and psychosocial functioning which ordinarily cannot be assessed directly by the prescribing physician. As stated by Conners and Rothschild (1968):

> What we actually observe is not a deficit in the process of learning but rather a failure of the child in the complex social matrix of the school world. Failure therefore, is partially a social value judgment and not a matter of fact. (p. 199)

Another facet of the problem of school–physician responsibility deals with the need for communication. Because there is reasonable likelihood that a given hyperactive child may not be optimally responsive to treatment, it is essential that the effects of the medication be monitored carefully. Unlike the circumstances that may exist in a clinical practice setting, many behavioral studies had the advantage of careful, periodic assessment by interdisciplinary teams of physicians, psychologists, educators, etc. As drugs presently are used clinically, such assessment does not always take place. Physicians and educators function in relative isolation of each other, with very little knowledge of each other's methods, findings, or terminology. There are serious questions as to whether physicians and schools are asking the right questions of each other, or even whether they are asking questions at all (Solomons, 1972; Weithorn & Ross, 1975). It is true that good research technique requires that teachers not be informed of which children in a study are on medication and which on placebo in order not to influence their evaluations. Some practitioners also advocate not informing the school that a child has been placed on medication for the same reason. Unfortunately, however, teachers' evaluations then cannot be focused on the specific target behaviors of the treatment. Thus, the need to objectify what are essentially qualitative judgments of behavior often is offset by the need to provide carefully monitored follow-up of treatment effects.

THE GOALS OF TREATMENT

In any treatment procedure, the goals must be clearly articulated so that the effects may be accurately assessed. With respect to criteria for drug treatment of hyperactivity, it is necessary to determine the extent to which the original symptoms require treatment. It is important to examine the validity, accuracy, and objectivity of the criteria for "too much activity" or "too little concentration." The ability to focus and maintain attention is a developmental process and it is not always possible to determine whether the allowable range of individual differences in the development of 6-, 7-, or 8-year olds has been overreached. Assessment of the effects of medication also is complicated by the fact that qualitative parental and teacher reports usually comprise the data not only for the initial referral, but also for determining the effectiveness of the treatment. Thus, before and after assessments are made by individuals whose own tensions, feelings, and attitudes are altered by the behaviors they are judging. It should be remembered that there are two aspects to the behavior of the hyperactive child: (a) he or she has difficulty coping, and (b) he or she is difficult to cope with. It is important to distinguish which of these two problems will be solved through the prescription of medication for a given child. A thorough review of the research has failed to reveal any studies in which children's observations of their feelings and reactions to drugs were part of the data reported. This information would be most informative, particularly were it to be compared to the reports of feelings and reactions of adults taking stimulant drugs.

Theoretically, successful treatment results in enhanced attention and the elimination of extraneous motor activity. This should lead to improved learning. However, research studies have not yielded data on actual learning improvement within the classroom setting. Despite Solomons' very salient suggestion that there be a Federal clearing house for clinical information on the efficacy of drug treatment (Solomons, 1972) there still is no such facility. Some learning functions have been shown to improve in a laboratory setting (Conners et al., 1964) but there is no evidence of a correlation between improvement in learning and simultaneous improvement in behavior. As a matter of fact there are some data which suggest that the optimal dosage for improved learning may not be the same as the optimal dosage for improved behavior. Sprague and Sleator (1973), using very low dosages[2] of methylphenidate on hyperactive children found that at .3 mg/kg,[2] short-term memory improved maximally, but that seat activity, as measured with a stabilimetric cushion, did not decrease maximally until dosages of .7 mg/kg. At the latter dosage, when seat activity was at its lowest level, task performance was no longer optimal.

In similar studies, using a picture recognition task as a measure of cognitive behavior and Conners' Teachers' Rating Scale (1969) as a measure of social behavior, Sprague and Sleator (1976) found that optimal social behavior occurred at dosages two to three times the dosage required for optimal cognitive behavior (see Figure 1). They stated:

[2]A kilogram is approximately equal to 2 pounds. Thus, a dosage level of .3 mg/kg. means approximately .3 mg for every 2 pounds of the child's weight. For a 50 pound child the dosage thus would be 7.5 mg. The AMA's recommended starting dosage of Ritalin is 5 mg (twice a day) with a maximum recommended dosage of 60 mg/day.

The zones of peak enhancement are not the same for both target behaviors. Thus, if one were to enhance the cognitive performance of a
hyperactive, distractible child, one would prescribe a dose of a stimulant
medication that falls within the optimal cognitive performance zone
(labeled optimal behavioral zone). But if one wanted to enhance the
mental health of the child's teacher in terms of optimizing the teacher's
rating of the child, which is based, we believe largely on the child's social behavior in the classroom, one would presribe a higher dose that
falls within the optimal social performance zone (labeled optimal titra-
tion zone). (p. 365)

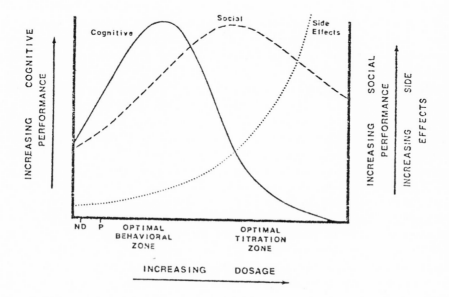

These data suggest that optimal learning may occur at dosages that
do not alter overt, observable behavior. Thus, reliance on behavioral
indices alone not only may fail to provide data on learning improvement but even may preclude more sensitive analysis of learning efficiency. The implications are that (a) some children whose behavior is
markedly improved actually may be on dosage levels that are too high
for optimal learning, and (b) some children who do not appear to be
behaviorally responsive to certain dosages actually may be able to
learn better despite the continued presence of hyperactivity.

ETHICAL CONSIDERATIONS

Several writers have addressed the issue of the possibility of in-
fringement on the rights of children (Grinspoon & Singer, 1973; Ladd,

1970). The Report of the Conference on Stimulant Drugs (1971) emphasizes the need for informed consent on the part of parents and children. While there undoubtedly are many instances in which parents and/or physician explain the purpose of medication to the child, there are many more in which neither the child nor the family has a full understanding of the issues.[3] It may be particularly true when prescriptions are given within large out-patient facilities of hospitals that primarily service children whose lives reflect the disruption engendered by poverty—such as broken families, inadequate parental supervision, successive placements in foster homes and institutions, etc. Unfortunately, it is also this population of children that often does not receive the benefit of sophisticated differential diagnosis to distinguish between hyperactivity caused by neurogenic factors and acting-out behavior caused by psychogenic factors.

Finally, drug treatment must be accompanied by provision of child and family with ancillary noneducational services. For example, in some cases supportive counseling or therapy may be needed if symptoms of hyperactivity result from emotional factors or are exacerbated by an unstable environment in which the child's problems are the focus or manifestation of underlying disturbances in family relationships. In other cases, the family may not be able to handle the supervision of medication nor the follow-up of behavioral change or medical side effects. In certain circumstances, a family may contain siblings or even parents who use or sell drugs. As Solomons (1972) has indicated, all these factors, where they exist, should be taken into consideration before medication is prescribed.

It would appear that along with the unquestioned beneficial aspects of medication for hyperactivity are the important questions of whether we have rushed precipitously into adopting a little-understood solution to a vaguely defined problem. In that regard, there is a need for additional effort on the part of both researchers and clinicians. While a great deal of the recent research has been excellent, there clearly should be investigations that include: (a) comparison of concomitant changes in classroom learning and overt behavior as a function of dosage levels; (b) specific distinguishing characteristics of good and poor responders to medication; (c) investigation of children's attitudes and emotional reactions to treatment itself; (d) combined pharmacological and behavioral studies; and (e) closer inspection of parallels between the responses to methylphenidate of normal adults and those of hyperactive children.

---

[3]One recently adjudicated issue (Roe *v.* Ingraham) involved legally mandated governmental record keeping of the names of individuals for whom prescriptions were written. Among the plaintiffs were the parents of a child receiving methylphenidate for hyperactivity.

In clinical practice, there is a need to be acutely aware of the problems surrounding referral, diagnosis, and drug treatment and follow-up. As stated earlier, these problems are not specific to stimulant drug treatment for hyperactivity, but are common to the entire area of clinical practice using psychotropic agents. However, professionals who work with children have an additional burden of responsibility because children frequently cannot provide informed consent to treatment and because they seldom are real participants in the decision-making process relating to the effects of the treatment.

REFERENCES

Bender, L., & Cottington, F. The use of amphetamine sulfate (Benzedrine) in child psychiatry. *American Journal of Psychiatry*, 1942 99, 116–121.

Bradley, C. The behavior of children receiving Benzedrine. *American Journal of Psychiatry*, 1937. 94, 577–585.

Bradley, C. & Bowen, M. Amphetamine (Benzedrine) therapy of children's behavior disorders. *American Journal of Orthopsychiatry*, 1941. 11, 92–103.

Cohen, D. Autism and aphasia as models of constitutional disability. Paper presented to International Association for Child Psychiatry and Allied Professions, Philadelphia, Pa., July 1974.

Conners, C. The effects of dexedrine on rapid discrimination and motor control of hyperkinetic children under mild stress. *Journal of Nervous and Mental Diseases*, 1966. 142, 429–433.

Conners, C. A teacher rating scale for use in drug studies with children. *American Journal of Psychiatry*, 1969. 125, 884–888.

Conners, C., Eisenberg, L., & Sharpe, L. Effects of methylphenidate (Ritalin) on paired associate learning and Porteus Maze performance in emotionally disturbed children. *Journal of Consulting Psychology*, 1964. 28, 14–22.

Conners, C. & Rothschild, G. Drugs and learning in children. In J. Hellmuth (Ed.), *Learning Disabilities* Vol. 3 Seattle: Special Child Publications, 1968.

Conners, C., Rothschild, M., Eisenberg, L., Schwartz, L.S., & Robinson, E. Dextroamphetamine sulfate in children's learning and achievement. *Archives of General Psychiatry*, 1969. 21, 182–190.

Conrad, P. The discovery of hyperkinesis: notes on the medicalization of deviant behavior. *Social Problems*, 1975. 23, 12–21.

Dykman, R.A., Ackerman, P.T., Clements, S.D., & Peters, J.E. Specific Learning Disabilities: An Attentional Deficit Syndrome. In H. Myklebust, (Ed.), *Progress in Learning Disabilities*. Vol. II. New York: Grune and Stratton, 1971.

Ebaugh, F. Neuropsychiatric sequalae of acute epidemic encephalitis in children. *American Journal of Diseases of Children*. 1923. 25, 89–97.

Eisenberg, L. Symposium: behavior modification by drugs—III. the clinical use of stimulant drugs in children. *Pediatrics*. 1972. 49, 709–715.

Feingold, B. Why Your Child is Hyperactive. New York: Random House, 1974.

Fish, B. The "one child-one drug" myth of stimulants in hyperkinesis. *Archives of General Psychiatry*, 1971. *25*, 193–203.

Fish, B. Stimulant drug treatment of hyperactive children. In D. Cantwell, (Ed.), The Hyperactive Child: Diagnosis, Management and Current Research, New York: John Wiley, 1975.

Freeman, R. Drug effects on learning in children: a selective review. *Journal of Special Education*, Fall 1966, 17–44.

Freeman, R. Review of medicine in special education. Another look at drugs and behavior. *Journal of Special Education*, Fall 1970, 377–384.

Froelich, R.E., & Heckel, R.V. The psychological effects of methylphenidate. *Journal of Clinical and Experimental Psychopathology and Quarterly Review of Psychiatry and Neurology*, 1962. *23*, 91–92.

Greenberg, L. & Lipman, R. Pharmocotherapy of hyperactive children: Current practices. *Clinical Proceedings of Children's Hospital of the District of Columbia*, 1971. *27*, 101–107.

Grinspoon, L., & Singer, S. Amphetamines in the treatment of hyperkinetic children. *Harvard Education Review* 1973. *43*, 515–555.

House of Representatives, Subcommittee of the Committee on Government Operations. 91st Congress, 2nd Session Sept. 29, 1970. Federal involvement in the use of behavior modification drugs on grammar school children of the right to privacy inquiry.

Kahn, E., & Cohen, L. Organic drivenness; a brain stem syndrome and an experience. *New England Journal of Medicine*, 1934. *219*, 748–753.

Ladd, E. Pills for classroom peace. *Saturday Review*, 1970. *53*, 66–83.

Lasagna, L. The pharmaceutical revolution; its implications on science and society. *Science*, 1969. *166*, 1227–1233.

Laufer, M. & Denhoff, E. Hyperkinetic syndrome. *Journal of Pediatrics*, 1957. *50*, 463–470.

Lennard, H., Epstein, L., Bernstein, A., & Ransom, D. Hazards in prescribing psychoative drugs. *Science*, 1970 *31*, 438–441.

Luria, A.R. The role of speech in the formation of mental processes. In A.R. Luria, (Ed.), The Role of Speech in the Regulation of Normal and Abnormal Behavior. Washington, D.C.: U.S. Dept. Health, Education and Welfare. Public Health Service, National Institutes of Health, 1966.

Magoun, H.W. The Waking Brain. Springfield, Ill.: Charles C. Thomas, 1963.

Needleman, H. Lead poisoning in children: neurological implications of widespread subclinical intoxication. In S. Walzer & P. Wolff, (Eds.), Minimal Cerebral Dysfunction in Children. New York: Grune and Stratton, 1973.

Paine, R. The contributions of neurology to the pathogenesis of hyperactivity in children. *Clinical Proceedings Childrens Hospital, Washington, District of Columbia*, 1963 *19*, 235–247.

Pavlov, I. Conditioned Reflexes. New York: Oxford Univ. Press, 1927.

Report of the Conference on the Use of Stimulant Drugs in the Treatment of Behaviorally Disturbed Young School Children. Washington, D.C.: January, 1971. Office of Child Development and Office of the Assistant Secretary for Health and Scientific Affairs, Department of Health, Education and Welfare. January, 1971.

Satterfield, J.M., Cantwell, D.P., & Satterfield, B.T. Pathophysiology of the

Hyperactive Child Syndrome. *Archives of General Psychiatry.* 1974. *31,* 839–844.

Solomons, G. Guidelines on the use and medical effects of psychostimulant drugs in therapy. *Journal of Learning Disabilities,* 1971 *4,* 471–475.

Solomons, G. Drug therapy and follow-up. Paper presented to N.Y. Academy of Sciences Symposium on Minimal Brain Dysfunction, New York, 1972.

Sprague, R. & Sleator, E. Drugs and dosages: implications for learning disabilities. In R.M. Knights & D. Bakker, (Eds.), The Neuropsychology of Learning Disorders. Baltimore: University Park Press, 1976.

Strauss, A., & Lehtinen, L. Psychopathology and Education of the Brain-Injured Child. Vol. 1. New York: Grune & Stratton, 1947.

Sykes, D., Douglas, V., Weiss, G., & Minde, K. Attention in hyperactive children and the effect of methylphenidate (Ritalin). *Journal of Child Psychiatry and Psychology,* 1971 *12,* 129–139.

Weiss, B., & Laties, V. Enhancement of human performance by caffeine and the amphetamines. *Pharmocology Review.* 1962 *14,* 1–36.

Weiss, G., Werry, J.S., Minde, K., Douglas, V. & Sykes, D. Studies on the hyperactive child V: The effects of dextroamphetamine and chlorpromazine on behavior and intellectual functioning. *Journal of Child Psychiatry and Child Psychology,* 1968 *9,* 145–146.

Weithorn, C.J., & Ross, R. Who monitors medication? Journal of Learning Disabilities, 1975 *8,* 59–62.

5

Drug Therapy for Hyperactivity: Existing Practices in Physician– School Communication

ROSLYN P. ROSS, Ph.D.

Increasing numbers of children are being diagnosed as having the hyperactive child syndrome. While many of these youngsters may encounter more than the usual difficulties in mastering the developmental tasks and reaching the expected milestones of infancy and early childhood, their difficulties usually do not become highlighted until entrance to school. Alternate educational and child-rearing strategies then are required to facilitate learning and growth in these children.

There has been a growing reliance on pharmacological treatment of the symptoms related to this syndrome during the last decade. There are two factors that are responsible for this growing reliance. The first factor is research findings that certain stimulant drugs, such as dextroamphetamine and methylphenidate, are effective in increasing focused attention and decreasing hyperactivity and distractibility in certain hyperactive children. The second factor is that theoretical explanations of the syndrome in terms of inferred central nervous system dysfunction have provided a rationale for the efficacy of stimulant medication in altering the behavior.

However, it is important to note that no matter how compelling these explanations in terms of central nervous system involvement are, little is actually known about the nature of the direct physiological action of the drugs on the central nervous system. Furthermore, while advances are being made in the understanding of biochemical mechanisms (i.e., brain functions, endocrine activity, amine metabolism), the relationships between biochemical events and observable behaviors are still inferred ones. As yet we do not know the biochemical correlates of normal affects and thoughts. In this vein, The Group for the Advancement of Psychiatry, Committee on Research (1975) sums up the current state of knowledge by stating that "the translation of psychologic conflict into cellular malfunction, or the reverse translation of disordered biochemical mechanisms into pathological behavior is still beyond us" (p. 17).

Thus, given our current limited state of knowledge about (a) the etiology of the hyperactive child syndrome, (b) the underlying biochemistry of complex observable behavior, and (c) the action of the stimulant drugs on the central nervous system, stimulant drug treatment for hyperactivity has the status of an empirical treatment that is effective but perhaps is not directly related to the etiology of the disorder. A problem that follows from this limited state of knowledge is that we cannot predict response to stimulant drugs in advance of a trial of the medication. The Report of the Conference on the Use of Stimulant Drugs in the Treatment of Behaviorally Disturbed Young School Children concluded in 1971 that stimulant medications are beneficial in only about one-half to two-thirds of the cases in which trials of the drugs are warranted. We cannot tell which hyperactive children will respond favorably. Appropriate dosage level and length of time for maintenance on medication also cannot be predicted in advance.

In addressing themselves to the problem of the idiosyncratic effects of the drugs on children, Satterfield, Cantwell and Satterfield (1974) were able to relate differential response to methylphenidate in a sample of hyperactive children to differences in central nervous system arousal as measured by galvanic skin response, EEG, and evoked cortical response. In a double blind technique, the best responders (judged by improvement in teacher ratings) were those who had abnormally low arousal levels. The authors hypothesize that insufficient CNS inhibition is associated with the low CNS arousal levels in the hyperactive children who respond favorably to stimulant medication and further that CNS arousal and inhibition vary together. Lack of inhibitory control over motor functions is posited as explaining excessive and inappropriate motor activity. Lack of inhibitory control over sensory function is thought to underlie distractibility. In commenting on their findings, Satterfield, Cantwell and Satterfield (1974) urge caution in interpreting them because they are based on small samples and weak, although significant, correlations.

Although findings of differential response to medication have been obtained, we cannot yet relate them to clinical practice in narrowing the target population for whom such drugs are initially prescribed. Another related problem is that judgments about response to medication are a function of the target behaviors under consideration. Sprague and Sleator (1973) and Sprague and Werry (1971) have presented data suggesting that optimal dosage for improved behavior may not be the same as optimal dosage for improved learning.

For all these reasons it is imperative that careful monitoring of the effects of stimulant medication takes place. The Report of the Conference on the Use of Stimulant Drugs (1971) stressed this need in the following statement:

> The decision to use drug treatment depends on the commitment to diagnose and to monitor the response to the treatment in the best tradition of medical practice. When there is informed parental consent, parents, teachers and professionals can collaborate in organizing and monitoring treatment programs. (p. 4)

The need for collaboration among parents, teachers, and professionals arises, among other things, from the fact that the target behaviors for which medication is prescribed occur outside the doctor's office and involve complex cognitive and psychosocial patterns of functioning not ordinarily assessed directly by physicians. It would follow that observations of behavior and learning should be made regularly and be reported to the prescribing physician by both family and school. In a study of follow-up procedures of private practitioners who had prescribed medication on the recommendation of the Iowa Hospital School, Solomons (1972) reported that 45% of the cases of 97 children were not monitored properly. A survey conducted among elementary school teachers in and around New York City by Weithorn and Ross (1975) yielded similar findings. In only 57% of the cases of 71 children was there some kind of contact between the school and the physician. This sample of teachers (a) expressed a need for further information about the nature of medication being used, (b) reported inadequate opportunity to exchange information with prescribing physicians and clinics, and (c) reported the most satisfactory adjustment in symptoms for which medication was prescribed when they had direct communication with physicians.

Because of the limited and selective nature of the samples in these two studies on monitoring, a more thorough investigation of current practices in (a) monitoring the effects of medication and (b) collaborative efforts of professionals and parents in this process was judged worthwhile.

THE GUIDANCE COUNSELOR SURVEY

A survey was conducted among guidance counselors, who are the primary liaison people between schools and the medical community in these matters. The survey focused on the nature and extent of the communication that was taking place. Five of the seven school districts in Queens, a borough of New York City, agreed to participate in the survey during the 1974–1975 academic year. A copy of the survey was sent to the guidance counselor in each elementary school in the participating districts. Returns were coded by the district guidance supervisors so that individual schools could not be identified. Returns were received for 66 schools with a total registration of 50,100 children. This represented a 55% rate of response to the survey.

INCIDENCE DATA

The data give only partial answers and probably represent an underestimate of the number of children actually on medication for the following reasons: (a) Some parents do not wish schools to be informed that their child is on medication. As a result, guidance counselors could report only on those children whom they knew to be on medication. (b) Many of the children receiving medication are in special classes. In some schools the regular guidance counselor did not service these classes and therefore could not report on them.

Of the 50,100 children enrolled in the schools from which reports were received, 441 children or .9% of the total enrollment were known to be on medication for hyperactivity. There were 274 children or 62% of the sample in special classes. The percentage of children known to be on medication in a school ranged from 0 to 10.7% with a median of .6%. The highest incidence, which was atypical, came from a school in which almost all youngsters in nine special classes were on medication.

An examination was made of the relationship between the percentage of children known to be on medication in a school and (a) size of the student body in a school, (b) guidance counselor case load, (c) socioeconomic status of the student body as estimated by the guidance counselor, and (d) ethnic composition of the student body as estimated by the guidance counselor. The significance of the relationships was tested by a chi square statistic. Median splits were used to designate the schools on the variables under consideration.

The findings indicate that there was no significant relationship between incidence and size of the student body or guidance counselor case load. There was a significantly lower incidence in schools that were below the median for socioeconomic status, χ^2 (1) = 3.94, $p <$ .05. There was also a significantly lower incidence in schools that had a predominantly nonwhite student body, χ^2 (1) = 4.06, p < .05. Thus, prevalence or incidence of known drug treatment for hyperactivity appeared to be greater for schools serving families that were predominantly middle class and/or predominantly white.

THE COMMUNICATION PROCESS

Most typically, guidance counselors learned that a child was on medication by being informed by parents (38% of the cases) or as a result of initiating an inquiry about a child who was having problems (32% of the cases). The prescribing physician was the original source of the information or the initiator of the communication process in only 17% of the cases. The remaining 13% of the cases tended to have this information in the records that formed part of the procedures preceding entrance into special education classes.

Because parents are primary informants, at least in the initial stages of communication, guidance counselor evaluations of parents' understanding and attitudes about this form of treatment take on particular significance. When asked to comment on their perception of parents, only 19% of the guidance counselors reported that they had found parents to be generally adequately or well informed about the nature of the medication and expected consequences. Guidance counselors also described parents as having generally negative and fearful feelings about their children being on medication (negative, 74%, positive, 26%). Thus, guidance counselors did not see parents as particularly effective informants for their purposes. In fact, they identified parents' lack of understanding as one of the problems in the use of medication.

This finding highlights, among other things, the importance of direct communication between the school and the prescribing agent. While guidance counselors reported that direct communication was relatively infrequent in the initial stage, they also reported an increase in communication when they specifically initiated it. Nevertheless, they felt there still was an insufficient exchange of information. Guidance counselors reported that they were not getting enough information and they were not being asked for enough information. For example, in one-half the cases there was no direct written or verbal exchange of information between the guidance counselor and the prescribing physician or just a brief notification that medication was being given. There had been one exchange of information for 12% of the children. There had been more than one exchange occurring on an irregular basis for 25% of the children and more than one exchange occurring on a regular basis for only 14% of the children.

Guidance counselors were also asked to rate the adequacy of the information they had for each child with respect to the nature of the drug treatment and expected consequences. (No distinction was drawn as to the source of the information and it could include written records and parent as well as physician informants.) They reported that in only one-third of the cases did they feel adequately informed and even in these cases, they often felt they had to make a determined effort to get the information. "You get information only if you ask the right questions" was one such comment.

Because the physician needs behavioral data on the child he or she is treating in order to adjust dosage level and to evaluate the appropriateness of drug treatment, the degree to which physicians and parents (who might be acting as intermediaries) were asking for feedback from the schools was also explored. Guidance counselors had been asked for detailed feedback on changes in behavior and learning in 35% of the cases, general feedback in 21% of the cases, and no feedback in 44% of the cases.

Among the guidance counselors who were able to report productive physician–school communication, there was repeated reference to the same two hospital clinics. Further investigation indicated that these two clinics had in common a structured reporting form requesting information from teachers which they sent out to the schools periodically. These reporting forms are the obvious result of an interdisciplinary effort to assess the effects of the medication.

In general, guidance counselors feel that drug treatment has not been accompanied by enough sharing of information with either schools or parents and they want more information. They want to know:

When a child is placed on medication and when dosage is changed
Name of medication and dosage
How often the medication is to be taken and for how long

Schedule of child's visits with the physician so they can help insure that visits are being kept

Reason for prescribing medication

Behavioral changes for which the school should look as signs of effectiveness

Behavioral signs that may be danger signals

When physicians want to be alerted or given feedback and what they want to know

They also want the physician's assessment of parental involvement and understanding so they may know whether there is any special support parents may need from the school in carrying out the treatment plan.

DO WE HAVE TRULY INFORMED PARENTAL CONSENT?

Survey data suggest a generally negative answer to this question. Parents were reported to be generally inadequately informed and to have predominantly negative and fearful feelings about their children being on medication. Parents fear addiction and adverse side effects, particularly from long-term use. As a consequence they may become erratic in giving the medication and may stop giving it without consulting a physician or informing the school. Several guidance counselors who reported generally positive feelings on the part of parents indicated that those who felt hesitant no longer medicated and therefore were not included in the sample. Similarly, some guidance counselors reported that they were no longer referring to agencies where the only treatment given the child was medication.

CHANGES IN BEHAVIOR AND LEARNING

Because of the idiosyncratic effects of the drugs, a decision to continue medication after an initial trial is dependent upon demonstrated effectiveness with respect to the symptoms for which it has been prescribed. Hence we should expect to find high levels of reported improvement for children who continue to be on medication. This did not appear to be the case. When asked to rate changes in behavior with respect to hyperactivity and distractibility, guidance counselors reported more appropriate behavior in only 62% of the cases. They reported that 32% of the children still seemed hyperactive and distractible and 5% seemed lethargic or sluggish. When it came to changes in learning and achievement, 32% were improved noticeably, 45% were improved slightly, and 23% were not improved.

The Report of the Conference on the Use of Stimulant Drugs (1971) placed the number of children for whom stimulant drugs potentially could be effective at about one-half to two-thirds of those for whom a trial of medication might be warranted. About the same number of children seem to be being helped in this sample. However, one wonders why medication has not been discontinued with the children who are not showing improvement. Could they all be at the initial stages of trial medication, undergoing dosage change and careful monitoring?

Another finding of some interest concerned the fact that guidance counselors found it more difficult to respond to the item referring to evaluating changes in learning and achievement after medication than to any other item on the questionnaire. This item was filled out for a noticeably smaller percentage of children than other items.

CONCLUSIONS

It would appear from the survey that present practices fall far short of meeting the criteria that have been established by the Report of the Conference on Stimulant Drugs (1971) for the use of stimulant drugs in the treatment of hyperactivity and related learning disturbances. The response to treatment is not being monitored adequately and therefore the variable idiosyncratic effects of the drugs are not being carefully assessed. Informed parental consent and involvement in the treatment is the exception rather than the rule. Collaboration among parents, teachers, and professionals in organizing and monitoring treatment problems is not taking place sufficiently.[1] Except in certain large institutional facilities that have interdisciplinary teams and research interests, physicians and educators function in relative isolation of each other, with very little knowledge of each others methods, findings or terminology.

The evidence that criteria for using these drugs are not being followed adequately raises the question of whether they are being mis-

[1]Following the completion of this survey there was a large-scale dismissal of guidance counselors from the New York City public schools because of financial problems. Given the amount of time that must go into monitoring, one can only wonder whether the decimated guidance staff is able to devote as much effort to this task as formerly. It does not seem likely.

used no matter what their therapeutic potential may be. One optimistic note that can be sounded is that current misuse in this sample does not seem to include the overuse of medication for control with economically disadvantaged groups. (Krager and Safer found substantially the same thing in a survey they conducted in suburban Baltimore County in 1974.) Nevertheless, concerns over the widespread acceptance of stimulant drugs would appear to be justified on the basis of the evidence that criteria for their use are not being followed adequately.

This situation can be remedied if physicians, school personnel, and parents recognize the need to establish and maintain structured communication. Physicians should prescribe medication for hyperactivity only when they are satisfied that both home and school are prepared to make a commitment to provide periodic feedback on behavior and learning.

The most effective means of providing relevant feedback between schools and physicians appears to be through direct communication—not through intermediaries, such as parents. Because maintaining such one to one communication is impractical over a long period of time, it is recommended that these initial contacts be followed by written reporting forms. The use of structured means of communication serves purposes in addition to economy of time. It has the advantage of directing both professions to impart information that has been judged to be relevant in a fashion that is understood by the other.

The Conner's Teacher Rating Scale (Conners, 1969, 1973; Sprague & Sleator, 1973; Safer & Allen, 1976) appears to be the instrument of choice for giving feedback to physicians on the dimension of hyperactivity. As shown in Figure 1, it is a ten-item scale which takes about 2 minutes to fill out. It is the most widely used scale and it has been standardized on school children in New York (Kupietz, Bailer & Winsberg, 1972) and Illinois (Sprague, Christenson & Werry, 1974) so that norms are available.

Unfortunately, a structured and standardized teacher rating form for learning changes still needs to be developed. Standard achievement tests are not sensitive enough to measure the effects of medication within relatively short periods of time. Laboratory tests that are sensitive to subtle learning performance changes are not applicable to the classroom setting.

Similarly, a structured reporting form for use by physicians still needs to be developed. However, even the use of such a form will not answer the needs for basic information on the nature of drug treatment that school personnel are expressing. These needs would be better served through in-service or university-based courses. An interdisciplinary approach to such instruction is recommended.

REFERENCES

Conners, C.K. A teacher rating scale for use in drug studies with children. *American Journal of Psychiatry*, 1969, *126*, 884–888.

Conners, C.K. Rating scales for use in drug studies with children. *Psychopharmacology Bulletin*, Special Issue (Pharmacotherapy of Children), 1973, 24–84.

Group for the Advancement of Psychiatry, Committee on Research. *Pharmacotherapy and Psychotherapy: Paradoxes, Problems and Progress*. New York: Brunner/Mazel, 1975.

Krager, J.M., & Safer, D.J. Type and prevalence of medication used in the treatment of hyperactive children. *The New England Journal of Medicine*, 1974, *291*, 1118–1120.

Kupietz, S., Bailer, I., & Winsberg, B.G. A behavior rating scale for assessing improvement in behaviorally deviant children: A preliminary investigation. *American Journal of Psychiatry*, 1972, *128*, 1432–1436.

Report of the Conference on the Use of Stimulant Drugs in the Treatment of Behaviorally Disturbed Young School Children. Washington, D.C.: Office of Child Development and Office of the Assistant Secretary for Health and Scientific Affairs, Department of Health, Education and Welfare, January 1971.

Safer, D.J., & Allen, R.P. *Hyperactive Children: Diagnosis and Management*. Baltimore: University Park Press, 1976.

Satterfield, J.M., Cantwell, D.P., & Satterfield, B.T. Pathophysiology of the hyperactive child syndrome. *Archives of General Psychiatry*, 1974, *31*, 839–844.

Solomons, G. "Drug therapy and follow-up." Paper presented at the meeting of the New York Academy of Sciences Symposium on Minimal Brain Dysfunction, New York, 1972.

Sprague, R.L., Christenson, D.E., & Werry, J.S. Experimental psychology and stimulant drugs. In C.K. Conners (Ed.), *Clinical use of stimulant drugs in children*. The Hague: Excerpta Medica, 1974.

Sprague, R.L., & Sleator, E.K. Effects of psychopharmacologic agents on learning disorders. *Pediatric Clinics of North America*, 1973, *20*, 719–735.

Sprague, R.L., & Werry, J.S. Methodology of psychopharmacological studies with the retarded. In N.R. Ellis (Ed.), *International review of research in mental retardation* (Vol. 5). New York: Academic Press, 1971.

Weithorn, C.J., & Ross, R. Who monitors medication? *Journal of Learning Disabilities*, 1975, *8*, 59–62.

CONNERS' ABBREVIATED TEACHER RATING SCALE

Child's Name _____

TEACHER'S OBSERVATIONS

Information obtained _____ By _____
                        Month   Day   Year

Observation	Degree of Activity			
	Not at all 0	Just a little 1	Pretty much 2	Very much 3
1. Restless or overactive				
2. Excitable, impulsive				
3. Disturbs other children				
4. Fails to finish things he starts, short attention span				
5. Constantly fidgeting				
6. Inattentive, easily distracted				
7. Demands must be met immediately—easily frustrated				
8. Cries often and easily				
9. Mood changes quickly and drastically				
10. Temper outbursts, explosive and unpredictable behavior				

OTHER OBSERVATIONS OF TEACHER (Use reverse side if more space is required.)

_____

_____

_____

_____

_____

Figure 1

6

DRUGS AND THE FAMILY

BETTIJANE EISENPREIS, M.S.

"The evidence indicates that a history given by parents concerning the behavior and activity level of their child is largely unreliable . . . Compared with fathers, mothers are more defensive, distorting and censoring their information. . . ."[1] Gerald Solomons, Paper delivered at a Conference on Minimal Brain Dysfunction, March 1972 (Solomons, 1973, p. 335)

Any serious consideration of such a weighty matter as drugs and the special child must take into account the fact that the special child, like all children, does not exist in a vacuum. He or she has teachers, classmates, friends, and various adults to whom he or she must relate. First and foremost, the child has a family; heading this family are one or two parents. While this statement may appear elementary in the extreme, it is surprising to note how often the parents' existence is overlooked or misinterpreted. Parents are often condescended to, are treated as a necessary evil or, worse, are considered the source of their child's problem. The purpose of this chapter is to present the

[1]"If a Boy Can't Learn," film by Lawren Productions, Inc., P.O. Box 1542, Burlingame, Calif., 94010.

subject of drugs and the special child in the context of the child's natural habitat, his or her family. By doing so, I hope to set the record straight.

DEFINITIONS AND PROCEDURES

For the purposes herein, the "special child" is one who is categorized either as having minimal brain dysfunction (MBD) or as being learning disabled. It is acknowledged that both terms are loose and have been variously defined. They are used for lack of more precise terms. Most of these children exhibit several of the following symptoms or behaviors: They are hyperactive; they are distractible, with very short attention spans. They are impulsive, unable to wait for gratification, and prone to temper tantrums. They "perserverate," repeat ideas and actions over and over, seeming to get stuck on one subject or one task. Often, they are perceptually impaired. They may have poor memory or auditory or visual impairment. Finally, their social development is often immature ("Do You Know this Child").

These characteristics must persist and they must exist in combination, usually three or more. The problems are not primarily emotional, although emotional difficulties may develop when such children try to perform tasks that they know they should be able to do and find that they cannot. Although these children are often retarded in development, they are usually of normal or above normal intelligence. Often the perceptual impairment just mentioned results in "specific learning disabilities," which according to one definition are:

> . . . a disorder in one or more of the basic psychological processes involved in understanding or using spoken or written languages. These may be manifested in disorders of listening, thinking, talking, reading, writing, spelling, or arithmetic . . . They do not include learning problems which are due *primarily* to visual, hearing, or motor handicaps, to mental retardation, emotional disturbance, or to environmental disadvantage. (Giles, 1971, p. 1)

"Drugs" as defined here are the so-called psychoactive medications used in treating MBD and related disorders. While megavitamin therapy is also used, that is a subject unto itself and is not dealt with here. The drugs discussed here are stimulants, tranquilizers, antidepressants, and the like.

A good part of the material for this chapter has been obtained from an informal poll of parents whose children have been diagnosed as having minimal brain dysfunction. A questionnaire was sent out, followed in several cases by conversations. The purpose was less to obtain objective data than to shed some light on the way that parents perceive problems and solutions and on right and wrong ways to approach families in order to help them. The parents queried were urban and middle class, all members of some organization devoted to promoting the welfare of their children, either the PTA of a special school or a parent–professional association. Most had one or more children in addition to the "special" child.

HOW IT BEGINS

Even a casual reading of parents' comments reveals feelings of doubt and uncertainty dating from early in the children's lives. "I was at my wit's end," says one mother. "We were all concerned," says another. Most of the children appeared to have problems before they reached school. It is not "scientific" to say so, but many parents appear to sense that "something is wrong" by the time the child is 2 or 3 years old. Many more suspect or fear that there is something amiss and try to reassure themselves that "he will outgrow it." The child may walk and talk late; he or she may be constantly in motion and never seem to need sleep; he or she may be a "loner," never playing with other children. Whatever the difficulty, parents often pray that next month or next year it will be gone. If there is a temptation to condemn this behavior, we must remember that rationalization is a legitimate, human means of coping with trouble.

Nevertheless, at some point all these parents faced the fact that their Johnny (or Susie—but fewer of these children appear to be girls) could not do something he or she should: read, talk properly, play, or sit still. And then the nightmare began: the pediatrician, the specialists, the tests. Maybe parents today face fewer hurdles than those who began several years ago. There may be more specialists, more knowledge, and more sympathy. The "state of the art" has grown in sophistication. Nevertheless, judging from the questionnaires, there is still a moment when parents must face terribly difficult decisions. Shall we allow the school to keep him or her back a grade? Shall we put him or her in psychological or psychiatric therapy? Shall we enter him or her in a special school or camp? And, of course, shall we allow him or her to take drugs?

Those decisions are no easier now than they were 10 or 15 years ago. The parent is tired and harassed with raising a difficult child and several others, just as difficult in their own "normal" way. Life is very complicated: you cannot leave this child with a sitter; cannot travel without making elaborate plans; cannot conduct a normal social life. You are hesitant to ask a friend to watch this child while you run to the market, even if you would gladly watch his or her child in return. Besides, it may not even be safe; the child may not understand or obey the stranger; he or she may impulsively dart after you into traffic; he or she may refuse to eat or sleep if deprived of his or her parents, even for a short time. When school time comes, you are constantly called for conferences with teachers or guidance counselors. You may be asked to withdraw him or her to transfer him or her to another class; he or she is a trial to you, to his or her teachers and classmates, to her or himself. The end result is a tired, resentful confused parent, guilty and even hating his or her own child. Oh, yes, you love the child. Of course you do. Only some days. . .

PARENTS IN THE MIDDLE

Not only do parents feel trapped and uncertain, but when they seek help, they find a bewildering lack of consensus. Often teachers, pediatricians, psychologists, and psychiatrists cannot agree on a course of treatment. The parent trying to map his or her next move finds both a conflict between disciplines and deep and bitter disagreement within disciplines. Fifteen years after minimal brain dysfunction and learning disabilities have become well-known, widely accepted terms, pediatricians can still be found who say "he'll outgrow it," teachers exist who are unaware of the difference between a lazy student and one who cannot learn. And as for specialists!—A very casual perusal of periodical articles directed to laymen is enough to send any concerned parent to his or her neighborhood witch doctor. Parents are told: drugs are the answer; drugs are not even a part of the answer; take him or her off all food additives; put him or her on megavitamins; take him or her to a psychiatrist; do not take him or her to a psychiatrist . . . and on, and on, and on.

In the area of drug therapy, the conflict is particularly acute. Because MBD and related problems are "invisible," it is difficult to make a firm diagnosis and even more difficult to arrive at a universal, or anywhere near universal, therapy. Still, certain drugs are frequently prescribed for certain symptoms associated with MBD. Most notable is Ritalin, prescribed to help hyperactive children focus better on one task at a time. Also, tranquilizers may be prescribed for the anxiety that often accompanies a perception that one is "special." Medication is usually prescribed in conjunction with other therapy: special education, pychiatric or psychological treatment, conferences and consultation with parents, etc. Rumors of abuse persist—horror stories of whole classes of children medicated to insure docility. While such abuses may exist, and if so they cannot be condoned, they are not within the scope of this chapter. The subject under discussion is the parents' role in deciding whether or not to allow their child to take drugs and the effect of that decision on family living.

THE PRESSURE OF TIME

Many pressures are applied to parents while they consider whether or not to agree to medication. There is pressure from school. Every child—and the handicapped are now included—has been assured a free, public education under the law. Nevertheless, a school can still apply pressure. The parent who believes that his or her child should study in a regular class can be told that, unless the child takes medication, he or she will be put in a class with emotionally disturbed or brain-damaged children. The parent who is convinced that his or her child is progressing in his education can be told that, without drugs, the child will not be promoted. Then, too, there is a more subtle pressure: an inference that the school knows better what is best for your child and that you are an uncooperative parent, blocking the child's progress for irrational, selfish reasons.

The pressure of time exacerbates parental doubts and anxieties. This pressure is especially acute when Ritalin or amphetamines are recommended. Stimulants are said to have a "paradoxical effect" on certain children, particularly those who are hyperactive. The following occurs in many cases:

> When stimulants are given in adequate doses, a favorable response— when it occurs—is rapidly obtained. Thus the child is able to adjust himself and organize his activities in the direction he wishes. The stimulant neither slows down nor peps up the child. Rather it mobilizes and increases his abilities to focus on meaningful stimuli and to organize his bodily movements more purposefully. Drug treatment should not be indefinite and is usually stoppped after age 11 or 12. ("Drugs and the Hyperactive Syndrome," 1971, p. 3)

Because the paradoxical effect seems to occur most often in children, it is logical to suppose that the therapy will no longer be effective when the subject is no longer a child. That is understandable. What is less helpful is the "last-chance" attitude of many physicians and others prescribing stimulant treatment. One mother said, "We really didn't want to put our son on drugs, but the school recommended them strongly and said to us, in effect, 'How can you deprive him of this help he needs and that he can only get now?' We consented very reluctantly because we knew it was now or never." Small doses were administered at first because the parents feared adverse side effects. When there were no results, the physician explained that the dosage was too small to do any good and that time was running out. The dosage was increased, with little effect, good or bad. Finally, after a 2 year trial, the parents were allowed to discontinue the drug. They did so with a sigh of relief.

To believe that time is such a very crucial factor, one must also believe that stimulants are or contribute to a "cure." They are not: parent after parent has reported that, once drug therapy is discontinued, they can discern no long-term benefit. Maturation, education, and other therapy may reduce or eliminate hyperactivity. Also, there is no minimizing the fact that the drug may allow a child to learn or prevent him from being irritable and distractible and thereby help him to acquire social skills. In this sense, it does have lasting effects. However, these medications are not "cures" in the sense that, if the child takes them before a certain age, they will cause his or her problem to go away. What they do is to help both parent and child to cope right now. The criterion should be: "Will it help him or her today?" not "Are there long-term benefits?"

Another false assumption is that the "paradoxical effect" is some sort of magic, that no other kind of medication but stimulants can help at all. This is not true: tranquilizers are sometimes effective. If a child is over 12 years old and if adolescence or other trauma begin to make his or her already difficult life more difficult, there are medications that can probably be of some help. Therefore, parents should be cautioned not to worry unduly about time. The cardinal rule is: It is your decision and, no matter how you decide, it is not irreversible. The parent should feel comfortable at all times and feel free to stop whenever he or she wishes. It must be remembered that:

> Drugs promise neither the passport to a brave new world nor the gateway to the inferno. Properly employed as a single component of a total treatment program, they can be helpful in realizing the goal of the healthy development of children. (Eisenberg, 1971, quoted in Solomons, 1973, p. 343)

WHEN MEDICATION WAS USED

A review of some of the cases reported in the questionnaire can give a picture of experiences typical of parents who have decided to allow medication, as well as those who have not. Details of cases described are changed to protect identities. The first, and largest, sample consists of children who have taken medication.

"It gave him a chance. Without it his life would have been hopeless," says Donald's mother, speaking of the medication that her son has been taking for over 9 years.

Donald's mother and father suspected in his first year of life that their son was not developing normally. Walking and talking came late, but besides that, he was abnormally irritable, restless, and active. He never sat still and almost never slept. Both parents found life with Donald extremely difficult, and when his little sister, a normal, active child, was born, their stamina was strained almost to the breaking point. Two pediatricians assured them that nothing was the matter. Then, a third pediatrician, a specialist in "special" children, conducted extensive tests and found evidence—both through an EEG (electroencephalogram) and in "soft neurological signs," symptoms that can be observed but do not show on an EEG—of minimal cerebral dysfunction. Medication, in conjunction with special education, was prescribed.

Donald's troubles were far from over, but the medication did help. "Life improved when he was placed on medication," says Donald's father. In fact, a visiting relative who frowned on the idea of putting children on drugs found that, when she was left alone with Donald, she had to resort to giving the medicine. The change in Donald—and in the relative—was dramatic. Donald immediately became cooperative, although in no way drugged or drowsy, and the doubtful lady became a convert.

In Donald's case, stimulants were prescribed: Dexedrine at first, then Ritalin when the effect of the Dexedrine wore off. Side effects were few, benefits great. Both parents pronounced themselves pleased with their decision and said that they would do the same again, if given a choice. To the question, "What comes now?" both replied a trifle uneasily. Donald is in his early teens; parents and physician concur that the medication must be tapered off and eventually discontinued. The therapy has been interrupted several times, especially in the summer when there is no school, without disastrous consequences. Nevertheless, they know the coming year will be one of trial and error. "We'll just have to play it by ear," says Donald's father. For this family, drugs have been a useful tool, enabling their child to learn and to function, giving them time to spend with him and with his sister. They are not anxious to give up this tool in their struggle to help their son achieve his full potential.

UNHAPPY PARENTS

Not all parents are as satisfied with the effect of medication as were Donald's. Only one mother in the sample reports that she was hesitant to allow medication at first but that it was she, not the physician, who asked that the dosage be increased. For the rest, initial reluctance to consent to drugs may foreshadow a less than happy experience with them for the entire family.

"It was a mistake," says Anne of the year which her son Mark spent on Ritalin. The medication had been prescribed at the insistence of the child's school because he was "having a great deal of difficulty in paying attention and would wander and daydream," although he was not hyperactive. For one year, Mark's parents grudgingly allowed him to take the drug. Always a small child, Mark's appetite was reduced, as is not uncommon with this drug. He became difficult to handle at mealtimes and had trouble sleeping. The family doctor, who had not recommended use of the drug, urged that Mark be taken off. After 1 year, Mark's parents decided that they would stop the therapy. Because the school insisted Mark remain on the drug, a placebo was given. "The school did not even know the difference," says Anne, which demonstrated to the already skeptical family that the benefits of the drug had been few, if any.

OTHER MEDICATIONS

Stimulants are the drugs that most people connect with MBD. However, the range of medications prescribed is staggering, especially considering how small a sample has been surveyed.

Two of the children took Thorazine for a considerable period of time. This drug is one of the phenothiazine family, drugs which "also produce a partial paralysis of the nervous system—a virtual chemical straitjacket indistinguishable from severe Parkinson's disease" (*Washington Star News,* 1972) in adults. However, a mother said that her child's physician had explained that the effects of the drug were much less dramatic when it was used for children. She said the drug was prescribed to make her child less anxious and apprehensive and that it achieved this end. "It just took the edge off," she said. Eventually, the effects of the Thorazine seemed to lessen and it was gradually discontinued, but she did feel it had been helpful and had had few bad effects.

A second mother whose child, John, took Thorazine was not nearly so sanguine. Describing herself as "extremely remorseful," she stated flatly that, given the choice, she would not now allow her child to take the drug. There were severe side effects, constipation and photosensivity. Because of the latter, John could only play outside for limited periods of time when the sun was shining. In addition, many medications had been tried before Thorazine and some of these had had nearly catastrophic side effects. Once John had become so lethargic that he had been unable to eat or attend school.

Why would parents submit a child to therapy that appears to be so undesirable? The answer is crucial to understanding the parent's predicament: John had already been expelled from one school because he was uncontrollable. At home, he was constantly in motion. He occupied his mother's entire, undivided attention, making it impossible for her to care adequately for her other child, a younger son. He rarely slept and despite the fact that his parents "spelled" each other at night, neither ever got sufficient rest. No babysitter could cope with John, so the parents never went out.

This description could lead to the conclusion that John's family consented to the use of Thorazine for their own benefit and not for his. This was not the case, for John was the worst sufferer. He was unhappy at school and at home, was isolated from his classmates and unable to get along with his brother. His life consisted of a series of "explosions" and temper tantrums; his extreme hyperactivity made any learning impossible. Thorazine produced a dramatic change: At a new, special class, John began to be able to pay attention, at least for short spans of time; he slept 8 hours each night; his temper was more under his control. Drastic though the therapy was, his ambivalent parents allowed its continuation until puberty. Yet it raised serious questions in their minds.

John's mother writes, "I am convinced . . . that drugs were too easy an answer." Torn by doubts as to whether one person should attempt to change the personality of another, she continues, "Ingenuity might have worked better than drugs, but the drugs were the only suggested solution, and I frankly didn't think to consider alternative answers."

Mellaril, also a phenothiazine, was prescribed in another instance. It had one undesirable side effect, producing an abnormally large appetite in an already heavy child. It did not produce marked improvement, although some was noted. Quite by accident, it was discontinued by a nurse in summer camp who did not understand that the child was to receive the medication. Because the child's parents believed the side effects of the drug outweighed its possible good effects, they kept him off. Because the school had insisted that the drug was helpful, they decided against telling their child's teacher, allowing her to assume that the medication was being given in the morning and evening, at home. After a suitable interval had elapsed and the school reported progress resulting in part from the medication, the parents informed the school that no medication had been given.

While stimulants and tranquilizers are the most frequently prescribed medications, they are by far not the only drugs used. A 1973 publication lists 18 different substances then prescribed in treating minimal brain dysfunction, and it is probable that the list has grown since that time (Millichap, 1973). Along with central nervous system stimulants and antianxiety and antipsychotic agents are antidepressants, antihistamines, and anticonvulsants. In referring to the last category, J. Gordon Millichap of Northwestern University Medical School says, "Reports of the efficacy of anticonvulsants in the control of hyperactivity are limited and are concerned primarily with trials in children whose behavior and learning problems are complicated by convulsive seizures" (p. 329).

The one anticonvulsant, Dilantin, that showed up in the sample was prescribed for a child who appeared to have no history of seizures. Christine's mother describes her problem as "probably brain damage; emotional and learning problems occurring as a result." It is true that no specific questions about seizures were asked, and this may be the reason that no information in that regard was volunteered. In any case, the mother reports that Dilantin was prescribed because a physician had said it was worth a try to see if anything would ". . . make her less withdrawn." Christine did not become less withdrawn. She did develop a rash, fever, and marked loss of equilibrium. Her concerned parents insisted that dosage be decreased, and when the symptoms persisted, terminated. However, drug therapy had lasted 3 months, producing much anxiety for the parents and little help for Christine.

TRIAL AND ERROR

Very few children arrive at the most effective drug on the first try. More often than not, parents describe a trial and error process that can be very disturbing, both to the child and to the whole family. Some drugs do not work; some work for a limited time and then "wear thin"; some have catastrophic side effects. Side effects reported include: loss of appetite, loss of equilibrium, excessive appetite, photosensitivity, anxiety, loss of sleep, rash, fever, and lethargy. However, there are many children who experience no adverse reactions at all. Also, it is apparent that gains often outweigh losses. Bad side effects are listed here only to warn parents that an initial trial period, which may be unpleasant, is involved. Families must be willing to endure such a period if they make the decision to try drug therapy. The initiation of medication should be scheduled at a convenient time—not when Johnny is just entering a new school or Grandma is coming from Peoria for a visit.

Also, it is important to remember that once a child is on medication, he or she must be carefully monitored. Even the advertisements for these drugs caution that children should receive frequent checkups and that medication should be interrupted from time to time to see whether it is still needed. Dosage may have to be adjusted or medications changed if side effects develop or if the child develops an immunity to the effect of one particular drug.

LONG-TERM GAINS

All parents were asked, "What do you see as long-term benefits?" The majority replied that there were few or none. Donald's mother, quoted earlier, was of the opinion that the immediate benefits of the drug, such as increased attention span and decreased irritability, gave rise to long-term benefits, such as increased learning in school and more friendships. Other parents said that, while the effects of the drugs were transient, they were still glad that medication had been tried. Perhaps medication had helped the child endure a particularly difficult period in his or her growing up. Often, parents voiced the opinion that the drugs had really had little benefit but that they were satisfied that they had left no stone unturned. One mother, whose son took Ritalin without effect, comments, "If something else appeared that might be helpful, we would try it."

Generally, parents who requested drug therapy or consented willingly to it seemed to be glad that they tried it, whether or not it worked. Parents who believed that they were "pressured" into putting their children on medication appeared more reluctant and less pleased with the results. "My feeling," says Anne, whose son Mark took Ritalin for a year, "is that the school recommended it as the easier way out than the one-to-one help he needed plus the extra attention, kindness and finding out just what it was that bothered him. . . ."

WHEN MEDICATION WAS NOT USED

No discussion of cases involving medication would be complete without some mention of cases in which medication was not recommended, or recommended but not accepted.

It is hard to get data on the large number of special children for whom drugs have not even been prescribed. The mother of one such child did answer the query by stating flatly that "not so much as an aspirin" had been suggested for her child's condition. Experience with special schools and camps and with parent groups demonstrates that many, many children are not on drug therapy and no such therapy has been recommended for them. Even the advertisement for Ritalin in a medical journal states that "Drug treatment is not indicated for all children with MBD," and appends a list of warnings for all those who do use it. If the drug is given, its use is to be interrupted from time to time to see whether it is still needed. Those critics who have suggested that all learning disabled children are automatically treated with drugs seem to be exaggerating.

Many parents for whose children medication was prescribed have decided against it. Fear of possible side effects, as well as doubts about whether the benefits would outweigh the risks, seemed to have motivated their decisions, regardless of whether pressure was applied. Fewer of this group responded to the questionnaire than did those whose children took drugs. However, this cannot be automatically interpreted as an indication that only a few parents decided against drug therapy. These parents may not have answered for a variety of reasons. They may be less interested in the subject of drugs than parents who have had the experience of giving medication to their youngsters. They may not feel a need to defend their decision or, conversely, they may feel uncomfortable about the decision and not want to discuss it.

Parents who did answer generally report no regrets. One mother says she is "happy" and would not change her decision. Another reported that, after a year of battling with a psychiatrist who wanted her child on medication, she was startled to hear the doctor announce, "It's a good thing *we* did not put Alan on drugs." Certainly it is clear that no one in the sample said anything like, "I shall always regret that I did not allow my child this chance."

SOME CONCLUSIONS

A quotation from a paper given at a Conference on Minimal Brain Dysfunction (Solomons, 1973) introduces this chapter; it is fitting that the same paper be invoked at the end. Especially considering the author's comment on parents, it is reassuring to read his conclusions:

1. Physicians are being pressured into the care of children with MBD.
2. Speaking generally . . . patients with MBD who are in drug therapy are not being adequately handled by the private practitioner.
3. . . . a regional facility is needed, where these children can have a multidisciplinary assessment . . . and long-term follow-up can be maintained.
4. Such centers should also be able to initiate and provide the necessary care to parents and other family members. . . .
5. Liaison could be maintained between the center and school personnel. . . .
6. Group sessions with parents and other involved family members could be carried out.
7. In some circumstances, organizations such as the Association for Children with Learning Disabilities and the Association for Retarded Children could be enlisted to help in specific programs. (p. 343)

The paper quoted was presented 5 years ago; many of its suggestions have been incorporated into programs. Some, unfortunately, have not. The level of cooperation between those involved with children who have MBD and related difficulties varies enormously according to geographical location and pure chance. Some parents are lucky: they find the right person or people to help them; but it is still largely a matter of luck. The significance of the seven points quoted above is that their author begins his paper by saying that parents cannot be trusted to give reliable histories of their own children. Nevertheless, even he acknowledges the necessity of close cooperation with parents and families. Parents are a fact of life. They are here to stay and if you can't beat them, you may as well join them.

The seventh point of these recommendations refers to certain organizations. Without going into detail, it should be explained that both groups mentioned are organizations of parents and professionals formed to work for children with specific disabilities. Both have a strong parent component. There are many other such organizations and they are becoming a potent force in advocating programs for handicapped children and adults. Their strength varies greatly from locality to locality, organization to organization, but they are a force to be reckoned with. As stated earlier, many of those polled in this chapter were members of such an organization. The amount of information, support, and strength that parents can gain from each other through these organizations cannot be underestimated. Whereas the author of the recommendations says that such groups can be helpful "in some circumstances," it may be that they can be helpful in many circumstances. Of course, the parents who join such a group have already come a long way: they acknowledge that they and their child have a problem and they are taking a giant step toward seeking a solution. In doing so, they are also offering their assistance to others. Professionals recommending medication to hesitant parents would do well to advise that they consult the local chapter of one of these organizations, when one exists in the area. In this way, parents can find out what others have done in similar circumstances and gain information and support for their own final decision.

Several points must be made in concluding this chapter. In reading them, professionals should remember that the author is a parent and is speaking unashamedly from the parents' point of view. Many of the findings of the chapter do have professional support and all are entitled at least to professional consideration.

1. An absolutely essential condition for successful use of medication is the parents' full knowledge and cooperation. While parents may consent reluctantly under pressure, it is these parents who have felt the most negative or ambivalent at the conclusion of therapy.

There were parents who reported negative feelings from start to finish, yet who admitted that the drugs had some beneficial effects, and there were others who were content to have tried, despite the fact that medication did not help. Still, it is important that parents feel satisfied with their decision. First, it is obvious that parental cooperation increases the chances of success. Parents who agree enthusiastically will make sure that medication is given as directed. They are more likely to be tolerant of the adjustment process, less hasty to stop giving the medicine because of slight side effects.

However, parental cooperation is needed because it is fundamentally, morally right that the parent have the ultimate responsibility for his or her child. The parent is the natural, proper guardian for the child. Not only is his or her consent needed, but his or her full, informed, and willing consent. It is needed for the child, for the parent, and for the rest of the family.

2. There is no "cure" for MBD and no absolute best therapy. Parents should be presented with all the alternatives and then left to draw their own conclusions. It is wrong to apply pressure on parents, to imply that they must decide at once and that the child cannot succeed without medication and will definitely succeed with it. Also, if the parent has some personal scruple against drugs per se, professionals should take that into consideration.

It seems to be true that medication given for MBD, by and large, has had few proven lasting bad effects. As far as we know at present, children do not become addicts in later life. However, widespread use of many of these medications is too recent for life-long follow-up to have been possible. Then, too, parents legitimately fear the effect on other children who may use their siblings' use of drugs as justification for their own experiments. Because the benefits of these drugs vary from case to case and seem to be transient at best, parental qualms deserve more weight. Drugs should be presented as one option, part of a total program.

3. Clearly there are some children who benefit from medication. Even in these cases, however, careful monitoring is necessary. Several years ago, a national magazine carried the story of a child who showed dramatic improvement under medication, then showed marked disturbance which disappeared when the medication was withdrawn (Bradbury, 1972). Follow-up cannot be overemphasized. Treatment cannot, and should not, be continued indefinitely.

4. Serious consideration should be given to the specific drug prescribed and its appropriateness to the particular condition. Although it is true that some medications seem to be helpful for certain conditions in some children, i.e., Ritalin for hyperactivity, it is equally true that the number of drugs prescribed and the number of symptoms for which they are prescribed is enormous. The survey raised many questions, such as: Why prescribe an anticonvulsant for a child with no history of seizures? Are the long-range effects of massive doses of Thorazine known? Have children who have taken Thorazine been followed through adulthood? Why would antihistimines be prescribed for MBD? If a child is subject to anxiety, could dosages of tranquilizers be limited to stress periods, such as exams or difficult social situations? Many of these questions were raised by the parents surveyed. A search for answers is needed.

5. "Minimal brain dysfunction" is a serious problem, for children and their families as well. The word "minimal" only refers to the fact that no definite lesion appears on an EEG and that the existence of a problem must be inferred from symptoms. Minimal brain dysfunction may be minimal compared to major brain injury, but it does cause major disruptions—in the child's ability to learn, to relate to others, and to live a normal life. Therefore, it is wrong to raise parents' hopes by suggesting that there is some magic age, such as 13 years, after which the problem goes away, and that all the child has to do is take a pill to make life tolerable for her- or himself and others until then. It is true, as one physician says, that,

> If the parent and teacher can bear with these children through their early childhood, they become easier to live with as they grow older and gain more control. They often succeed in college and in adulthood, where one need not be so much like one's neighbour and where competition is not so great (Bakwin, p. 4)

This is a far cry from saying that all problems will disappear. Which problems disappear and to what extent is an individual matter, dependent on many factors. Whereas it is true that early diagnosis and treatment are invaluable, it is also true that parents should be given a full picture of the possibilities, both good and bad, and be told how difficult it really is to predict with accuracy. If medication is not given when a child is 10 years old and he or she seems to need it at 16 years, there are many drugs that are still applicable. Also, one should not lose all hope because third grade was a disaster; tenth grade may be better. There is a film, "If a Boy Can't Learn" which tells the true story of a learning-disabled 17-year-old whose problem was not diagnosed until then but who was enabled by proper teaching to graduate from high school. Parents should know that new decisions can be made at any time if necessary; few decisions are as irreversible or as momentous as they may seem. While this may sound gloomy (the problems do not vanish entirely), it is also hopeful (there is always time to change course and try again).

6. Finally, a word to professionals: Do not underestimate parents. It is amazing that they can do what they do and surprising how understanding they can be, given the full story. Living with some of these children is a feat that should not be discounted. Loving them is difficult, if not almost impossible at times. Yet parents do it every day and never think twice about it. What they need from you is assurance that you are doing your homework. Is sufficient research being done to follow-up the children of this generation who have been placed on intensive drug therapy? Are new methods of treatment being sought continuously? What about preventive measures—are obstetrical methods in this country as good as they could possibly be? (Birth complications proved to cause brain damage must be reduced.)

Parents continue to do their job—they have no choice. Professionals must do theirs and not regard the parent as "the enemy." Parents are a valuable source of information and of assistance. To no one else in the world is the "special" child so truly "special" as to his or her parent, who is also teacher, advocate and friend.

REFERENCES

Bakwin, R.M. *The Brain Injured Child (Cerebral Damage)*. Reprinted by The New York Association for Brain Injured Children, 305 Broadway, New York, N.Y. 10007.

Bradbury, W. An Agony of Learning. *Life,* October 6, 1972, 57–68.

Do You Know This Child. Pamphlet published by the New York Association for Brain Injured Children, 305 Broadway, New York, N.Y. 10007.

Drugs and the Hyperactive Syndrome. Reprinted from *American Education*, U.S.

Dept. of Health, Education & Welfare, Office of Education, Vol. 7, No. 5, June 1971, in NYABIC, Vol. 12, No. 4, Fall 1971, p. 3.

Eisenberg, L. Principles of Drug Therapy in Child Psychiatry with Special Reference to Stimulant Drugs. *American Journal of Orthopsychiatry, 41,* 371–379.

Giles, M.K. (Ed.). *For Parents of Children with Learning Disabilities.* Center for Learning Disabilities, Rose F. Kennedy Center for Research in Mental Retardation and Human Development, Albert Einstein College of Medicine, Bronx, New York, February 1971.

"If a Boy Can't Learn" Lawren Productions, Inc., P.O. Box 1542, Burlingame, Calif. 94010. (film)

Millichap, J.G. Drugs in management of minimal brain dysfunction. In F. de la Cruz, B.H. Fox, & R.H. Roberts, (Eds.), *Minimal Brain Dysfunction. Annals of the New York Academy of Sciences,* 1973, *205,* 321–334.

Solomons, G. Drug Therapy: Initiation and Follow-Up. In F. de la Cruz, B.H. Fox, & R.H. Roberts, (Eds.), *Minimal Brain Dysfunction.* New York: New York Academy of Sciences, 1973.

Washington Star News, Nov. 5, 1972; reprinted in *Congressional Record,* Oct. 9, 1973.

7

HYPERACTIVE CHILDREN AT RISK

KAREN PREIS, M.D.
HANS R. HUESSY, M.D.

INTRODUCTION

Today, it is accepted that the "hyperactive" or MBD (minimal brain dysfunction) syndromes represent one of the most common behavior problems in childhood and account for a high percentage of referrals to child guidance clinics (Rogers, Lilienfield & Pasamanick, 1955; Chess, 1960; Laufer & Denhoff, 1957; Werner, Bierman, French, Simonian, Connor, Smith & Campbell, 1968). These behaviors have been described in the scientific literature since 1902 and have been recognized in all areas of the world *(Report on the Conference of Stimulant Drugs,* 1971). The most common complaint made of these children is that they are extremely overactive or restless. In addition, the child is often unable to sustain attention for more than a short period of time and is extremely impulsive and highly distractible. Even though of normal intelligence, "hyperactive" children often do poorly in school as a result of their inattention and impulsiveness. These children present a complex challenge to their families, educators, pediatricians, child psychiatrists and psychologists, and neurologists.

Estimates of prevalence vary. The work of Stewart, Pitts, Craig

129

and Dieruf (1966) indicates that 4% of first grade students in the St. Louis school system suffer from "hyperactive" behavior disorders. They found a prevalence of 1 per 25 students, which agreed with opinions of kindergarten and first grade teachers with whom the authors spoke, in that on the average there was one "hyperactive" child in every class. Prechtl and Stemmer (1962) found a higher prevalence in their study of Dutch children. They termed their syndrome the "choreiform syndrome," which they defined as behavior problems associated with minimal choreiform movements detectable using electromyography. Today these children would be diagnosed as having MBD. They found this syndrome present in 20% of elementary grade school boys and 10% of girls. The syndrome was severe in 5% of the boys and 1% of the girls.

Huessy, in his epidemiologic study examining the natural course of "hyperactive" behavior disorders in childhood, noted that 10% of second grade students in rural Vermont schools manifested symptoms consistent with the "hyperactive" syndrome (Huessy & Gendron, 1970). Huessy discussed this high prevalence. If learning disorders caused by severe lack of stimulation in early childhood are omitted, there are numerous studies indicating a 10% incidence of behavior disorders and a 10% incidence of learning disorders in the United States elementary school population. As a result of some overlap between these groups, he concluded that it was probable that 15% of all children had one or another, or both, of these types of problems.

There seems to be a definite sex ratio. Estimates of males to females being affected range from four to one (Huessy & Gendron, 1970) to nine to one (Werry, 1968a).

HISTORICAL BACKGROUND

The hyperactive child syndrome was probably first described in 1845 by Heinrich Hoffman, a German physician. In his children's book he told the story of "Fidgety Phil" in pictures and verse. His humorous stories spoke of the following:

Fidgety Phil,
He won't sit still;
He wriggles, and giggles. . .

The naughty, restless child
Growing still more rude and wild.

Since the time of Heinrich Hoffman it has become evident that this is not a humorous problem. The children's story is entertaining, but the real-life story for these children and their families is far more serious.

Research on the etiology of the "hyperactive" and "minimal brain dysfunction" syndromes has taken two parallel and, at times, mutually exclusive areas of examination. One area of research relates the symptoms to evidence of some kind of organic central nervous system damage or dysfunction, while the other explains everything by psychodynamic factors.

The behavioral symptoms which would be included under the diagnosis of the "hyperactive" syndrome have been noted to occur with central nervous system disorders. Still (1902) was probably the first to describe the behavioral symptoms, particularly lack of impulse control, seen in children with brain damage. His report was followed by studies of changes of behavior in individuals who had sustained injuries to their brains after they had reached adulthood. In the 1920s, the literature began describing "the nervous conditions" in children that affected learning and caused behavior disturbances (Burr, 1921; Miles, 1921). Subsequently Ebaugh (1923) reported on changes in behavior of children who had previously had encephalitis. This was followed by the work of Kahn and Cohen (1934) and of Bond and Smith (1935), which described certain behavioral sequelae observed in children who had been victims of encephalitis lethargica and other central nervous system injury.

There have been many studies that have attempted to link specific central nervous system infections, trauma, and epilepsy with resulting changes in behavior and learning ability (Hohman, 1922; Sherman & Beverly, 1923; Bond, 1932; Blau, 1937; Lurie & Levy, 1942; Wagenheim, 1954; Ounsted, 1955; Thurston, Middlekamp, & Mason, 1955; and Johnson, 1960). No specific central nervous system disease was found to be specific for "hyperactive" behavior disorders.

The theory for the organic etiology of these "hyperactive" behaviors was given dramatic impetus in 1937 when Charles Bradley, of the Emma Pendleton Bradley Home in Rhode Island, showed that amphetamine significantly modified the behavior of children with this symptom constellation. With stimulant medication the children became calmer, their behavior improved, and their learning disabilities decreased. The use of barbiturates made these children's problems worse. The causal association between the "hyperactive" behaviors and the postulated organic etiology led to the first diagnostic labels for these syndromes: "Postencephalitic behavior disorder," "organic drivenness," "minimal brain injury," "brain damage," and "association deficit pathology." After Bradley (1957), Laufer and Denhoff (1957), and Denhoff, Laufer, and Holden (1959) coined the term "hyperkinetic impulse disorder," the behaviors associated with the "hyperactive" syndrome came to be held as a legitimate diagnostic sign of brain damage in children.

From the 1940s to the 1960s there was prolific research into brain function and its relation to psychological dysfunction and to the education of children with brain dysfunction and damage (Werner & Strauss, 1941; Strauss & Werner, 1942; Werner & Thuma, 1942; Strauss, 1944; Strauss & Lehtinen, 1947; Gesell & Amatruda, 1941; Strauss & Kephart, 1955; Ingram, 1956; Levy, 1959, 1966).

There has been extensive investigation to detect subtle, organic insults that may be affecting behavior. The major focus has been on perinatal insults (Pasamanick, Rogers, & Lilienfeld, 1956; Clements, 1966; Burks, 1960). Werry, Weiss, and Douglas (1964) noted that disorders of pregnancy such as bleeding, toxemia, high blood pressure during pregnancy, birthweight of under 5 pounds, any cerebral trauma, unconsciousness, and any type of anoxia requiring active medical intervention, tended to occur more frequently during the pregnancies and deliveries of hyperactive children than among a control group. From a review of the birth records of children with behavior disorders, Knobloch and Pasamanick (1966) demonstrated an association between prematurity and complications of pregnancy and delivery, and behavior disorders. They found a variety of psychological, behavioral, and neurological problems in children demonstrating behavior disorders and reading disabilities, as well as in children suffering from cerebral palsy, epilepsy, and mental deficiency. The highest association of these complications was found for children who were "hyperactive, confused and disorganized."

Other research, however, has shown contradictory results (Stewart et al., 1966). Minde, Webb, and Sykes (1968) studied the birth records of 56 hyperactive children and compared them with 56 controls, with respect to 23 different prenatal and perinatal complications. They found that the only significant difference was that more "hyperactive" than normal children were born following an abnormally short or long labor which was further complicated by the use of forceps. There was no evidence that the mothers of hyperactive children suffered from or were more predisposed to have difficulties producing brain damage in their offspring than were the mothers of normal children. Their findings were supported by a 10 year follow-up study of the children of the Kauai pregnancy study, which indicated that there were no differences found between children with and without perinatal complications who were living outside of institutions, in the proportion of poor grades or in the incidence of language, perceptual, and emotional problems. It was concluded that many more children were affected by unfavorable environment than by severe perinatal stress (Werner et al., 1968).

Despite the dramatic evidence of an association between "hyperactive" behavior disorders and central nervous system damage and disease, other investigators were beginning to note that there were many children who suffered these same behavioral, social, and emotional disabilities who did not have any neurological stigmata or strikingly abnormal electroencephalographic signs that would permit a solid diagnosis of brain damage (Eisenberg, 1957; Chess, 1960; Stewart et al., 1966; Minde et al., 1968). One of the first authors to express this concern was Childers (1935) who stated that in his experience only a minor proportion of the cases of "hyperactivity" that he saw were directly related to a definite neurological disease. He began to focus attention on the psychological and sociological factors that might be etiologic in this syndrome, in particular the lack of security which he perceived in these children. The psychoanalytic literature began to state that most behavioral disturbance in children could be explained on the basis of early repeated traumatic events in childhood, in particular, disturbances in the mother–child relationship. There is an abundance of literature discussing the psychodynamic etiology for "hyperactive" behaviors and learning impairment (Pearson, 1954; Rexford & Van Amerongen, 1957).

As a result of this purely psychodynamic or psychosocial approach, many children were not diagnosed correctly, the neurological component to their difficulty was missed, and they were declared to be untreatable. This difficulty in accurate diagnosis is quite understandable because many of the behavioral difficulties included in the "hyperactive" syndrome can be explained in many cases on a purely psychodynamic basis. It is often not easy to recognize the organic dysfunction. It is still not possible to discuss with great accuracy how subtle organic and central nervous system deviation affects psychological symptoms and personality structure.

In addition, the psychodynamic explanation was given support from the observations that some children who had had a dramatic central nervous system injury had absolutely no behavioral sequelae. It became increasingly evident that behavioral sequelae of brain damage in childhood could be extremely diverse. It could vary from an absence of behavioral disturbance to apparent behavioral disturbance, to the presence of mental subnormality or serious disorganization of social, intellectual, and interpersonal functioning indistinguishable from the major psychoses of childhood (Birch, 1964; Thomas, Chess, & Birch, 1968; Wender, 1971; Chess, 1972; Shaffer, 1973). The result of these findings was a subtle shift in terminology from "minimal brain damage" to "minimal brain dysfunction" (Clements & Peters, 1962).

Several authors have raised concern about the danger of the use of the term "minimal brain dysfunction" and "mild brain damage." They think that the terms have been used too often as all-inclusive labels for a heterogeneous group of children whose behavior difficulties may or may not have an organic basis. The risk is that even though there is no direct evidence of central nervous system pathology, the presence of the brain disorder may be automatically inferred from the child's behavior. This could result in an inexact and excessive diagnosis that would equate "hyperactivity" with "minimal brain dysfunction" (Birch, 1964; Chess, 1972). As a result, some authors avoid this problem by using the term "hyperactive behavior" disorder rather than the term "minimal brain dysfunction." They will only use the term "minimal brain dysfunction" if they can document some evidence of cerebral malfunctioning on electroencephalogram, soft neurological signs, or psychological tests indicative of specific organically based learning difficulties.

Just as the organic hypothesis has not held true as etiologic for all children with hyperactivity, neither does the psychogenic hypothesis. While a significant number of families of hyperactive children appear abnormal from a psychiatric point of view, there is a surprising number who also appear essentially normal. Werry, Weiss, Douglas, and Martin (1966) and Stewart et al. (1966) found the frequency of psychiatric disorders in the families of "hyperactive" and control children to be similar. They concluded that hyperactivity could apparently occur in the absence of any parental abnormality and vice versa. Furthermore, the coexistence of parental pathology and "hyperactivity" in a child could be just as easily explained by a genetic hypothesis as by a psychodynamic one.

Malone (1963), in his South End Family Project, noticed disturbed children from disorganized families who demonstrated all of the common behavioral symptoms associated with the "hyperactive" syndrome. Most clinicians today recognize the difficulty in making the diagnosis of "hyperactivity" in "deprived" children. Malone's work highlights this difficulty in sorting out the effects of family disorganization, inadequate environmental stimulation, negative environmental influences, poor nutrition, and inadequate schooling.

In addition, Werry (1968b) postulates that there may be confusion between the "hyperactive" syndrome and the pure motor hyperactivity that can exist in the absence of any other emotional or behavioral problems, or indeed, any other abnormalities, be it either a neurological deficit or a learning problem. He thinks that for some children who are being classified under the "hyperactive" syndrome the learning and behavioral difficulties are secondary to pure differences in motor activity level.

The literature on the "hyperactive" syndrome of childhood and "minimal brain dysfunction" is a prolific one. The syndrome or syndromes has been the subject of several recent clinical investigations (Bradley, 1957; Laufer & Denhoff, 1957; Burks, 1960; Stewart et al., 1966; Werry, 1968a; Gross & Wilson, 1974). Numerous reviews have been published on the syndromes of the "hyperactive" child and "minimal brain dysfunction" (Pincus & Glaser, 1966; Stewart, 1970; Marwitt & Stenner, 1972; Huessy, 1973; Wender & Eisenberg, 1974; Safer & Allen, 1976). Recent research is attempting to discover biochemical abnormalities of the central nervous system (Safer & Allen, 1976).

There is also an extensive literature on the treatment of these children. After Eisenberg, Conners, and Sharp (1965) published their study, which demonstrated that the "hyperactive" child was generally unresponsive to psychotherapeutic approaches, there was an increased research on the psychophysiological, behavioral modification, counselling, psychoeducational, and remedial education approaches. These different approaches can be applied singularly or together to help these children and their families, and are thoroughly reviewed by Safer and Allen (1976).

Even though the literature is extensive, a great deal of further investigation is expected. If the "hyperactive" or "minimal brain dysfunction" syndrome were only a problem of childhood or adolescence that was of short duration there would not be the concern that there is today. In the 1950s it was generally accepted that the hyperkinetic syndrome and "minimal brain dysfunction" syndromes diminished with age (Bradley, 1957; Lytton & Knobel, 1958). It was taken for granted that the responsibility of physicians and educators was to stand by the parents in the early difficult years, while reassuring them that their child would "outgrow" this problem. Laufer and Denhoff (1957) stated, "In later years, the syndrome tends to wane spontaneously and disappear. We have not seen it persist in those patients followed to adult life." As a result, children and their families waited impatiently for the arrival of puberty and the "cure" that this would bring.

Recent evidence, however, indicates that this is not the case. Laufer (1962) and Anderson and Plymate (1962) indicated that "minimal brain dysfunction" persisted into adolescence. It is becoming increasingly clear that for some children, the symptoms from which they are suffering will be a lifelong disability. The results of clinical and empirical investigations are indicating the major problems of

these children are short attention span and impulsivity, which interfere not only with the child's academic life, but also with social and
emotional learning. The recognition of the symptoms of the "hyperactive" and "minimal brain dysfunction" syndromes in adolescents and
in adults, and the data from retrospective and prospective studies indicate
that although young adults and teenagers have less motor hyperactivity and restlessness, the educational, social, and emotional problems persist.

Between 4 and 20% of school age children are potentially at high
risk for difficulties. Today, there are real problems for these children,
their parents, their siblings, their peers, and their teachers. Tomor-
row, the problems continue for these "grown-up" hyperactives, their
spouses, their friends, their employers, and perhaps their own children. The remainder of this chapter will delineate the long-term
implications for these children that result from having the psychological, academic, and/or social manifestations of "hyperactivity" or
"minimal brain dysfunction" in childhood.

TERMINOLOGY AND CLINICAL ORIENTATION OF THE AUTHORS

As a result of the confusion in terminology that exists in this literature, we have found it necessary to categorize the many behavioral
manifestations reported in the literature into some form of standardized nomenclature. This was done in order to have meaningful data
to compare, as well as to allow for reasonable organization. The decision to place behaviors into either the "hyperactive" or the MBD
category reflected our clinical orientation.

Throughout this chapter the term "hyperactive" is used to indicate
the "hyperkinetic reaction of childhood and adolescence" as defined
by the current American Psychiatric Association diagnostic nomenclature (DSM II, 1968), and the "hyperkinetic syndrome" which is being
proposed by the World Health Organization (Rutter, Lebovici, Eisenberg, Sneznevskij, Sadoun, Brooke, & Lin, 1969). Both of these terms
imply a long-term pattern of behavior in childhood and adolescence
characterized by motor restlessness, short attention span, poor impulse control, learning difficulties, and emotional lability. Both of
these terms stress that it is a constellation of symptoms and not
necessarily a discreet disease entity which is being described by these
terms. This is a more general term than MBD.

MBD will be used to indicate "minimal brain dysfunction" as defined by a Public Health Service Committee, led by Clements (1966):

> This term as a diagnostic and descriptive category refers to "children of near-average, average or above average intellectual capacity with certain learning and/or behavior disabilities, ranging from mild to severe, which are associated with deviations of function of the central nervous system. These deviations may manifest themselves by various combinations of impairment in perception, conceptualization, language, memory, and control of attention, impulse or motor function. . . . These aberrations may arise from genetic variations, biochemical irregularities, perinatal brain insults, or other illnesses or injuries sustained during the years critical for development and maturation of the central nervous system, or from unknown causes." (Pps 9–10.)

MBD implies a detectable neurological dysfunction which is manifest in either specific cognitive function testing and/or on physical examination, and which is associated with the behavioral manifestations of "hyperactivity," and an IQ of ≥ 80. It is very probable that some of the children diagnosed as "hyperactive" really suffer from MBD, but the data given in the literature and/or the nature of the study do not give sufficient information to further refine the diagnosis to MBD.

The authors believe that the children, adolescents, and adults classified as "hyperactive" and MBD represent individuals suffering from "clinical syndromes." There is a concurrence of a set of signs and symptoms that characterize and distinguish these two groups of individuals from others. The individuals suffering from either of these "clinical syndromes" if followed over time are shown to have an increased risk for both present and later academic, social, and behavioral problems.

We do not believe that either "hyperactive" individuals or individuals diagnosed as MBD suffer from a disease. There is no study that unequivocally identifies changes in structure or function of the central nervous system, or other body organs, which would explain this behavior.

The "clinical syndromes" we are discussing are still very general categories. Future research is anticipated to define these "clinical syndromes" more precisely. There may be many subgroups of the MBD and "hyperactive" syndromes. Current research indicates that for some of these children the behavioral, educational, social, and emotional difficulties that are observed are the result of some pre- or perinatal insult; for others the direct result of central nervous system infection, trauma, or other insult; for others a developmental lag in central nervous system maturation; for others abnormalities of central nervous system neurotransmitters; for others a metabolic imbalance such as hypoglycemia; for others a breakdown in family and social stability; for others a purely psychogenic basis; for others the result of some pattern of genetic inheritance; and for others a combination of these factors.

The authors will utilize the term MBD when they note "soft" neurological signs described in the studies reviewed. "Soft" neurological signs are variable and lack correlation with anatomical lesions. These include difficulties in fine motor coordination, visual–motor coordination imbalance, choreiform movements, clumsiness, poor speech, and problems of left–right discrimination. If there are hard neurological signs indicative of brain damage, the individuals will be reported as suffering from brain damage.

Reports of abnormal electroencephalograms (EEGs) will not alone place a child in the MBD category as opposed to the "hyperactive" category. Abnormalities in the EEG can be found in "hyperactive" children and children with other psychiatric disturbances, as well as in normal children. In addition, "hyperactive" and MBD children can have a normal EEG. The majority of EEG studies to date have been shown to be inconclusive in that the abnormalities are nonspecific. We only obtain EEGs if the history is suggestive of seizures or episodic behavior.

We lean toward a diagnosis of MBD versus "hyperactivity" when minor congenital anomalies are present (Waldrop, Penderson & Bell, 1968). These stigmata have also been noted in schizophrenic children and overlap with some of those seen in mongolism. They include the following: anomalies of the epicanthus, hyperteleorism, absent or nonpendant lower earlobe, high arched palates, short and curving fifth fingers, single palmar crease, abnormally long and webbed third toe, abnormal space between the first and second toe, and strabismus. All of these come about in the first trimester of pregnancy and are often related to viral infection during that time.

Psychological test results alone do not place a child in the MBD category. There are no psychological test findings pathonomonic of either "hyperactivity" or MBD. Variability of subtest scores and other signs of organicity on testing—i.e., perserveration, concreteness, stereotyped and poorly conceived mental processes—support the diagnosis of organic dysfunction and lead us to consider that the child may have MBD versus "hyperactivity."

We distinguish between the categories of "hyperactivity" and MBD because our clinical impression is that the two syndromes have different responses to medication and different prognoses. Much of the confusion in the literature is a result of studies that have investigated both of these syndromes as if they were equivalent, with the result that the interventions have not been able to be correlated with outcome in any meaningful way.

The problem of categorizing children as "hyperactive" versus MBD is further compounded by the fact that the literature often reflects the orientation of the reporter and does not include important data that a professional in another speciality would collect. The educators often report on school performance without including physical assessment, the emotional climate of the family, or the socioeconomic status of the family. The pediatricians are more likely to report the child as demonstrating a deviation in development because a large part of their work deals with the variability and unpredictability of children's development. They often do not consider that the etiology may be psychogenic or sociogenic. The psychiatrist, however, may assume that the problem is psychogenic or sociogenic and may fail to consider that the behavior disorder may be secondary to an abnormality of the central nervous system. The neurologist is often uncomfortable stating that the child has any organic impairment unless he or she has the classical neurological signs of damage, i.e., sensory defects, motor abnormalities, abnormalities of gait, and reflex changes. The psychologist sometimes will identify the children only on the basis of test results.

Confusion also results from the fact that the behavioral manifestations of both "hyperactivity" and MBD vary depending on the individual's age (Figure 1) and the expression of these behaviors varies depending upon the setting. The family is usually aware of all the behavioral manifestations in that they see the child at all times of day in a variety of situations. The educator who observes the child in the classroom is familiar with most of the difficulties, especially the learning problems and the difficulties that these children have in a group setting. The physician or psychologist, however, who evaluates the child in a highly structured, minimally stimulating "one-to-one" setting may see no evidence of "hyperactive" behaviors.

The problem is further complicated in that the "hyperactive" child's behavior shows marked variability from day to day. Parents often describe their child as being "two different people" or as having "Jekyll and Hyde" personalities. Their school work may vary from day to day, week to week, and, in some cases, even year to year. A seemingly "good" year for a child interspersed among preceding and succeeding "poor" years is most often related to a firm, patient teacher who understands the child, combined with a highly structured classroom.

In addition, there are several other conditions that must be ruled out before one can make the diagnosis of either MBD or "hyperactivity"; the diagnosis of reactive disorders, childhood and adolescent depressions, and anxiety neuroses must be excluded. The children, adolescents, or adults must have difficulties which pervade all aspects of their lives; problems in one sphere only would tend to favor other psychiatric diagnoses. The structure and stability of the family and school must be accurately assessed in order to determine whether

Figure 1. Behavioral symptoms of "hyperactive" children.

INFANCY	PRE SCHOOL	ELEMENTARY SCHOOL
Restlessness	*Into everything*	*Short attention span*
Irritability	Short attention span	Daydreams (girls)
Irregularity	*Destruction*	Can't sit still (boys)
Excessive crying	Can't sit still	Low frustration tolerance
High fevers	Temper tantrums	*Overreacts*
Poor eater	Speech problems	*Learning problems*
High activity	Gets to sleep or	Doesn't complete tasks
	Wakes up very early	Class clown
	Cruel to animals	Aggressive
	Aggressive	Poor peer relations
	Impulsive	Impulsive
	Trouble with groups	Poor self-image
	Mood swings	
	Fire setting	
	Enuresis	

HIGH SCHOOL	ADULTS
Educationally retarded	Easily distractable
Poor attention span	Impulsive
Lack of motivation	*Short fuse*
Unreliable	Explosive
Aggressive	Sleep problems
Impulsive	Mood swings
Overreacts	*Trouble with lasting relationships*
Struggles with authority	*Can't relax*
Delinquent activity (boys)	Stretches the truth
Promiscuity (girls)	Trouble with groups
Mood swings	Alcohol abuse
Lies	Overly dramatic
Accident prone	*Poor self-image*
Suicidal gestures	Exposes self
Poor self-image	Poor job performance
School dropout	Frequent arguments or fights
Alcohol abuse	

these are etiological or contributory factors to the symptoms. The psychological symptoms must be assessed to ascertain whether they are the result of a purely psychodynamic problem or whether they are reactive symptoms brought about by the difficulties that the child suffers in his or her day-to-day life as a result of being "hyperactive." Careful history must rule out fatigue, hunger, or drug abuse as a cause of these behaviors. Physical examination and neurological examination must rule out other causes of behavior and/or learning problems. Unfortunately, the literature in this field does not always allow for these distinctions.

There is a need for multidisciplinary research that assesses *all* the variables and follows these children over time. The limited assessments have resulted in multiple theories regarding etiology. The multiple theories have resulted in limited, fragmented, or incomplete therapy for these children. Each theory may have its validity for a small "subgroup" of children. There may be many different "subgroups" that have a final common pathway of behavioral expression; what we see may represent individualized, unique interactions among biological, psychological, and social factors.

Evidence for Risk of Future Difficulties

Evidence that children diagnosed as "hyperactive" or MBD are at risk for future emotional, academic, and social difficulties is obtained from six sources:

1. Epidemiological study of the natural history of children with "hyperactive" behaviors.
2. Retrospective studies of adults whose histories have indicated "hyperactivity" or MBD in childhood.
3. Prospective studies of children diagnosed as "hyperactive" or MBD.
4. Identification of adolescents who manifest the symptoms of "hyperactivity" or MBD.
5. Identification of adults who manifest the symptoms of "hyperactivity" or MBD.
6. Studies of the blood relatives of "hyperactive" children.

Study of the natural history

As a result of the growing interest in the "hyperactive" syndrome, minimal brain dysfunction (MBD), and learning disabilities, it became important to know something of the natural history of these disorders. In 1964, Dr. Hans Huessy, while serving as a consultant to the Counseling Service of Addison County, Inc., Vermont, developed a checklist that consisted of the 14 problems that appeared to be most often mentioned by the teachers when he was consulting with the schools. He administered this checklist to a random sampling of schools in the county. The teachers filled out the questionnaire on 1113 students in grades 1–6, approximately 44% of the total student body in these grades ($N = 2524$). He noted four problems that were the most frequently reported: slow learner, but probably not retarded; fidgety; short attention span; and interrupts class. His data indicated the following: There were fewer problems in the first grade in all categories; during the second grade the most problems were present, especially in learning areas; during the third grade all problems except for interrupting in class seemed to be lowest, and by the fourth grade there was again an increase in learning problems which tapered by the fifth grade (Figure 2).

He also noted that half of the underachievers in the sample seemed to demonstrate symptoms of "hyperactivity." He was impressed by the change in symptom patterns over time, as well as by the high proportion of "hyperactive" children who seemed to be referred to the clinic. Therefore, in 1965, he began a longitudinal population study in order to ascertain the natural history of children with both the behavioral and academic difficulties associated with the "hyperactive" and MBD symptoms. He designed a questionnaire to document the kinds of behaviors that were usually associated with

Figure 2. Major problems displayed by 1113 school children (grades 1–6) in Addison County, Vermont. (——) Slow learner, probably not retarded; (++++) fidgety; (– – –) short attention span; (•••••) interrupts class.

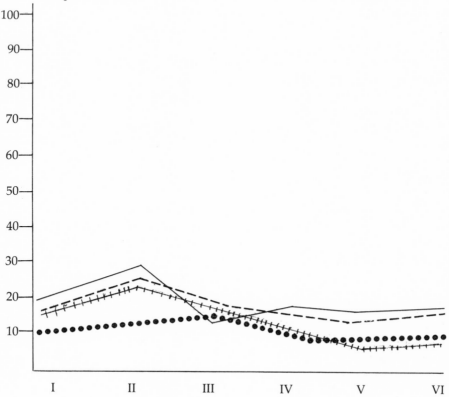

Figure 3. Huessy psychiatric history.

Birthday:_____

Name:_____

Sex:_____

I. SOCIAL MATURITY:

REMARKS

1. Degree of participation in group activities.
   □ ABOVE AVERAGE
   □ AVERAGE
   □ BELOW AVERAGE
   □ POOR
   □ NONE

2. Relationship to adults and children on a one to one basis.
   □ ABOVE AVERAGE
   □ AVERAGE
   □ BELOW AVERAGE
   □ POOR
   □ NONE

3. If below average on either ratings 1 or 2, does he/she do better in one to one relationships than in group settings?
   □ YES   □ NO

4. Amount of aggressive behavior.
   □ NONE
   □ OCCASIONAL
   □ AVERAGE
   □ MORE THAN AVERAGE
   □ CONSTANT

5. Impulsivity.
   □ RARELY
   □ OCCASIONAL
   □ AVERAGE
   □ FREQUENT
   □ CONSTANT

6. Frustration tolerance.
   □ UNUSUALLY HIGH TOLERANCE
   □ FAIRLY HIGH TOLERANCE
   □ AVERAGE TOLERANCE

☐ MODERATELY LOW TOL-
ERANCE
☐ VERY LOW TOLERANCE

7. Overall emotional mood.
☐ FLUCTUATES APPROPRIATE
TO SURROUNDINGS AND
SUBJECT MATERIAL WITH
KEEN INTEREST
☐ FLUCTUATES APPROPRIATE-
LY, BUT LESS INTENSELY
THAN ABOVE
☐ FLUCTUATES ACCORDING TO
INTEREST AND STIMULI
☐ REQUIRES ADDITIONAL
STIMULUS TO GET DESIRED
RESPONSE
☐ SEVERE FLUCTUATIONS IN
MOOD, FROM ECSTASY TO
DEEP DESPAIR WITH LITTLE
STIMULUS

8. Parents and other teachers
report problems with this
child with frequent crisis
situations occurring.
☐ NEVER
☐ RARELY
☐ FREQUENTLY
☐ QUITE FREQUENTLY
☐ CONSTANTLY

II. NERVOUS AND MUSCULAR DEVELOPMENT:

1. Coordination and agility.
☐ SUPERIOR
☐ GOOD
☐ AVERAGE
☐ POOR
☐ VERY POOR

2. Fine muscle tremor and/or
twitches of face, hands
and arms are noted (i.e.
fidgity).
☐ NEVER
☐ RARELY
☐ OCCASIONALLY

☐ FEQUENTLY
☐ CONSTANTLY

3. Speech and ability to express himself are
☐ SUPERIOR
☐ ABOVE AVERAGE
☐ AVERAGE
☐ BELOW AVERAGE
☐ POOR

4. Writing ability is
☐ EXCELLENT
☐ ABOVE AVERAGE
☐ AVERAGE
☐ POOR
☐ UNREADABLE

III. PERFORMANCE:

1. Spatial perception and ability to see and correct errors.
☐ SUPERIOR
☐ ABOVE AVERAGE
☐ AVERAGE
☐ POOR
☐ VERY POOR

2. Reading level according to age and grade.
☐ SUPERIOR
☐ ABOVE AVERAGE
☐ AVERAGE
☐ BELOW AVERAGE
☐ VERY RETARDED

3. Mathematics level according to age and grade.
☐ SUPERIOR
☐ ABOVE AVERAGE
☐ AVERAGE
☐ BELOW AVERAGE
☐ VERY RETARDED

4. Spelling level according to age and grade.
☐ SUPERIOR
☐ ABOVE AVERAGE

☐ AVERAGE
☐ BELOW AVERAGE
☐ VERY RETARDED

5. Performance in general is
☐ SUPERIOR
☐ ABOVE AVERAGE
☐ AVERAGE
☐ CONSISTANTLY POOR
☐ VERY UNPREDICTABLE AND ERRATIC

IV. GENERAL ATTITUDE AND BEHAVIOR:

1. Activity and energy level seems
☐ ABOVE AVERAGE AND WELL ORGANIZED
☐ AVERAGE
☐ ANNOYING AND FAIRLY POORLY ORGANIZED
☐ LOW ENERGY AND POORLY ORGANIZED
☐ CONSTANT MOTION AS THOUGH DRIVEN

2. Interest span
☐ CONCENTRATES TO THE EXCLUSION OF OUTSIDE DIS-TRACTIONS
☐ COMPLETES TASKS WELL
☐ NEEDS URGING TO STICK WITH A TASK
☐ IS EASILY DISTRACTED
☐ JUMPS FROM ONE ACTIVITY TO ANOTHER WITHOUT COMPLETING ANY (SHORT INTEREST SPAN)

3. In permissive or group ac-tivities
☐ REMAINS ORGANIZED AND LEADS
☐ COOPERATIVE WITH OTHERS AND LEADERS
☐ BEHAVIOR VARIES LITTLE FROM STRUCTURED SETTING

☐ TENDS TO BE OVEREXCITED
  AND LOSE CONTROL
☐ BECOMES EXCITED TO THE
  ECSTATIC POINT

4. Personality
  ☐ LOVEABLE
  ☐ LIKEABLE
  ☐ NEUTRAL
  ☐ OFTEN ANNOYING
  ☐ UNPREDICTABLE

5. Intelligence (your judge-
   ment, not I.Q.)
  ☐ SUPERIOR
  ☐ ABOVE AVERAGE
  ☐ AVERAGE
  ☐ BELOW AVERAGE
  ☐ VERY DULL

these syndromes, as well as, the signs of learning disabilities (see Figure 3). This questionnaire was completed by the teachers and assessed social maturity, neuromuscular development, academic performance, and general attitudes and behaviors of the children. No neurological data were obtained, and it was not possible to further refine the diagnosis to MBD. Some of the children he studied probably had MBD.

Since the time of Dr. Huessy's work, a questionnaire designed by Conners (1969) has been commonly used in similar research. The Huessy questionnaire and the Conners questionnaire were filled out on a group of over 300 children, and a positive correlation of .77 was found between the two, with the Huessy questionnaire identifying some learning problems not identified by the Conners questionnaire (Perault & Novotny, 1974).

In 1966, the Huessy questionnaire was completed on 100% of the second grade pupils in several rural schools in Vermont (Huessy & Gendron, 1970). The total sample was 501 second grade students. The same questionnaire was filled out on the same children when they were in the fourth grade (1968), and fifth grade (1969). In the ninth grade the school records were reviewed (1973).

The raw scores on the Huessy questionnaire were scaled to percentiles and the upper 20% were designated as "hyperactive." The same children were rated on the same instrument by different teachers each year. It was felt that this factor would serve to prevent a teacher–child personality interaction from establishing a child as "hyperactive." Various checkback procedures were done asking teachers to identify problem children in their class.

In a follow-up examination, if a teacher had any of the subjects in his or her class, he or she was asked to fill out a questionnaire for all of his or her students. Because many of the high scorers had been labeled as problems by the teachers, the problem of a self-fulfilling prophesy was present. However, it was felt that the questionnaire did not lead to "labeling" as such. There obviously could not be any control for the possible effect of such "labeling" done by the teachers on their own. These questionnaires were never scored by the teachers and the teachers never learned of the children's scores. The questionnaires never became a part of the children's school record.

The results obtained after following these children for 2½ to 3 years after the initial assessment indicated that the behaviors associated with both the "hyperactive" syndrome and MBD followed the familiar standard curve of distribution. They represent the upper end of the curve. There was no break between the children with and without this behavioral constellation (Huessy & Gendron, 1970; Huessy, Marshall & Gendron, 1973). The scores had originally been obtained on 501 second graders. Seventy-one (71) children had been lost by the fourth grade. The lost scores, however, showed no unusual distribution.

A significant finding was that "hyperactive" behaviors and learning problems were not stable over time. One-third to one-half of the "hyperactive" group stopped being "hyperactive" 2½ to 3 years later. This was felt to be in line with the general decrease in unacceptable behavior with increasing age in children. These children, however, had been replaced by a new group of "hyperactive" children who had not shown such symptoms 2½ to 3 years before. The new high scorers had behavior patterns indistinguishable from the patterns of the original high scorers (see Figure 4 and Table 1). The ratio of boys to girls for the behavior problems was 4 to 1. The data indicated that in the group that had deteriorated, more boys had deteriorated. In the group that had improved, more girls had moved out of the "hyperactive" group.

Recently data have been obtained on the same group of children in the ninth grade (1973). The same trends persist. Some children move out of the hyperactive group. However, by the fifth grade the picture seems quite constant. Again, there is a better prognosis for the girls than the boys. Those children that were diagnosed in the second, fourth, and fifth grades seemed to have the worst outcome, followed by those children diagnosed in the fourth and fifth grades, or the fifth grades only. These children are experiencing academic as

FIGURE 4

HUESSY STUDY OF NATURAL HISTORY OF
"HYPERACTIVE" BEHAVIORS.

Flow diagram of 352 cases which were available for all 3 studies.
Numbers indicate frequency by sex for each group. Explains groups in
table 1.

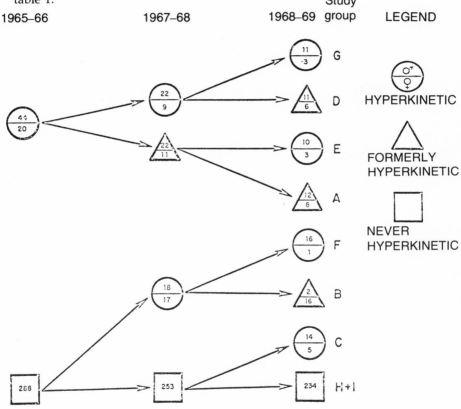

Table 1

HUESSY STUDY OF NATURAL HISTORY OF "HYPERACTIVE" BEHAVIORS

Group	Above 80 Percentile	No. children	%boys	Mean IQ scores	Grade Point average	% of group in remedial: Math	English	% of group in advanced: Math	English	% of children who repeated one or more grades	% of children with poor or very poor social adjustment
A	2nd Grade only	17	60	97.8	2.22	47	24	6	6	47	0
B	4th grade only	14	57	97.3	1.89	25	16	17	0	43	23
C	5th grade only	17	76	98.4	1.93	31	50	0	0	29	59
D	2nd and 4th grades	13	62	90.0	1.95	45	18	0	0	82	25
E	2nd and 5th grades	10	70	83.9	1.90	44	55	0	0	67	20
F	4th and 5th grades	14	93	96.9	1.68	33	75	0	0	62	54
G	2nd, 4th, and 5th grades	10	100	90.0	1.48	44	67	0	0	33	70
11	Identified Children	95	73	95.3	1.90	38	42	5	1	50	35
11	Controls Percentile	45	67	107.3	2.76	2	14	27	23	11	7
H	0–30	22	68	114.1	2.97	0	5	36	32	0	0
I	40–70	23	65	100.7	2.55	5	23	18	14	22	13

Figure 5

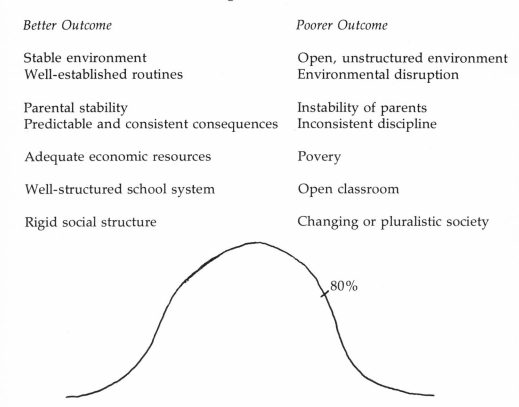

Better Outcome	Poorer Outcome
Stable environment	Open, unstructured environment
Well-established routines	Environmental disruption
Parental stability	Instability of parents
Predictable and consistent consequences	Inconsistent discipline
Adequate economic resources	Povery
Well-structured school system	Open classroom
Rigid social structure	Changing or pluralistic society

80%

well as behavioral difficulties in school (Figure 5; Huessy & Cohen, 1976). The data on specific difficulties that these children are experiencing are discussed in greater detail in the section reviewing prospective studies on "hyperactive" children.

There were several conclusions from this study: (1) The Huessy questionnaire predicted "hyperactive" behavior disorders 3 years later with about 60% accuracy. (2) It appears that the behaviors characteristic of both the "hyperactive" child syndrome and MBD are not stable over time. The children who demonstrate these behaviors begin their lives, for reasons unknown to us at present, along the upper limits of the standard distribution curve for this type of behavior. Whether they move farther toward the extreme end of the curve and have problems or move to the center and become "just active children" seems to be the result of various environmental determinants at home and in school. Those factors which seem to influence outcome are summarized in Figure 6. (3) The natural history study, although it does not shed any light on etiology, indicates that there may be at least two possible subgroups of children. The children identified in the second grade may have a primary etiology for their problems. The appearance of another group of children in the fourth and fifth grades who have not had symptoms in the second grade indicates that environmental factors may be primary in the etiology of these children's difficulties.

Figure 6

The 35% of the "hyperactive" children with social problems in ninth grade:

Suspended
Placed on social probation
Assigned detention

Offenses committed: Teachers considered them:

Truancy   Loud
Tardiness   Inattentive
Smoking in school   Uncooperative
Cutting classes   Lazy
Forging passes   Sneaky
Stealing   Immature
Discharging fire extinguishers   Annoying
Disrupting the classroom   Inconsiderate
Defying school authorities   Unpredictable
                                       Defiant
                                       Easily discouraged
                                       Easily distracted

                                       In addition, teachers noted:

                                       Daydreaming
                                       Fooling around
                                       Disturbing others
                                       Seeking attention
                                       Responding poorly to disci
                                           pline
                                       Unable to sit still, concentrate,
                                           settle down, and/or follow
                                           directions

None of the records of the control population contained comments similar to these descriptions.

Retrospective studies

There has been a growing interest in adult adaptation of children identified as having behavior disorders. Data on the relationship between childhood disorders and adult adaptation can be obtained in one of two ways. The early medical and psychiatric records of individuals who are experiencing difficulty as adults can be reviewed. The second method is one that arbitrarily defines a period of time, reviews those chart records for evidence of certain behavioral difficulties, and then follows up these identified children to see what their adaptation as adults has become. This second type of research, because of the new confidentiality procedures, is unfortunately no longer possible.

One of the classic works utilizing this second method of study was that of Lee M. Robins (1966). She reviewed 524 child guidance clinic patient records and compared them to 100 nonpatient controls. She followed up these patients 25 to 30 years later. She attempted to correlate childhood behavior with adult diagnoses. The results of her study indicated that only 8% of the control subjects had seemingly disabling symptoms, as compared with 34% of the patient group. Thus, the rate of adult disability was just about four times greater than among the controls. In her study, the number and type of symptoms present at the time of the initial referral correlated with adult outcome. Antisocial behaviors seem to be the best predictors of adult psychopathology.

Many researchers assume that the children involved in her study who at the age of 12 years had trouble with the law were most likely "hyperactive." She found that for those children who had been referred to the clinic because of antisocial behavior, 50% had been jailed as adults versus 13% of those who had been referred to the clinic because of nonantisocial behavior, versus 0% in the control population. The adult outcome regarding school performance, psychiatric illness, and antisocial acts is summarized in Table 2.

Robins also found that of 76 girls referred to the child guidance clinic because of antisocial behavior, 20 would be diagnosed as hysterical personalities as adults. These data add evidence to later research (studies discussed under the Blood Relatives of "Hyperactive" Children), which finds a relationship between alcoholism, sociopathy, hysteria, and hyperactive behavior disorders of childhood. Guze, noting that hysterical personalities predominantly, if not exclusively, are disorders of women, while sociopathy is predominantly a disorder of men, has suggested that "Depending upon the sex of the individual, the same etiologic and pathogenic factors may lead to different, though sometimes overlapping clinical pictures" (Cloninger & Guze, 1970).

Karen Preis, M.D., and Hans R. Huessy, M.D.

Table 2

	90	524	14	83	64	84
Number: Study Year study: Authors:	1956 Morris et al.	1966 Robins	1967 Menkes	1971 Mendel- son et al.	1971 Weiss et al.	1974 Huessy et al.
Neurological damage			55%	None	None	
EKG Abnormality					25%	
Speech Deficit				20%		
Clumsy				40%		
Soft signs			73%		None	
Hyperactivity (17%)			21%	71%	30%	75%
Abstractibility				77%	46%	
Aggression (4%)				51%	20%	
Mood adjustment	20.5%			55%		
Home adjustment						
Good				22%	31%	5%
Satisfactory				46%	49%	45%
Poor		15%		32%	20%	50%
School						
Poor				46%	80%	60%
Repeat 1 grade				58%	70%	
Drop out (4%)				2.4%		21%
Antisocial (2%)						
Acts		45%				
Police contact	83%		57%	25%		26%
Court contact (12%)	10%		10%	18%	15%	
Jail (0.5%)		50%	5%			13%
Psychiatric illness						
Self-Supporting		75%	56%			
Emotional disorder	32%	34%	60%	54%		
Psychosis	18%		28%	1.5%		
State (0.2%)			7%	2.4%		13%
Hospital						

*Normal population data for adolescents.
**Normal population data for adults.

Another study similar to Robins' was conducted by Mellsop (1972), who followed up 3370 children who had been referred to the Department of Psychiatry between the years 1945 and 1954. He found that the group of children with behavior disorders had a fourfold increase in their chance of being adult psychiatric patients. He noted that children with personality and conduct disorders similar to those found in children suffering from the "hyperactive" syndrome, were likely to have a poor prognosis.

Menkes, Rowe, and Menkes (1967) studied 14 children who had

been seen at the Johns Hopkins Hospital 25 years before. The authors had been looking for children who would have been classified as falling into the category of the "hyperactive" child with MBD. All of these children had presented with "hyperactivity" and learning difficulties. They all showed evidence of one or more of the following nonbehavioral criteria for brain dysfunction: clumsiness of fine movement, visual–motor deficit, and impaired or delayed speech. Under "hyperactivity" they included distractibility, short attention span, emotional lability, impulsivity, and low frustration threshold. None of the children that they studied were psychotic and there were no patients with seizures or IQ levels of less than 70. Ten of the patients in their review would be diagnosed as suffering from brain damage rather than brain dysfunction. Eight of the children today would be diagnosed as having MBD.

Patients were followed up 14 to 20 years later. The follow-up included a complete psychosocial interview, an evaluation of the patient's personal medical history, an assessment of his or her present mental functioning, and an assessment of current socioeconomic status, a battery of psychological tests and a complete neurological examination. At the time of reexamination, four patients were in institutions with a diagnosis of psychosis, two were clearly retarded and living dependent lives with their families, and only eight were self-supporting. Of these eight who were self-supporting, however, four had spent some time in institutions; two in institutions for delinquent boys, one in a hospital for the retarded, and one in a jail.

As adults, eight of the 11 patients who were examined neurologically had definite evidence of neurological dysfunction, one had equivocal evidence, and only two had none. In most cases the abnormalities found included terminal intention tremor and coordination difficulties, as demonstrated by poorly performed rapid alternating movements and impaired tandem gait. Three of the adults still claimed that they were restless. In the 11 other adults the signs of hyperactivity had disappeared. Three adults did not remember when this had occurred, while eight others felt that it occurred between 8 and 21 years, with the majority occurring between 12 and 14 years. These data are summarized in Table 2.

Menkes et al. (1967) was very concerned by the data which indicated that children who had the behaviors of the "hyperactive" syndrome of childhood associated with neurological dysfunction had a high degree of psychosis as adults. They suggested that perhaps this indicated that

in part, the diagnostic criteria were not rigorous enough to exclude children that presented a picture of brain dysfunction on a purely psychiatric basis. On the other hand, it may well reflect the natural history of the syndrome of "hyperactivity" with minimal brain dysfunction of childhood. The latter possibility is exemplified by the fact that two other patients, at present psychotic, were found on examination to have definite neurological abnormalities. Birch (1964) pointed out that among the behavior syndromes which may accompany central nervous system dysfunction are some which are indistinguishable from the childhood psychoses. It is likely that organic disturbances in body boundaries, and interpretation of sensory input data can result in a self-reinforcing process, with maladaptation and alienation leading to a clinical picture identical with a so-called "functional" psychosis. (p. 398)

Additional support for the theory of the relationship between the symptoms of MBD in childhood and adult psychoses is obtained from the work of Kupfer, Detre, and Koral (1975). They investigated 174 adult psychiatric out-patients who represented nine major diagnostic categories. They found that there were certain links between childhood difficulties and life-long personality traits, as well as adult psychiatric symptomatology. Their findings suggested that the childhood traits related to adult schizophrenia might be manifestations of childhood MBD. They also concluded that because they obtained the early childhood history from the patients themselves, it was possible that the data were distorted. Their work, however, does represent an area that needs further investigation.

Morris, Escoll, and Wexler (1956) retrospectively studied 90 children who had been admitted to a psychiatric hospital for severe acting-out. These children had normal intelligence and there was no evidence of psychosis or overt brain damage. At the time of first being seen they were described as disobedient and markedly restless. The follow-up 21 years later indicated that for the 68 who were 18 years or older, 12 had become psychotic, 10 were diagnosed as borderline, 7 had acquired a criminal record, and only 14 were described as doing well. These data are summarized in Table 2.

Borland and Heckman (1976) studied 20 men who had conformed to the diagnostic criteria for the "hyperactive" child syndrome 20 to 25 years earlier. They interviewed these men and their brothers. Their results indicated that a large majority of men who were "hyperactive" had completed high school, and each was steadily employed and self-supporting. Half of the men who were "hyperactive" continued to show a number of symptoms of "hyperactivity." Nearly half of these men had problems of a psychiatric nature and despite normal intelligence scores and levels of education had not achieved a socioeconomic status that was equal to that of their brothers or their fathers. The authors concluded that some of the emotional problems in everyday living may result from the persistence of symptoms of "hyperactivity" into adulthood and that most of the social and psychiatric consequences of the disorder relate to its presence in childhood, as well as to its persistence in adulthood.

A retrospective study that almost qualifies as a prospective follow-up study was done by Mendelson, Johnson, and Stewart (1971). The authors followed up 83 patients 2–5 years after they were first seen in a psychiatric clinic where they had received a diagnosis of "hyperactivity." They were not able to use uniform criteria for selection because the symptoms associated with the hyperactivity had not been recorded systematically on the chart. These children, however, were all continuing to be followed in the same clinic where the investigators were working. The children were by this time young adolescents. They excluded any children with evidence of brain damage or an IQ less than 70, but it is impossible to tell from the data whether they were talking about "hyperactive" children or children suffering from MBD. Unfortunately there was no control group in this study. Overall they noted that 55% were improved, while 35% were the same or worse. The major symptoms currently complained about were overactivity (71%), distractibility (77%), impulsiveness (84%), and irritability (67%). Thirty-two percent were still experiencing difficulties at home, while 46% were experiencing difficulties in school. Only 8% had major improvement in their function with regard to the major symptoms, relationships at home, and relationships at school. Fourteen percent had improvement in their major symptoms at home but were still having trouble at school, while 10% had shown improvement in their major symptoms but were still experiencing trouble in school and at home. For 22% of the children there had been no change, either in major symptoms, relationships at home, or relationships at school.

The same authors noted the most frequent complaints from the mothers at the time of follow-up was "a rebellious attitude." Mothers also complained that schoolwork was not being done (22%), that the overactivity was a serious problem (12%), that peer relationships were seriously disturbed (12%) and that antisocial behavior was a major concern (8%). The mothers complained of no difficulty in only 10% of the children.

One of the most striking findings of their study was that many of the children were involved in delinquent behavior as adolescents (see Table 3). In addition, chronic low self-esteem appeared to be the most serious aspect of the children's problems in the 25% who had a poor outcome.

The results of these studies attempting to correlate early childhood behavior with adolescent and adult outcome led the way for several major prospective studies of children diagnosed as suffering from the "hyperactive" syndrome or MBD of childhood.

Table 3
Antisocial Symptoms at Follow-Up

Symptom	% of children
Frequent lying	83
Incorrigible	66
Cursing excessively	59
Fighting	51
Stealing	51
Destructive	52
Bad associates	34
Threatening to kill parents	34
Excessive drinking	15
Recklessness and irresponsibility	22
Running away	18
High sex interest	18
Setting fires	15
Poor employment record [a]	13
Carrying weapon	7
Drug abuse	5

[a]History of being fired because of irresponsible actions or failing to show up for work.

Prospective studies of children diagnosed as "hyperactive" or MBD

Prospective long-term follow-up of children diagnosed as "hyperactive" is being conducted by researchers at the Montreal Children's Hospital and at the University of Vermont College of Medicine.

Weiss, Minde, Werry, Douglas and Nemeth (1971) were the first to report on a prospective follow-up of their "hyperactive" children. The children were selected for having a diagnosis of "hyperactivity" between the ages of 6 and 13 and IQ greater than 84. They had no major brain damage or dysfunction, such as epilepsy or cerebral palsy; there were no children who were psychotic; and they were living at home with at least one parent. Ninety-two percent of their sample were boys. The mean age at the initial referral was 8.7 years, and the mean age at follow-up, 4–6 years later, was 13.34. They noted that "hyperactive" children were still less able to concentrate on their schoolroom tasks than were the normal controls. The poor concentration was now the chief complaint made by 46% of the mothers. Motor hyperactivity seems to have dropped substantially. 20% of the children were still rated by their mothers as being excessively aggressive. On psychiatric evaluation no children were psychotic at the 5-year follow-up, although three did show some schizoid traits. These three had had similar pathology 5 years previously, but at this time it had probably been obscured by the severe hyperactivity. The most common pathological trait reported by 70% of the mothers was emotional immaturity. It was associated with a lack of ambition and a severe lack of ability to maintain goals (30%). The authors were also impressed by the unexpected sadness of mood which developed during the interviews as the children talked about themselves. It seems that the children were highly aware of their many past and continuing failures and marked by low self-esteem.

One of the striking findings was the degree of antisocial behavior that these children demonstrated. Twenty-five percent had a history of acting-out antisocial behavior with ten having had actual court referrals. At initial evaluation only two of the 16 children had given a history of antisocial behavior. (These and the following data are presented in Table 2.)

These authors also noted that poor academic functioning was the feature that most clearly characterized the group as a whole and was present in 80% of the children. Only 13 (20%) had not repeated at least one grade or were achieving average or above average in their schoolwork. Seventy percent had repeated at least one grade, versus 15% of the control children, and one-half of these had repeated two or more grades. Only three children (5%) were doing above average work, those being the ones previously described with schizoid traits, who also had WISC IQs greater than 125.

These authors continued their investigation of these children and selected a subgroup of 20 adolescents to study in greater detail (Minde, Weiss & Mendelson, 1972). Weiss et al. (1971) had noticed a significant decrease in the target symptoms of hyperactivity, distractibility, aggressivity, and excitability. When Minde et al. (1972) matched 20 of these adolescent "hyperactives" with normal controls on the basis of age, sex, socioeconomic standards according to the measures of Hollingshead and Redlich, and full-scale IQ on the WISC, the "hyperactive" youngsters scored significantly higher on all four target symptoms than did their normal peers ($P < .001$). This was regardless of whether they had or had not taken medication.

They also noted that 20 of these children had improved on one target symptom, whereas only two had shown improvement on two target symptoms. At the time of follow-up three children still had problems with "hyperactive" behavior, eight with distractibility, ten with aggressive behavior, and three with excessive excitability.

Minde et al. (1972) noted that the decrease in target symptoms did not appear to have any influence on the emotional adjustment of the children. They assessed fixed parameters to determine emotional outcome: (1) present complaint, (2) peer interaction, (3) relationship to authority, (4) antisocial behavior, (5) object relationships, and (6) sexual adjustment. A child was designated as well adjusted if he or she was doing well in five out of the six areas and as poorly adjusted if he or she were having difficulties in four out of the six areas. Twenty-eight out of the 91 children were assessed as having good outcomes, 41 out of the 91 as being in between, and 18 out of the 91 as having poor outcome. There were not sufficient data to assess emotional outcome in four of the 91. Many of the children who had been diagnosed as well adjusted initially showed poor outcome at follow-up and definite schizoid characteristics. These children did well on target symptoms but poorly behaviorally and were thought by the authors to possibly represent a small, distinct group of "hyperactive" children (Weiss et al., 1971; Minde et al., 1972).

Huessy, Metoyer, and Townsend (1974) reported on an 8–10 year follow-up of 84 children who had been diagnosed as having behavior disorders in rural Vermont. They noticed that 75% of the individuals still complained of symptoms of motor hyperactivity. Forty-five percent of their patients would be classified as having had a satisfactory home adjustment, and 50% had a poor home adjustment. Five out of the 84 were happily married themselves and two out of the 84 were unhappily married. There had been two engagements within the population that they followed. One had been maintained while the other one had been broken. In addition, 60% of the subjects had very poor school performance and 21% of the subjects had dropped out of school versus a dropout rate in the state of Vermont of 4%. Again, a striking predominance of antisocial behavior was noted in that 13% of the population had spent some time in a correction facility and 13% of the population had been in-patients at the state mental hospital. The average age at the time of diagnosis for these subjects had been from 3 to 16 years and the range at follow-up was from 9 to 24 years of age. These data are summarized in Table 2.

Huessy and Cohen (1976) have reported on 7-year follow-up of children identified as having the behavioral symptoms associated with the "hyperkinetic syndrome" and MBD. These children were originally diagnosed as "hyperactive" (greater than the eightieth percentile) in the second grade. Currently these children are being followed in the twelfth grade, but these data are not yet ready to report. Their study indicated that if the child was identified at any time other than the second grade he was definitely at risk for later behavioral and/or educational problems. The children were identified in the second, fourth, and fifth grades and it was noted that 33% of these children ended up repeating at least one grade and that 70% were having problems in the area of social adjustment. Children identified in the second grade only had 47% of whom repeated a grade, but none of them showed a poor social adjustment. "Hyperactive" children were also noted to have substantially lower mean point averages in achievement scores, when they were matched with other children.

Overall, 35% of the "hyperactive" children were having social problems in the ninth grade. These problems are summarized in Figure 6. The majority of these children were often suspended, placed on probation, and/or assigned detention. It was striking that none of the records of the control population contained comments similar to these.

There were two striking findings from this study. (1) Those children without any evidence of problems in the early grades (zero to the thirtieth percentile) did not develop any problems by the ninth grade and (2) 65% of the children, who had earlier been placed at risk because they were identified as having behavioral symptoms associated with the "hyperactive" syndrome and MBD in childhood, were doing quite well. The authors concluded that many therapies in the past had been content with 60 or 70% good outcome, and they felt that nature does that well by itself.

In the future, the outcome for the children involved in Huessy's prospective study will be collated with their degree of adaptation in the twelfth grade. In addition, another prospective study is being done by Riddle and Rapaport (1976) at Georgetown University. They have followed 72 hyperactive boys for 2 years now. The mean age at follow-up is 10.2 years. Their data seem to follow the same trend in that the patient group continues to manifest behavioral and academic difficulties. It is hoped that they will be able to continue following this group of children into adolescence and adulthood.

Identification of adolescents who manifest the symptoms of "hyperactivity" or MBD

Identification of "hyperactivity" persisting into adolescence and the high association between antisocial behaviors and adolescent "hyperactivity" have led investigators to take a very hard look at antisocial and delinquent adolescents to ascertain whether they may, indeed, be suffering from the "hyperactive" or MBD symptoms.

Since Bradley's work in 1937, amphetamine has been used in a variety of behavior disorders. There were early, uncontrolled studies utilizing amphetamine in delinquent populations (Korey, 1944; Hill, 1947). Few of these studies indicated that the children might have characteristics similar to those of the "hyperactive" child. The results of these investigations indicated that many of the antisocial behaviors were reduced with the use of stimulant medication.

Childers (1935) reported on 10 children, eight boys and two girls, who were primarily considered hyperactive when first referred to his clinic several years earlier. When they returned for a restudy after an interval of several years it was because of involvement in delinquent behaviors. On the initial visit they were 8.6 years of age and at the time of follow-up were 15.8 years of age. He had noticed that the motor hyperactivity was gone but that they were still overtalkative and all were involved in aggressive types of delinquency. The boys were involved in recurrent stealing and the girls in sexual misconduct. They were very sullen and resentful and complained of being picked on. He posed the question whether delinquency was either an outcome or a concomminant problem for the "hyperactive" child.

Anderson and Plymate (1962) gave detailed descriptions of the behavioral, emotional, social, and academic problems of children who had been diagnosed as having MBD in adolescence. They also suggested these children were more at risk for having difficulties of an antisocial nature. They gave no data as to the number of cases on which they were reporting. Laufer (1962) simultaneously drew attention to the fact that adolescents with MBD were still experiencing difficulties. His work also was more descriptive than statistical, and we have no idea as to the number of children he was discussing. It is, however, striking to note how little attention was paid to the results. Currently, some clinicians will still tell parents that their child will most likely outgrow the problem and that they need not worry. Many clinicians still are hesitant to mention that "hyperactivity" may persist for fear of discouraging the parents and the children.

"The impulse ridden character disorder" has long been associated with juvenile delinquent acts. Kaufman, Durkin, Frank, Heims, Jones, Ryter, Stone, and Zilbach (1961) reviewed this literature. On close examination, many of the children described as coming under this diagnostic entity could be classified as suffering from the "hyperactive" or MBD syndrome. Healy and Bronner (1936) found that delinquents, when compared to sibling controls, demonstrated significantly more cross and fussy behavior in infancy and more enuresis, restlessness, hyperactivity, and impulsiveness in childhood. These are the same childhood history characteristics as found in 37 "hyperactive" children studied by Stewart et al., (1966).

Eisenberg, Lachman, Molling, Lockner, Mizeile, and Conners (1963) performed a double blind study and noted that dextroamphetamine improved the performance on all parameters of behavior in institutionalized delinquent boys. The study had definite statistical limitations and did not report all of the symptoms they were monitoring, but it did lead investigators to be concerned with the relationship between delinquents and "hyperactive" children.

Recent work by Maletzky (1974) indicates that there may be a subpopulation of delinquents who are indeed suffering primarily from the "hyperactive syndrome" of adolescence. He performed a double blind study on adolescent males who had been referred to a psychiatric outpatient clinic as a result of antisocial behavior. He studied 14 matched pairs between the ages of 13 and 18, who were not psychotic, had no documented disease of the central nervous system including epilepsy, and who were not retarded. Although this was just a preliminary study he noted a significant improvement in behavior with marked diminution in antisocial acts ($p < .001$). In addition, the adolescents did not develop any tolerance to the amphetamine nor were there any reports from their parents of euphoric effects. Thus, he concluded there was no evidence of drug intoxication. In reviewing the 22 pretreatment variables, he found that a history of "hyperactivity" as a child was significantly correlated to the response to dextroamphetamines. His findings lend support to the notion that "hyperactivity" of childhood may persist as delinquency of adolescence in some individuals.

Ascertaining the relationship between "hyperactivity" and juvenile delinquency is not purely an academic pursuit. The evidence is demonstrating that the juvenile delinquent population is at high risk for future psychiatric disorder. A recent retrospective study of a delinquent population reported on children referred to the New Haven, Connecticut Juvenile Court 20–25 years ago. The researchers noted that the incidence of psychiatric hospitalization and/or treatment was found to be significantly greater than that of the general population of Connecticut ($P < .001$) and significantly greater than the incidence in a demographically similar random sample from the New Haven area ($P < .001$) (Balla, Lewis, Shanok, Snell, & Henis, 1974).

There are many areas of overlap in the life histories of delinquent and "hyperactive" children (Preis, 1976). "Hyperactive" children and juvenile delinquents are described as children who "aren't able to postpone gratification." Both juvenile delinquent and "hyperactive" children have multiple behavior problems. Both are often unable to integrate themselves within the social system of the school and their peer group. The sociological theories of delinquency (Cloward & Ohlin, 1960; Cohen, 1966; Miller, 1959) describe the problem of predelinquents in their adaptation to social norms. These theories discuss how, because the adolescents are not able to fit in with the group, they pull away from the group to establish peer relationships in the subculture of delinquency. This same theory could apply equally well to the "hyperactive" child who is not able to fit in with the group.

Both the "hyperactive" child and the delinquent as described by Aichhorn (1935) have disturbed family relationships. Laufer, Denhoff and Solomons (1957) discuss the weak ego of the "hyperactive" child which renders him or her unable to appropriately handle information through autonomous ego function. Redl and Wineman (1957), in their classic description of the delinquent child, stress how the therapist must act as an ego supplement for this child. Literature on delinquency is replete with discussions of the parents of the delinquents having very ambivalent attitudes toward their children. The unpredictability of the irritable, overly active, difficult infant who oftentimes later goes on to become a "hyperactive" child can create this very same ambivalent parent–child relationship.

Barcai (1971), using the Finger Twitch Test with a group of children 10–12 years of age, was able to isolate a group of behavior problem children who responded favorably to stimulant drugs in much the same manner as the "hyperactive" child. Wolff and Hurwitz (1966) discovered a choreiform syndrome which was similar to that measured by the Finger Twitch Test in 15% of children in regular school, as compared to 45% of children in schools for delinquents. Their data also had an interesting age trend. Among the group from 11 to 14 years of age who were delinquent, there was a 45% incidence of the choreiform syndrome; in the 14–17 year olds, only 37% displayed this syndrome. In addition, both delinquents and "hyperactive" children have marked difficulties in academic progress. Hurwitz, Bibace, Wolf and Rowbotham (1972) found that juvenile delinquents and boys with learning disabilities did poorly on motor tests and demonstrated greater difficulties with sensory motor and symbolic sequencing than did normal boys. These boys with learning disabilities, as well as the juvenile delinquents they described, demonstrated symptoms of the "hyperactive" child syndrome. This seemingly high relationship between learning disabilities and delinquent behavior has recently drawn intense government attention (Murray, 1976).

Healy and Bronner (1936) postulated that delinquency was a last-resort lifestyle for self-expression and self-actualization. This theory would fit quite well for the "hyperactive" child who is unsuccessful in social and educational relationships and unhappy with her or himself. He or she can improve his or her low self-esteem and in some ways achieve a form of social recognition by becoming involved in antisocial behaviors. In addition, the "hyperkinetic" child's isolation and frustrated need for accepting relationships would make him or her a likely candidate for joining an established delinquent group which stressed impulsivity, immediate gratification, and denial of drive postponement as part of the group ethos.

Despite the recognition of "hyperactive" adolescents; the recognition that 30% of psychiatrically disturbed adolescents had soft neurological abnormalities as compared to approximately 5% of the control population (Hertzig & Birch, 1968); and that approximately one-half of adolescent underachievers have clear-cut signs of MBD in early childhood (Hammar, 1967), there has been much debate as to whether adolescents should receive medication. Some individuals feel that adolescents will no longer respond to medication or that the adolescent is more likely to abuse drugs. Oettinger (1973) has been the most outspoken in favor of routinely using stimulant drugs in the treatment of adolescent "hyperactives" and states that he has been doing so for the past 30 years. Recently, Gross and Wilson (1974) have reported that they also prescribe stimulants until age 16.

Safer and Allen (1975) reported the treatment of "hyperactive" adolescents and noted the therapeutic response to stimulants did not significantly change from age 6 to age 16. They also noted that teenage "hyperactive" children were as inattentive as younger "hyperactive" children, although they were less aggressive and less overactive. They did not find that the mean dose of stimulant medication needed to achieve a successful classroom response for the school-age "hyperactive" child was significantly increased with age. There was no abuse of stimulants by the "hyperactive" teenagers. Earlier, Mackay, Beck and Taylor (1973) found methylphenidate (Ritalin) was effective in treating ten adolescents age 12 to 18 years who were suffering from what we would now call MBD. The response of adolescents to stimulant medication is consistent with the observation that pubescence and adolescence are not necessarily correlated with neurological maturity (Weiss et al., 1971; Wikler, Dixon, & Parker, 1970). It is believed that many adolescents with "hyperactivity" may be suffering from neurophysiological lag and can therefore benefit from stimulant medication. None of the above authors has observed the emergence of any form of psychological or physiological dependence as a consequence of stimulant medication. On the contrary, the adolescents tent to discontinue medication as soon as it fails to be helpful.

Identification of adults who manifest the symptoms of "hyperactivity"
or MBD

The identification of adolescents who are suffering from MBD and the "hyperactive" syndrome of childhood led investigators to search out the presence of these syndromes in adult populations. Evidence of "hyperactive" symptoms and MBD persisting in adulthood has come from three sources: research into the psychopathic personality, identification of adult patients who have the same symptoms, and interviews with parents who have children suffering from "hyperactivity" and MBD who describe themselves as having been "hyperactive" children and as still having the symptoms.

Investigation into the "psychopathic" personality has led to the recognition of the "hyperactive" or MBD syndrome in adults. McCord and McCord (1964) describe a psychopath as "an a-social, aggressive, highly impulsive person who has little or no guilt, and is unable to form lasting bonds of affection with other human beings." Similar criteria have been proposed by Cleckley (1964). Several investigators believe that this term "psychopath" has tended to include a heterogeneous group, having in common only a history of antisocial behavior (Karpman, 1948).

Blackburn (1975) attempted to classify the "psychopathic" personality. He found four major subgroups within this diagnostic category. Two of these subgroups conformed with the more classic definition of the "psychopath" as described by McCord and McCord. Both of these groups were hostile, aggressive, impulsive, and undersocialized. They differed from one another only by the degree of guilt they experienced. Findings were very similar in that they resembled those behavioral characteristics defined by Quay (1964) among young offenders. The behaviors described by Blackburn are those very consistent symptoms of "hyperactive" behaviors. It is not possible from the data that he gives to state whether the preincarceration histories are consistent with the "hyperactive" or MBD syndrome. This is an area that needs much further investigation, particularly in light of the report of Barcai and Rabkin (1974). They describe the case of a 20-year-old woman who was referred because of antisocial behavior and a clear-cut, early history of the "hyperactive" disorder of childhood. She was still evidencing difficulty with impulse control and short attention span, and she responded very nicely to dextroamphetamine. A review of impulse disorders describes a subgroup of individuals who demonstrate the symptoms of both "hyperactive" child syndrome and MBD in adulthood (Frosch & Wortis, 1954).

In 1968, Hartocollis attempted to ascertain the relationship of organicity and adult psychiatric disorder. The group of the adult patients he studied did not have hard neurological signs, but had psychological test findings similar to those that could be seen in children with the MBD syndrome. They were not the psychological test findings characteristic of patients with documented neurological damage. He found that the early histories of these patients had much in common: difficult gestation and/or birth, feeding difficulties, clumsiness, hyperactivity, temper tantrums, and aggressiveness. The latency

age behavior of these adults was clearly hyperactive, and deviant adolescent behavior included lying, petty thievery, and quarrelsome, aggressive behavior. Although the adults had different presenting clinical pictures, they all had very similar abnormalities. As adults they
were overactive, concrete in their thinking, had reading difficulties,
extreme lability of mood, irritability, excitability, sometimes violent
outbursts, and attempts at suicide. Diagnoses included schizophrenia
(8/15), depression (4/15), and infantile personalities (2/15). He concluded that adult in-patients who had organic impairment on the
basis of psychological tests represented a possible common pathway
for children who had suffered from MBD.

Quitkin and Klein (1969) pursued the relationship between childhood and adult MBD. They examined adult pyschiatric in-patients
under the age of 25 years and found that 30% had a definite history
of soft neurological signs and/or motor hyperactivity, impulsivity,
clumsiness, and other problems suggestive of MBD. These adult in-
patients fell into two major diagnostic groupings: impulsive–destructive
and the awkward–withdrawn. The former group included mainly
emotional character disorders, while the awkward–withdrawn subgroup constituted individuals suffering from process schizophrenia
and schizoid and passive–dependent character disorders. These findings are interesting in light of the work of Blackburn (1975), alluded to
earlier. One of four subgroups under his diagnostic category
"psychopath" would coincide with the awkward–withdrawn characteristics described by Quitkin and Klein.

Bach-y-Rita, Lion, Climent, and Ervin (1971) reported on a 2-year
study of 130 patients with a chief complaint of explosive, violent behavior. In reviewing the early childhood histories of these individuals,
they felt that many demonstrate currently, as well as in the past,
symptoms and signs of MBD. Unfortunately they did not present the
data in such a way as to show what percentage of their patients were
felt to have their difficulty as a result of adult MBD.

We think there are two points that deserve discussion. One, the
increased prevalence of neurological signs in a psychiatrically disturbed population does not document that neurological impairment
causes psychiatric illness. It is entirely possible that both the neurological soft signs and the psychological problems are a common manifestation of an underlying disease process. Second, the increased prevalence of a "hyperactive" or MBD history among psychiatric patients
does not imply that all children suffering from these disorders become
psychiatrically disturbed adults. This retrospective data combined
with prospective data do indicate, however, that a percentage of
them, yet to be accurately defined, are at risk for adult psychiatric
disease.

The most striking indication of the presence of "hyperactive" and MBD syndromes in adulthood is the *de novo* diagnosis in adults. Arnold, Strobl, and Weisenberg (1972) describe a 22-year-old black male who walked into their office after having seen a medical film on the "hyperkinetic" syndrome, stating "I believe I am, and was, a hyperkinetic person." His early history was consistent with that of the "hyperactive" syndrome and he currently was experiencing difficulty with hyperactive motor behavior and concentration. He was treated in a double blind fashion with dextroamphetamine. The results indicated that while on dextroamphetamine he had improved concentration, reduced anxiety, and increased depression. There was no evidence of euphoria from the medication. Simultaneously, Shelley and Riester (1972) described 16 cases at an Air Force training base of adults who presented symptoms of MBD. The patients were aged 18 to 23 years. They had soft neurological signs, visual perceptual abnormalities, as well as difficulties coping with the basic tasks of military training. The majority of them had had a decrease in motor hyperactivity, impulsivity, and aggressiveness over the years. Their speech disturbances had tended to disappear with increasing age. All of the patients of this group had been able to graduate from high school and a few from college, prior to their entering the Air Force. At this point in time the individuals did not have marked difficulty in getting along with their peers, nor did they have any serious psychiatric maladjustments. The major difficulty which they experienced was coping with the Air Force situation, which demanded precise, effective visual–motor performance. History obtained from their parents indicated that this had been a life-long problem for them and substantiated the fact that these children had suffered from short attention span, motor hyperactivity, easy distractibility, and impulsiveness. This study is one of the few which shows that the outcome may not be as poor as the other studies have indicated.

Once the syndrome was accepted as a legitimate diagnosis in adults, many cases began to be reported in the literature. Jeans (1974) reported on two adult patients he had seen in his psychiatric practice who he felt were suffering from "hyperactivity" of adulthood. Both of these individuals had been referred because of anxiety and depression. Both responded well to methylphenidate and were able to work in psychotherapy. Morrison and Minkoff (1975) describe three cases of adults who they felt currently demonstrated symptoms of "hyperactive" behavior disorder, and their histories were consistent with the histories of children with the "hyperactive" behavior disorder. They suggested that the diagnostic category of explosive personality might be a sequel to the "hyperactive" child syndrome, or that the "hyperactive" child syndrome might be one subgroup under this diagnostic category. One of their cases had Halstead–Reitan neuro-psychological battery results revealing severe impairment suggestive of MBD.

Mann and Greenspan (1976) hypothesize that adults who had MBD as children constitute a distinct diagnostic entity which may exist alone or with a variety of other psychiatric symptoms. They felt that patients with ABD, or "adult brain dysfunction'" as they called it, shared a basic impaired inability to focus attention effectively. They present data on two adults who had different personality structures, symptoms, and behavioral patterns but who shared a basic impairment in the ability to focus attention. Both of these patients responded immediately to imipramine. The attention deficit was corrected, with remarkable improvement in the presenting symptoms, as well as increased ability to work in therapy leading to changes in personality structure and behavior.

The most extensive report of adult "hyperactivity" is the work of Huessy and Blair (1977). They began to look for "adult hyperkinetics" in the summer of 1974. They collected psychosocial, medical, family, educational, history of signs and symptoms of MBD and drug response data on 64 patients who were thought to be hyperactive. The files of these patients showed complete or nearly complete data in all cases. Unavailable information usually pertained to medical and family histories.

The patients they were studying were given medication trials during the course of treatment as residents of Spring Lake Ranch, a therapeutic community (51 cases) or as clinic out-patients (13 cases). The clinical sample consisted of 32 males and 32 females who ranged in age from 18 to 46 years with a mean of 25.4 years. At least 26 showed a definite behavioral history suggesting childhod "hyperactivity." Four of these had been treated with medication as children. Twelve had had learning disabilities while in school. Sixty-four percent had completed high school, while 43% had attended college, but only two percent had completed college. One had some graduate training, and seven were still in school. Six had attended special schools as children.

Fifty-one of the subjects had been in-patients in a psychiatric hospital at least once (Spring Lake Ranch excluded), and many had accumulated multiple diagnoses during that time. Thirty-four had been labeled schizophrenic, notably paranoid (14) and chronic (9). Sixteen were labeled as having depressive disorders (two manic depression). Fourteen had been diagnosed as personality disorders. Thirty-six had previously received phenothiazine therapy with variable success. Nine subjects had strong evidence of central nervous system organicity, e.g., epilepsy, narcolepsy, or atypical EEG. Nine had histories of difficult births or early accidents and illnesses that suggested possible brain damage.

There was a high prevalence of psychiatric disorder in the subjects' families. Thirty-three subjects had 59 reports of primary relatives with a psychiatric disorder. Twenty-three subjects had 30 reports of primary relatives with the "hyperactive" associated disorders of alcoholism or sociopathy. Thirty-five subjects had 90 reports on any relative with a psychiatric disorder. No family data were available on 13 of the 64 subjects. Twenty-five subjects had 52 reports of any relative with "hyperactive" associated disorders.

Imipramine was the drug of first choice because of reluctance to use stimulant drugs with unstable patients. Other drugs used in the study were methylphenidate, dextroamphetamine, methamphetamine, pemoline, and diphenylhydantoin. The results of this study indicated that 49 of the 64 subjects (25 male, 24 female) showed a positive response to at least one of the drugs. Improvement was noticed in 76.6% of the clinical sample, once the drug of choice had been identified. Unfortunately no significant relationship was found between a positive response to a specific medication and any one symptom or historical factor. Therefore, the authors were unable to devise a scheme by which the drug of choice could be reliably selected beforehand. This duplicates previous experience with children. Except for pemoline (Cylert), the drugs showed their effect within an hour.

Huessy & Blair (1977) concluded that medication was effective in treating "adult hyperactivity" and MBD. Medication, however, can only control these symptoms, and it is therefore necessary for the patient to continue a regular drug regimen. They noted that it is very difficult to get "adult hyperactives" to maintain a consistent drug regime as out-patients. It seems that the calming effect of these drugs cause the patients to experience new emotions that they may find difficult to manage. Many patients elected to discontinue drug therapy in order to avoid these emotions. This is in marked contradistinction to the usual drug abuser, who uses drugs to try to "tune out." When medication has the desired effect on "adult hyperactives," it causes them to "tune in."

We (1977) believe that a crucial dimension in "hyperactivity" and MBD has to do with the individual's relationship to time. Both the children and the adults live in the moment. It seems that with the medication working on "tuning in," it prevents the individuals from being able to live in the moment. We conclude that if one has not grown up with an internal tolerance for stress and frustration, when the medicine suddenly gives one this privilege, it is not particularly attractive. Cappella, Gentile, and Juliano (1977) found that there is a marked difference in time perception between normal and "hyperactive" children. The time seems to pass much more slowly for the "hyperactive" child. When asked to press a button, when they felt that 7, 15, and 30 seconds had elapsed, "hyperactive" children overestimated the time period. They pressed it at 10.8 versus 6 seconds (7 seconds), 23.08 versus 11.93 seconds (15 seconds), and 50.84 versus 26.56 (30 seconds).

It seems that with the "adult hyperactive" or MBD, drug abuse is not the problem. Discontinuance of drug use is. Goldman, Dinitz, Lindner, and Foster (1976) noted the same finding in the sociopaths who they had treated with imipramine who showed markedly improved behavior. They all refused to continue taking the medication at the end of the study.

Huessy & Blair (1977) emphasize that with the disappearance of symptoms the adult patient is not suddenly well. He is still an individual who has been handicapped in the development of social skills throughout his lifetime, and needs support in this area. In their sample, there was a marked failure on the part of the majority of subjects to develop long-lasting, close friendships as children. They concluded that extensive research was needed to learn to classify the adult patients more adequately, to learn how to help them overcome their social deficits, and to learn to differentiate symptoms from habits. It appeared that drugs were clinically useful in the treatment of "hyperactivity" and MBD in adults.

Studies of blood relatives of "hyperactive" children

Evidence of an association of behavior problems of childhood with specific psychological difficulties in their families has been accumulated during the last 70 years. In 1902, Still noted "disorders of intellect, epilepsy, or moral degeneracy" in the families of 17 of his original 20 cases. Another study of children with behavior disorders, some of whom could be identified as being "hyperactive," found that 8.6% had a family history of alcoholism, versus 1% in the total population (Gunnarson, 1946). Morris et al. (1956) studied a group of children with "aggressive behavior disorders." These children resembled "hyperactive" children, although there was a high percentage of children who could be diagnosed as sociopathic. Forty-seven percent of their parents had a psychosis, neurosis, alcoholism, or other personality disturbance. Hallgren (1950) and Frisk, Wegelius, Tenhunem, Widholdm, and Hortling (1967) reported behavioral difficulties associated with dyslexia and an increased prevalence of "hyperactive" behaviors among the nondyslexic siblings. Mendelson et al. (1971), in their study of "hyperactive" children, noted that 22% of the fathers and 4% of the mothers were problem drinkers. They also noted that 10% of the mothers, 21% of the fathers, and 37% of the siblings had learning or behavior disorders as a child.

Dennis P. Cantwell (1972) and James R. Morrison and Mark A. Stewart (1971) have presented data that indicate that the "hyperactive" child syndrome may be transmitted genetically or socially from parent to child.

Cantwell (1972) looked at the parents of 50 white children who had been diagnosed as "hyperactive" and 50 control children. The children had been diagnosed as "hyperactive" using the criteria of Stewart, Thach, and Friedin (1970) which required definite evidence of hyperactivity and distractibility, and the presence of any six of the other 28 symptoms found to be most characteristic of the syndrome. Both the "hyperactive" children and the control children were between 5 and 9 years of age, were attending school, had no sensory deficits, and had a full-scale IQ greater than 80 (WISC). They came from intact families with both parents living at home.

The parents were evaluated using a standardized clinical interview, and carefully defined diagnostic criteria. Ten percent of the parents of "hyperactive" children were thought to have been hyperactive themselves, and all of these parents were psychiatrically ill with alcoholism, sociopathy, or hysteria. In addition, nearly half the parents of "hyperactive" children had some psychiatric diagnosis. This was a significant difference when compared to the parents of the control children ($P < .005$). Fathers in both groups tended to be more ill than the mothers. There was a significant difference in the greater prevalence of alcoholism, sociopathy, hysteria, and probable hysteria in the parents of "hyperactive" children. Suicide attempts and psychiatric care were also more frequent in the parents of "hyperactive" children ($P < .001$). A striking finding was that the parents of most of the control group were free of psychiatric illness.

Morrison and Stewart (1971), using the same criteria as Cantwell, studied the parents of 59 children diagnosed as "hyperactive" and 41 control children matched with them for age and sex. The children were all white and their age varied from 6 to 18 years. Parents were interviewed in a standardized clinical interview and data were also obtained on other first and second degree relatives.

Their results were very similar to those of Cantwell. Again, 10% of the parents of "hyperactive" children were found to have been hyperactive themselves when they were children. There was not, however, a statistically significant difference in the prevalence of hyperactivity in the parents of "hyperactive" children versus parents of control children. They found that 20% of "hyperactive" children had a parent who had been "hyperactive," versus 5% for the control children, suggesting an association between hyperactivity in the parent and child. When hyperactivity was assessed in aunts and uncles or for aunts, uncles, and parents, the families of "hyperactive" children showed a highly significant greater prevalence of hyperactivity than control families ($P = .001$). These authors also noted a high prevalence of psychiatric disorder in the hyperactive parents of "hyperactive" children. Seventy-five percent of these hyperactive parents had definite psychiatric illness.

In addition, one-third of the parents of "hyperactive" children had some psychiatric diagnosis as compared to one-sixth of the control parents ($P = .025$). The parents of the "hyperactive" children had twice as much alcoholism as the controls. There was a significantly higher prevalence of the combination of alcoholism, hysteria, and sociopathy in the parents of "hyperactive" children ($P < .01$). In 21 of the 59 families that had a "hyperactive" child, at least one parent was alcoholic, hysteric, or sociopathic. Only four of the 41 control families were so affected ($P < .025$).

The "hyperactive" children were also more likely than controls to have a first or second degree relative with alcoholism ($P < .025$). Cantwell's research (1972) had also indicated increased alcoholism ($P < .001$) and sociopathy ($P < .001$) in second degree male relatives, and hysteria ($P < .001$) in second degree female relatives of "hyperactive" children.

Both studies indicate that the parents of the "hyperactive" child had a high prevalence of psychiatric illness, most frequently alcoholism, followed by an excess of hysteria and sociopathy. Both studies indicate the fathers have more psychiatric illness than the mothers, and that the "hyperactive" parents of the "hyperactive" children seem to be at high risk for psychiatric disability.

Other recent studies have indicated an association between alcoholism, hysteria, and sociopathy. Guze, Wolfgram, McKinney, & Cantwell (1967) found a high prevalence of hysteria in the female relatives of convicted male criminals, and of alcoholism in their male relatives. Woerner and Guze (1968) noted a high rate of alcoholism and sociopathy in male relatives of hysterics. Cloninger and Guze (1970) found a striking association between hysteria and sociopathy in convicted women criminals. Cantwell (1972) noted that in his study group there was a higher prevalence of alcoholism and sociopathy than in the group studied by Morrison and Stewart (1971). He attributed this to the increased prevalence of alcoholism and sociopathy in a military population.

Both Cantwell (1972) and Morrison and Stewart (1971) felt the results of their studies were consistent with either an environmental or a genetic origin. The results were consistent with findings of other studies regarding transmission of disordered behavior from parents to child. Rutter (1966), after studying the children of physically and mentally ill (but not alcoholic) parents, suggested that psychiatric illness in the parent has a nonspecific, disturbing effect on the environment which produces symptoms in the child. He was not able to find a specific mental or physical illness in the parent that was associated with a specific disorder of child behavior. He did note, however, that children of mentally ill parents were "aggressive, anxious, and disobedient."

There are several possible explanations for these associations. The parents of a "hyperactive" child may be sensitized to the diagnostic symptoms and be more likely to report similar behaviors in themselves or other family members. The learning theorist might argue that a parent might teach a child by modeling the hyperactive behaviors or by selectively reinforcing active behavior. Morrison and Stewart (1971) thought that the high prevalence of alcoholism would favor a genetic pattern. Cantwell (1975) reviews the studies to date and concludes that the generation-to-generation transmission is more likely genetic than environmental. He suggests that there might be a "sub-group of hyperactive children" who had a genetic transmission, or that there might be "several genetically distinct sub-groups of hyperactive children."

Silver (1971) noted data that suggested the possibility of inherited traits in family members that could produce nervous systems with "maturational lags" characterized by altered cognitive, perceptual, and memory functions. He indicated the need for further study in the genetic aspects of hyperactivity.

In an attempt to explore the genetic hypothesis, Warren, Karduck, Bussaratid, Stewart, and Sly (1971) studied the chromosomes of 96 children (82 boys and 14 girls) diagnosed as having the "hyperactive" child syndrome. They found no evidence of sex chromosomes aneuploidy (i.e., an extra X or an extra Y chromosome) or other chromosome abnormality. They concluded that a recognizable chromosome abnormality is not a major cause of the genetic transmission of the "hyperactive" child syndrome.

The best way to separate genetic and environmental issues is to study children, siblings, and parents living separately. If the behaviors are present in different environments, then they are more likely caused by genetic factors. Safer (1973) studied 14 children with a diagnosis of "hyperactivity" whose siblings or half-siblings had been reared in foster homes. He found that 50% of full siblings in contrast to only 14% of the half-siblings were characterized by short attention span, repeated behavior problems, and a diagnosis of "hyperactivity" as judged by an independent rater.

Morrison and Stewart (1973a) examined the legal parents of 35 adopted, "hyperactive" children. Their hypothesis was that if they could demonstrate an excess of alcoholism, hysteria, and sociopathy in these adopting parents, then an environmental transmission of the behavior disorder would seem most likely. Likewise, if they found adopting parents (or extended family members) to have a low prevalence of these same psychiatric illnesses, then the genetic transmission of hyperactivity would be strengthened. They used the same criteria for the diagnosis of the hyperactive child syndrome as they had in their previous article (1971). The children had had no contact with their biological parents since birth and had been permanently placed by the age of 2.5 years.

They interviewed the adoptive parents of 35 "hyperactive" children, the biological parents of 59 "hyperactive" children, and the biological parents of 41 control children. They were able to obtain only very limited information about the biological parents of the adopted "hyperactive" children. The children were similar in all aspects. The adoptive parents were 3–5 years older than the other parents. The adoptive homes had fewer children in them when compared to the biological and control groups. The adopting parents were significantly higher in economic status than the biological parents but were similar to the control parents.

The results offer striking evidence for a genetic hypothesis. Diagnoses of sociopathy and hysteria are confined entirely to the biological parents of "hyperactive" children $(P < .05)$. This group also had a higher prevalence of alcoholism, although it was significantly different only between biological fathers and adopting fathers. The prevalence of alcoholism was twice as high in the biological relatives of "hyperactive" children $(P < .05)$. The parents of the adoptive group and the control group had one-half as many psychiatric disorders as the biological parents. The presence of hyperactivity was again found to be greater in the biological parents: 12.8% of the biological fathers versus 3.4% of the adoptive fathers and 0.8% of the control fathers; and 2.6% of the biological mothers versus 0.8% of the adopting mothers and 0.8% of the control mothers. The data strengthens the genetic hypothesis, but further investigation needs to be done looking at two different populations of adopted children with the same disorder.

Further investigation using this "adoption study method" is beginning to be done in an attempt to shed light on the genetic hypothesis. These studies involve comparing incidence estimates for two kinds of adopted children: children whose biological parents have psychiatric illness and children whose biological parents are healthy. If the incidence of a disorder is significantly higher in adopted away children whose biological parents are psychiatrically ill, this is taken as evidence for genetic factors playing a role in the development of the disorder.

Recently concern has been expressed that the lack of information about most parents who give their children up for adoption can result in including many parents at high risk for psychiatric disturbances in the control group. This could introduce considerable bias against a genetic hypothesis, because high risk among the control group of adopted children would make it difficult to find a still higher risk among the children whose biologic parents were ill. As a result of lack of information, control groups for these adoption studies are often selected with the only criteria being that there is no documented record of a psychiatric diagnosis.

Recent research supports the possibility of this bias existing (Horn, Green, Carney, & Erickson, 1975). When they compared pregnant unwed mothers (363) with married pregnant women (28) and 18-year-old women (2054), the unwed pregnant mothers had significant $(P < .001)$ elevation of five of the nine clinical scales of the Minnesota Multiphasic Personality Inventory (MMPI). Elevations on psychopathic deviancy (Pd) and schizophrenia (Sc) were particularly substantial, followed by elevations in paranoia (Pa), psychasthenia (Pt), and hypomania (Ma). If these mothers had been the control group for an adoption study, their offspring would probably show a greater incidence of the disorders than in the general population. Thus, a genetic hypothesis could be lost as a result of this sampling error. Huessy postulates, on the basis of his clinical experience, that hyperactive adolescents are more likely to produce illegitimate children. This might lead to more "hyperactivity" in adopted children. These data stress the need to select control groups that are truly representative of the general population.

Cantwell (1975) and Morrison and Stewart (1973b, 1974) have discussed the possible genetic mechanisms that may be involved in the "hyperactive" child syndrome. Both review the evidence to date and suggest that a polygene mode of inheritance is most likely. A single gene autosomal pattern is not possible because of the higher prevalence of this disorder in boys. The transmission pattern from father to son reported in all of the studies is against a sex-linked inheritance. Single dominant transmission does not seem probable in that one of the parents always should be "hyperactive" and there should not be generational skipping. This has not yet been demonstrated to be the case. A simple recessive trait is possible, in that there are reports of hyperactivity in the siblings, but is ruled out because this implies that parents or other relatives should not be affected. The data to date show a marked prevalence of hyperactivity in both the parents and close relatives. They conclude that the high male-to-female ratio and the transmission from either or both parents raise the possibility that "we are dealing with some sort of genetic–environmental– endocrinologic interaction, in short, polyfactoral transmission" (Morrison & Stewart, 1974b). A polygene inheritance would imply that more than one gene was involved in the transmission of the disorder, and that the disorder would only be seen when the correct number or correct combinations of genes was present. A more definitive answer to the genetic mechanism will probably be obtained by analysis of twins with "hyperactivity."

In summary, the data indicate that there is a significantly high prevalence of psychiatric illness in the biological parents of "hyperactive" children and that there seems to be a generation-to-generation transmission of hyperactivity. The risk for the "hyperactive" child may be serious psychiatric illness in adulthood, as well as the possibility of transmitting the same emotional, academic, and social disabilities to his or her own children.

CONCLUSION

The results of all the studies previously reviewed indicate that some children do not outgrow the "hyperactivity" or MBD syndrome and that as adults they are still experiencing emotional, social, behavioral, and academic difficulties.

There have been many attempts to correlate outcome with a variety of factors. Menkes et al. (1967) was unable to find any correlation between the patient's social adjustment as adults and the early home environment. He felt that in order to elicit prognostic factors in the home environment, a much larger sample would be needed because the classification of "favorable" or "unfavorable" was too general a category. Minde et al. (1972) saw no statistically significant differences in five aspects of family functioning: marriage relationship, childrearing practices, maternal deprivation, emotional climate at home, and parental mental health. There was evidence, however, that psychologically children changed their families, and that the poorer outcome group made their families generally worse and had a negative effect on the child-rearing practices, as well as the emotional climate of the home. They did not notice any effect on the parent–parent bond, which they felt resisted corruption by these children. This is an important finding in that clinically, when we evaluate children, it is necessary to assess which has come first—the child's "hyperactivity" or the family problems. Mendelson et al. (1971) had also evaluated the families for emotional problems, as well as problems that the parents had had in earlier childhood, but he could not correlate these factors with outcome.

Oettinger (1973) suggests that high social class and high IQ affect outcome positively. Information is available suggesting that IQ and psychological adjustment of high-risk infants is affected by life experience. Knobloch and Pasamanick (1967), found that the school-age IQ of neurologically impaired children, as well as normal infants, was correlated with parental social class. Those children in the highest social class had IQs at approximately two standard deviations above those of the lower class children. Similarly, Drillien (1964) found that premature infants were three times as likely to show "maladjusted" classroom behavior when exposed to medical and/or psychosocial stress. Huessy, Metoyer, Townsend (1974) in their 10-year follow-up found no relationship of social class to outcome. He did not assess IQ in relationship to outcome.

The predominance of the diagnosis of "hyperactivity" in males versus females raises a very important question. Huessy and Cohen (1976) showed that the three groups of "hyperactive" children with poor social adjustment (Group C, G, and F, Figure 4 and Table 1) had fewer girls than any other groups. Furthermore, 60% of the "hyperactive" children who had had both excellent grade point averages and no record of being discipline problems in school were girls. This raises a very large question that still remains to be answered. Is there some difference in the maturation of the central nervous system between boys and girls, or are these differences in outcome between boys and girls the result of different expectations that our society places on boys and girls?

Mendelson et al. (1971) thought that there were differences noted in the relationship to age of presentation and their outcome. They found that the older children were more likely to have school behavior problems as a chief complaint ($P < .05$). In addition, the older children were more likely to have trouble with the police or likely to be overconcerned with sex ($P < .01$), or likely to have been truant ($P < .01$), to have skipped class ($P < .01$), to have kept bad company ($P < .05$), to have been discipline problems ($P < .05$), and to have poor relationships with the teacher ($P < .05$). Huessy and Cohen (1976) indicated that those children identified on successive occasions in the elementary school years (Group G), or those children who were identified late in the fourth and the fifth grade (Group F) or just in the fifth grade (Group C), were at greater risk for academic and social problems. Children identified in the second grade only (Group A) seemed to have a better prognosis than children identified later.

There have been no studies to date that have indicated a relationship between therapy, either psychological, pharmacological, psychotherapeutic, and educational, singularly or in combination, which have been shown to alter outcome. Minde et al. (1972) in their follow-up study of 91 children over a 5-year period noted that two-thirds of their children had moderate to severe learning problems. Twenty-eight out of the 91 had received some help over the 5-year period. Twenty-one of these 28 had received greater than 25 hours of remedial help. However, the selection was very arbitrary as to who was going to get the remedial education. In addition, these children had not been given remedial help by teachers who were specifically trained in special education techniques. They were not able to see any improvement in these children's function as assessed on psychological tests. They felt that this lack of any reasonable effect from remedial therapy was difficult to evaluate, except to say that many of the children so treated had presented with such severe learning problems that they may well have been beyond conventional assistance.

Menkes et al. (1967) found no relationship between outcome and treatment but felt their sample size was too small. Minde et al. (1972) assessed the present complaints that the children were having, the quality of their peer interactions, the relationship to authority, antisocials behaviors demonstrated, the quality of their object relationships, and their sexual adjustments. The well-adjusted child was defined as one functioning well in five out of six of these areas. Although 28 out of the 91 of the children were assessed as having a good outcome, Minde et al. concluded that the psychological adjustment did not appear to be dependent on the duration of drug taking because the correlation between the duration of pharmacotherapy and outcome was not statistically significant. Huessy et al. (1974) were unable to relate drug response or length of psychopharmacological therapy to final outcome. It is important to note that in most of these studies there is not adequate documentation of which children with which problems have taken what drugs for what period of time. Future researchers need to keep very careful records, not only on the criteria for the diagnosis, so that we may sort out the "hyperactivity" versus MBD, but also to detail the amount of pharmacological, psychological, and educational therapy that children are given. Without this comprehensive research we will not be able to identify those children at greatest risk or in any meaningful way be able to correlate treatment with outcome.

The studies reviewed were far from conclusive and raised many questions yet to be answered. How can we learn to distinguish the children likely to remain "hyperactive" from those likely to improve spontaneously? Which factors contribute to improvement? Whereas motor hyperactivity itself may disappear in puberty, other, perhaps more serious, features of this syndrome may not. In addition, studies imply that not only do the psychological abnormalities associated with "hyperactivity" and MBD persist, but that these abnormalities may change their form. We need to explore what types of "hyperactivity" and MBD children later go on to have psychiatric disabilities. The "hyperactive" and MBD syndromes may sometimes be an early manifestation or precursor of better recognized psychiatric disorders of adolescence and adulthood and span the range from academic underachievement to infantile and impulsive character disorders, hysteria, alcoholism, sociopathy, and schizophrenia. There is increasing evidence suggesting that there may be many factors in common between a number of seemingly disparate diagnostic categories. To date, the fate of the most common and the least seriously affected "hyperactive," inattentive child who is amiable and has minor learning difficulties is unknown.

We suggest early identification and long-term, multimodal therapy—educational, psychological, and pharmacological—for as long as indicated, even into adult life, in the hopes of modifying what appears to be a more serious prognosis than has been previously suspected.

REFERENCES

Aichorn, A. *Wayward Youth*. New York: Viking Press, 1935.

Anderson, C.M., & Plymate, H.B. Management of the brain-damaged adolescent. *American Journal of Orthopsychiatry*, 1962, *32*, 492–501.

Arnold, L.E., Strobl, D., & Weisenberg, A. Hyperkinetic adult: Study of the "paradoxical" amphetamine response. *Journal of the American Medical Association*, 1972, *222*, 693–694.

Bach-y-Rita, G., Lion, J.R., Climent, C.E., & Ervin, F.R. Episodic dyscontrol: A study of 130 violent patients. *American Journal of Psychiatry*, 1971, *127*, 1473–1478.

Balla, D., Lewis, D.O., Shanock, S., Snell, L., & Henise, J. Subsequent psychiatric treatment and hospitalization in a delinquent population. *Archives of General Psychiatry*, 1974, *30*, 243–245.

Barcai, A. Predicting the response of children with learning disabilities and behavior problems to dextroamphetamine sulfate. *Pediatrics*, 1971, *47*, 73–80.

Barcai, A., & Rabkin, L.Y. A precurser of delinquency: The hyperkinetic disorder of childhood. *Psychiatric Quarterly*, 1974, *48*, 387–399.

Birch, H.G. (Ed.). *Brain damage in children—the biological and social aspects*. Baltimore: Williams and Wilkins Co., 1964.

Blackburn, R. An empirical classification of psychopathic personality. *British Journal of Psychiatry*, 1975, *127*, 456–460.

Blau, A. Mental changes following head trauma in children. *Archives of Neurological Psychiatry*, 1937, *35*, 723–769.

Bond, E. Postencephalitic, ordinary and extraordinary children. *Journal of Pediatrics*, 1932, *1*, 310–314.

Bond, E.D., & Smith, L.H. Post-encephalitic behavior disorders. *American Journal of Psychiatry*, 1935, *92*, 17–33.

Borland, B.L., & Heckman, H.K. Hyperactive boys & their brothers: A 25 year follow-up study. *Archives of General Psychiatry*, 1976, *33*, 669–675.

Bradley, C. The behavior of children receiving benzedrine. *American Journal of Psychiatry*, 1937, *44*, 577–585.

Bradley, C. Characteristics and management of children with behavior problems associated with organic brain damage. *Pediatric Clinics North America*, 1957, *4*, 1049–1060.

Burks, H.F. The hyperkinetic child. *Exceptional Children*, 1960, *27*, 18–26.

Burr, C.W. The nervous child. *New York Medical Journal*, 1921, *114*, 205.

Cantwell, D. Psychiatric illness in the families of hyperactive children. *Archives of General Psychiatry*, 1972, *27*, 414–417.

Cantwell, D.P. Genetics of hyperactivity. *Journal of Child Psychology and Psychiatry and Allied Disciplines*, 1975, *16*, 261–264.

Capella, B., Gentile, J.R., & Juliano, D.B. Time estimation by hyperactive and normal children. *Perceptual and Motor Skills*, 1977, *44*, 787–790.

Chess, S. Diagnosis and treatment of the hyperactive child. *New York State Journal of Medicine*, 1960, *60*, 2379–2385.

Chess, S. Neurological dysfunction and childhood behavioral pathology. *Journal of Autism and Childhood Schizophrenia*, 1972, *2*, 299–311.

Childers, A.T. Hyper-activity in children having behavior disorders. *American Journal of Orthopsychiatry*, 1935, *5*, 227–243.

Cleckley, H. *The Mask of Sanity*. St. Louis: Mosby, 1964.

Clements, S. Minimal Brain Dysfunctions in Children. NINDB Monograph No. 3. Washington, D.C.: United States Public Health Services, 1966, 9–10.

Clements, S.D., & Peters, J.E. Minimal brain dysfunction in the school-age child. *Archives of General Psychiatry*, 1962, *6*, 185–197.

Cloninger, C.R., & Guze, S.B. Psychiatric illness in female criminality: The role of sociopathy and hysteria in the antisocial woman. *American Journal of Psychiatry*, 1970, *127*, 303–311.

Cloward, R.A., & Ohlin, L.E. *Delinquency and opportunity: A theory of delinquent gangs.* New York: Free Press, 1960.

Cohen, A. *Deviance and control.* Englewood Cliffs, N.J.: Prentice-Hall, 1966.

Conners, C.K. A teacher rating scale for use in drug studies with children. *American Journal of Psychiatry*, 1969, *126*, 884–888.

Denhoff, E., Laufer, M.W., & Holden, R.H. The syndromes of cerebral dysfunction. *Journal of the Oklahoma State Medical Association*, 1959, *52*, 360–366.

Diagnostic and Statistical Manual of Mental Disorders DSM-II. Washington, D.C.: American Psychiatric Association, 1968, p. 50.

Drillien, C.M. *The growth and development of the prematurely born infant.* London: E. & S. Livingstone, Ltd., 1964.

Ebaugh, F.G. Neuropsychiatric sequelae of acute encephalitis in children. *American Journal Diseases of Children*, 1923, *25*, 89–97.

Eisenberg, L. Psychiatric implications of brain damage in children. *Psychiatric Quarterly,* 1957, *31,* 72–92.

Eisenberg, L., Conners, C.K., & Sharpe, L. A controlled study of the differential application of outpatient psychiatry treatment for children. *Japanese Journal of Child Psychiatry,* 1965, *6,* 125–132.

Eisenberg, L., Lachman, R., Molling, P.A., Lockner, A., Mizeile, J.D., and Conners, C.K. A psychopharmacologic experiment in a training school for delinquent boys: Methods, problems, findings. *American Journal of Orthopsychiatry,* 1963, *33,* 431–446.

Frisk, M., Wegelius, E., Tenhunem, T., Widholm, O., & Hortling, H. The problem of dyslexia in teenagers. *Acta Paediatrica Scandinavica,* 1967, *56,* 333–343.

Frosch, J., & Wortis, S.B. A contribution to the nosology of the impulse disorders. *American Journal of Psychiatry,* 1954, *111,* 132–138.

Gesell, A., & Amatruda, C. *Developmental diagnosis.* New York, Paul B. Hoeber, Inc., 1941.

Goldman, H., Dinitz, S., Lindner, L.A., & Foster, T.W. "Drug Treatment of the Sociopathic Offender." Read before the 140th meeting of the American Association for the Advancement of Science, San Francisco, California, February, 1974.

Gross, M.B., & Wilson, W.C. *Minimal brain dysfunction.* New York: Brunner/ Mazel, 1974.

Gunnarson, S. Some types of nervous disorders in children and their prognosis; investigation based study of hospital material, followed up by subsequent examination. *Acta Paediatrica,* 1946, *33,* (Suppl. 4), 1–76.

Guze, S.B., Wolfgram, E.D., McKinney, J.K., & Cantwell, D.P. Psychiatric illness in the families of convicted criminals: A study of 519 first-degree relatives. *Diseases of the Nervous System,* 1967, *28,* 651–659. Pg. 54.

Hallgren, B. Specific dyslexia (congenital word-blindness), *Acta Psychiatrica Scandinavica,* 1950 (Suppl. 65), 1–287.

Hammar, S.L. School underachievement in the adolescent: A review of 73 cases. *Pediatrics,* 1967, *40,* 373–381.

Hartocollis, P. The syndrome of minimal brain dysfunction in young adult patients. *Bulletin of the Menninger Clinics,* 1968, *32,* 102–114.

Healy, W., & Bronner, A.F. *New light on delinquency and its treatment.* New Haven: Yale University Press, 1936.

Hertzig, M.D., & Birch, H. Neurologic organization in psychiatrically disturbed adolescents. *Archives of General Psychiatry,* 1968, *19,* 528–537.

Hill, D. Amphetamines in psychopathic states. *British Journal of Addiction,* 1947, *44,* 50–54.

Hohman, L.B. Postencephalitic behavior disorders in children. *Johns Hopkins Hospital Bulletin,* 1922, *33,* 372–375.

Horn, J.M., Green, M., Carney, R., & Erickson, M.T. Bias against genetic hypothesis in adoption studies. *Archives of General Psychiatry,* 1975, *32,* 1365–1367.

Huessy, H.R. Minimal brain dysfunction in children (hyperkinetic syndrome): Recogniztion and treatment. *Drug Therapy,* September 1973, 52–63.

Huessy, H.R. The adult hyperkinetic. *American Journal of Psychiatry.* 1974, *131,* 724–725.

Huessy, H.R., & Blair, C.L. *Clinical trials of drug therapy in sixty-four adults with symptoms and/or childhood histories of minimal brain dysfunction.* Submitted for publication.

Huessy, H.R., & Cohen, A.H. Hyperkinetic behavior and learning disabilities followed over seven years. *Pediatrics*, 1976, *57*, 4–10.

Huessy, H.R., & Gendron, R.M. Prevalence of so-called hyperkinetic syndrome in public school children of Vermont. *Acta Paedopsychiatrica*, 1970, *37*, 243–248.

Huessy, H.R., Marshall, C., & Gendron, R. Five hundred children followed from grade two through grade five for the prevalence of behavior disorder, *Acta Paedopsychiatrica*, 1973, *39*, 301–309.

Huessy, H.R., Metoyer, M., & Townsend, M. 8–10 year follow-up of 84 children treated for behavioral disorder in rural Vermont. *Acta Paedopsychiatrica*, 1974, *40*, 230–235.

Hurwitz, I., Bibace, R.M.A., Wolff, P.H. & Rowbotham, B.M. Neuropsychological function of normal boys, delinquent boys, and boys with learning problems. *Perceptual Motor Skills*, 1972, *35*, 387–394.

Ingram, T.T.S. A characteristic form of overactive behavior in brain damaged children. *Journal of Mental Science*, 1956, *102*, 550–558.

Jeans, R.F. Two patients belie theory that adults don't suffer from MBD. *Roche Report: Frontiers of Psychiatry*, October 1974, 5–6.

Johnson, E. A study of psychological findings of 100 children recovering from purulent meningitis. *Journal of Clinical Psychology*, 1960, *16*, 55–58.

Kahn, E., & Cohen, L.H. Organic drivenness—a brain-stem syndrome and an experience. *New England Journal of Medicine*, 1934, *210*, 748–756.

Karpman, B. The myth of the psychopathic personality. *American Journal of Psychiatry*, 1948, *104*, 523–534.

Kaufman, I., Durkin, H., Frank, T., Heims, L.W., Jones, D.B., Ryter, Z., Stone, E., & Zilbach, J. Delineation of two diagnostic groups among juvenile delinquents: The schizophrenic and the impulse-ridden character disorder. *American Journal of Orthopsychiatry*, 1961, *29*, 292–318.

Knobloch, H., & Pasamanick, B. Prospective studies on the epidemiology of reproductive casualty. *Merrill-Palmer Quarterly of Behavior and Development*, 1966, *12*, 27–43.

Knobloch, H., & Pasamanick, B. Prediction from the assessment of neuromotor and intellectual status in infancy. In Zubin, J. and Jervis, G.A. (Eds.), *Psychopathology of mental development*. New York: Grune & Stratton, 1967.

Korey, S. The effects of benzedrine sulfate on the behavior of psychopathic and neurotic juvenile delinquents. *Psychiatric Quarterly*, 1944, *18*, 127–137.

Kupfer, D.J., Detre, T.P., & Koral, J. Relationship of certain childhood "traits" to adult psychiatric disorders. *American Journal of Orthopsychiatry*, 1975, *45*, 74–80.

Laufer, M.W. Cerebral dysfunction and behavior disorders in adolescents. *American Journal of Orthopsychiatry*, 1962, *32*, 501–506.

Laufer, M.W., & Denhoff, E. Hyperkinetic behavior syndrome in children. *Journal of Pediatrics*, 1957, *50*, 463–474.

Laufer, M.W., Denhoff, E., & Solomons, G. Hyperkinetic impulse disorder in children's behavior problems. *Psychosomatic Medicine*, 1957, *19*, 38–49.

Levy, S. Post-encephalitic behavior disorder—a forgotten entity: A report of 100 cases. *American Journal of Psychiatry*, 1959, *115*, 1062–1067.

Levy, S. The hyperkinetic child—a forgotten entity. Its diagnosis and treatment. *International Journal of Neuropsychiatry*, 1966, *2*, 330–336.

Lurie, L.A., & Levy, S. Personality changes and behavior disorders of children following pertussis—report based on study of 500 problem children. *Journal of the American Medical Association,* 1942, *120,* 890–894.

Lytton, G.J., & Knobel, M. Diagnosis and treatment of behavior disorders in children. *Diseases of the Nervous System,* 1958, *20,* 5–11.

MacKay, M., Beck, L., & Taylor, R. Methylphenidate for adolescents with minimal brain dysfunction. *New York State Journal of Medicine,* 1973, *73,* 550–554.

Maletzky, B.M. d-Amphetamine and delinquency: Hyperkinesis persisting? *Diseases of the Nervous System,* 1974, *35,* 543–547.

Malone, C.A. Some observations on children of disorganized families and problems of acting out. *Journal of the American Academy of Child Psychiatry,* 1963, *2,* 22–49.

Mann, H.B., & Greenspan, S.I. The identification and treatment of adult brain dysfunction. *American Journal of Psychiatry,* 1976, *133,* 1013–1017.

Marwit, S.J., & Stenner, A.J. Hyperkinesis: Delineation of two patterns. *Exceptional Children,* 1972, *38,* 401–406.

Mellsop, B. 1972. Psychiatric Patients as Children & Adults: Childhood Predictions of Adult Illness. *Journal of Child Psychology & Psychiatry.* 1972, *13,* pg. 91–101.

McCord, W., & McCord, J. *The psychopath: An essay on the criminal mind.* New York: Van Nostrand, 1964.

Mendelson, W., Johnson, N., & Stewart, M. Hyperactive children as teenagers: A follow-up study. *Journal of Nervous and Mental Diseases.* 1971, *153,* 272–279.

Menkes, M.M., Rowe, J.S., & Menkes, J.H. A twenty-five year follow-up study on the hyperkinetic child with minimal brain dysfunction. *Pediatrics,* 1967, *39,* 393–399.

Miles, R.S. Common nervous conditions of children. *Archives of Pediatrics,* 1921, *38,* 664.

Miller, W. Lower class culture as a generating milieu of gang delinquency. *Journal of Social Issues,* 1959, *14,* 5–19.

Minde, K., Webb, G., & Sykes, D. Studies on the hyperactive child: VI prenatal and paranatal factors associated with hyperactivity. *Developmental Medicine and Child Neurology,* 1968, *10,* 355–363.

Minde, K., Weiss, G., & Mendelson, N. A 5-year follow-up of 91 hyperactive children. *Journal of the American Academy of Child Psychiatry,* 1972, *11,* 595–610.

Morris, H., Jr., Escoll, P., & Wexler, R. Aggressive behavior disorders of childhood: A follow-up study. *American Journal of Psychiatry,* 1956, *112,* 991–997.

Morrison, J.R., & Minkoff, K. Explosive personality as a signal to the hyperactive child syndrome. *Comprehensive Psychiatry,* 1975, *16,* 343–348.

Morrison, J.R., & Stewart, M.A. A family study of the hyperactive child syndrome. *Biological Psychiatry,* 1971, *3,* 189–195.

Morrison, J.R., & Stewart, M.A. The psychiatric status of the legal families of adopted hyperactive children. *Archives of General Psychiatry,* 1973, *28,* 888–891. (a)

Morrison, J.R., & Stewart, M. A Bilateral inheritance as evidence for polygenicity in the hyperactive child syndrome. *Journal of Nervous and Mental Diseases,* 1974, *158,* 226–228.

Morrison, J.R., & Stewart, M.A. Bilateral inheritance as evidence for polygenicity in the hyperactive child syndrome. *Journal of Nervous and Mental Diseases*, 1974, *158*, 226–228.

Murray, C.A. *The link between learning disabilities and juvenile delinquency: Current theory and knowledge.* Superintendent of Documents, U.S. Government Printing Office 027-000-00479-2, April 1976. Pg. 41.

Oettinger, L. General discussion. *Annals of the New York Academy of Science*, 1973, *205*, 345. (a)

Oettinger, L. Presentation given at Claremont Reading Conference, Claremont, California, February 9, 1973. (b)

Ounsted, C. The hyperkinetic syndrome in epileptic children. *Lancet*, 1955, *2*, 303–311.

Pasamanick, B., Rogers, M., & Lilienfield, A.M. Pregnancy experiences and the development of childhood behavior disorder. *American Journal of Psychiatry*, 1956, *112*, 613–618.

Pearson, G. *Psychoanalysis and the education of the child.* New York: W.W. Norton, 1954.

Perault, P., & Novotny, M. *Early Diagnosis of Minimal Brain Dysfunction in Children.* University of Vermont research project, 1974.

Pincus, J.H., & Glaser, G.H. The syndrome of "minimal brain dysfunction" in childhood. *New England Journal of Medicine*, 1966, *275*, 27–35.

Prechtl, H.F.R., & Stemmer, C.J. The choreiform syndrome in children. *Developmental Medicine and Child Neurology*, 1962, *4*, 119–127.

Preis, K. "Minimal Brain Dysfunction and Juvenile Delinquency." Paper presented at Symposium on Minimal Brain Dysfunction at the University of Vermont College of Medicine, April 1976.

Quay, H.C. Dimensions of personality in delinquent boys as inferred from the factor analysis of case history data. *Child Development*, 1964, *35*, 479–484.

Quitkin, F., & Klein, D.F. Two behavioral syndromes in young adults related to possible minimal brain dysfunction. *Journal of Psychiatric Research*, 1969, *7*, 131–142.

Redl, F., & Wineman, D.T. *The aggressive child.* Glencoe, Ill.: The Free Press of Glencoe, 1957.

Report of the Conference on the Use of Stimulant Drugs in the Treatment of Behaviorally Disturbed Young School Children. *Psychopharmacology Bulletin*, 1971, *7*, 23–29.

Rexford, E.N., & Van Amerongen, S.T. The influence of unsolved maternal oral conflicts upon impulsive acting out in young children. *American Journal of Orthopsychiatry*, 1957, *27*, 75–87.

Riddle, K.D., & Rapoport, J.L. A 2 year follow-up of 72 hyperactive boys. *Journal of Nervous and Mental Diseases*, 1976, *162*, 126–134.

Robins, L.N. *Deviant children grown up: A sociological and psychiatric study of sociopathic personality.* Baltimore: Williams & Wilkins Co., 1966.

Rogers, M.E., Lilienfeld, A.M., & Pasamanick, B. Prenatal and paranatal factors in the development of childhood behavior disorders. *Acta Psychiatrica et Neurologica Scandinavica*, 1955 (Suppl. 102), 1–157.

Rutter, M. *Children of sick parents.* London: Oxford University Press, Inc., 1966.

Rutter, M., Lebovici, S., Eisenberg, L., Sneznevskij, A.V., Sadoun, R., Brooke, E., & Lin, T.Y. A tri-axial classification of mental disorders in childhood. *Journal of Child Psychology and Psychiatry*, 1969, *10*, 41–61.

Safer, D.J. A familial factor in minimal brain dysfunction. *Behavioral Genetics*,

1973, *3,* 175–186.

Safer, D.J., & Allen, R.P. Stimulant drug treatment of hyperactive adolescents. *Diseases of the Nervous System,* 1975, *36,* 454–457.

Safer, D.J., & Allen, R.P. *Hyperactive children.* Baltimore: University Park Press, 1976.

Shaffer, D. Psychiatric aspects of brain injury in childhood: A review. *Developmental Medicine and Child Neurology,* 1973, *15,* 211–220.

Shelley, E.M., & Riester, A. Syndrome of minimal brain damage in young adults. *Diseases of the Nervous System,* May, 1972, 335–338.

Sherman, M., & Beverly, B.I. The factor of deterioration in children showing behavior difficulties after epidemic encephalitis. *Archives of Neurological Psychiatry,* 1923, *10,* 329–343.

Silver, L. A proposed view on the etiology of the neurological learning disability syndrome. *Journal of Learning Disabilities,* 1971, *4,* 6–15.

Stewart, M.A. Hyperactive children. *Scientific American,* 1970, *222,* 94–98.

Stewart, M.A., Pitts, F.N., Craig, A.G., & Dieruf, W. The hyperactive child syndrome. *American Journal of Orthopsychiatry,* 1966, *36,* 861–867.

Stewart, M.A., Thach, B.T., & Freidin, M.R. Accidental poisoning and the hyperactive child syndrome. *Diseases of the Nervous System,* 1970, *31,* 403–407.

Still, G.F. Some abnormal psychical conditions in children. *Lancet,* 1902, *1,* 1077–1082.

Strauss, A.A. Ways of thinking in brain-crippled deficient children. *American Journal of Psychiatry,* 1944, *100,* 639–647. Pg. 4.

Strauss, A.A., & Kephart, N. *Psychopathology and education of the brain-injured child; Vol. II, progress in clinic and theory.* New York: Grune & Stratton, 1955. Catalogued under Strauss and Lehtinen.

Strauss, A.A., & Lehtinen, L. *Psychopathology and education of the brain-injured child.* New York: Grune & Stratton, 1947. Serves as Vol. I.

Strauss, A.A., & Werner, H. Disorders of conceptual thinking in the brain-injured child. *Journal of Nervous and Mental Disorders,* 1942, *96,* 153–172.

Thomas, A., Chess, S., & Birch, H.G. *Temperament and behavior disorders in children.* New York: New York University Press, 1968.

Thurston, D., Middlekamp, J., & Mason, E. The late effects of lead poisoning. *Journal of Pediatrics,* 1955, *47,* 413–423.

Wagenheim, L. The effect of childhood disease on IQ variability. *Journal of Consulting Psychology,* 1954, *18,* 354.

Waldrop, M.F., Pedersen, F.A., & Bell, R.Q. Minor physical anomalies and behavior in preschool children. *Child Development,* 1968, *39,* 391–400.

Warren, R.J., Karduck, W.A., Bussaratia, S., Stewart, M.A., & Sly, W.S. The hyperactive child syndrome: Normal chromosome findings. *Archives of General Psychiatry,* 1971, *24,* 161–162.

Weiss, G., Minde, K., Werry, J.S., Douglas, V., & Nemeth, E. Studies on the hyperactive child: VIII. Five-year follow-up. *Archives of General Psychiatry,* 1971, *24,* 409–415.

Wender, P.H. *Minimal brain dysfunction in children.* New York: John Wiley & Sons, 1971.

Wender, P.H., & Eisenberg, L. Minimal brain dysfunction in children. in Arieti, S. (Ed.), *American Handbook of Psychiatry.* Vol. II. New York: Basic Books, Inc., 1974. Pp. 130–146.

Werner, E., Bierman, J., French, F., Simonian, K., Connor, A., Smith, R.S.,

& Campbell, M. Reproductive and environmental casualties: A report on the ten-year follow-up of children of the Kauai pregnancy study. *Pediatrics,* 1968, *42,* 111–117.

Werner, H., & Strauss, A. Pathology of figure ground relation in the child. *Journal of Abnormal Social Psychology,* 1941, *36,* 58–67.

Werner, H., & Thuma, B. A deficiency in the perception of apparent motion in children with brain injury. *American Journal of Psychology,* 1942, *55,* 58–67.

Werry, J.S. Studies on the hyperactive child: IV An empirical analysis of the minimal brain dysfunction syndrome. *Archives of General Psychiatry,* 1968, *19,* 9–16. (a) Pg. 9. (Quote)

Werry, J.S. Developmental hyperactivity. *Pediatric Clinics of North America,* 1968, *15,* 581–599. (b)

Werry, J., Weiss, G., & Douglas, U.I. Studies on the hyperactive child—I. Some preliminary findings. *Canadian Psychiatric Association Journal,* 1964, *9,* 120–130.

Werry, J.S., Weiss, G., Douglas, U., & Martin, J. Studies on the hyperactive child III. The effect of chlorpromazine upon behavior and learning. *Journal of the American Academy of Child Psychiatry,* 1966, *5,* 292–312.

Wikler, A., Dixon, J., & Parker, J. Brain function in problem children and controls: Psychometric, neurological, and electroencephalographic comparisons. *American Journal of Psychiatry,* 1970, *127,* 634–645.

Woerner, P.I., & Guze, S.B. A family and marital study of hysteria. *British Journal of Psychiatry,* 1968, *114,* 161–168.

Wolff, P.H., & Hurwitz, I. The choreiform syndrome. *Developmental Medicine and Child Neurology,* 1966, *8,* 160–165.

8

Long Term Effects of Stimulant Therapy for HA Children: Risk Benefits Analysis

RICHARD P. ALLEN, Ph.D.
DANIEL J. SAFER, M.D.

In the past few years the increasing use of stimulant medication as a maintenance therapy for hyperactive children (Krager and Safer, 1974) has led to a situation where nearly one percent of our elementary school-age children are receiving stimulant drug treatment on a long term bases of two or more years. Attention should, therefore, increasingly focus upon the long term effects of this therapy. Accordingly, we shall attempt to summarize and evaluate the reported findings of long term benefits and side effects of stimulant therapy for hyperactive children. A basic assumption underlying addressing the issue of long term effects of the medication is that this type of therapy requires continued medication use in order to continue effectiveness. The treatment plan for hyperactive children, therefore, generally involves medication administration for one or more years to manage school problems. The evaluation of the effects and risks of stimulant treatment must, therefore, be based upon a similar long term time period.

At the outset it should be clear this chapter concerns stimulant treatment for developmental hyperactivity in children. In this paper, as in our previous work, developmental hyperactivity is abbreviated as hyperactivity or, simply, HA (Safer and Allen, 1976). The diagnosis of developmental hyperactivity can be difficult, but when one obtains a detailed, year by year, home and school history, the task is far simpler and there is a high degree of diagnostic reliability. Hyperactivity represents a failure to control motor activity which persists year after year and should not be confused with restlessness associated with a transient situational reaction. The diagnosis requires an historical account of overactivity in situations requiring motor inhibition, preferably dating from the early childhood years. These children are often not overactive in one-to-one situations and when activity is appropriate, as in play. When environmental demands for persistent attention increase, the problem increases. Thus, the first grade may be the initial setting where HA becomes problematic.

Although nearly 100% of developmentally hyperactive children will be overactive in a given class, when diagnosed only 14% of the children judged by the teacher to be overactive have the HA problem. Similarly, while approximately 85% of HA children are inattentive, only about 13% of the inattentive children are also hyperactive. With relation to learning impediments, about 80% of HA children show an appreciable learning lag, whereas only 39% of children with prominent learning lags are HA (Safer and Allen, 1976).

The natural prevalence of HA is about 4 to 5% of the school-age children with a four-to-one male-to-female ratio. There is a strong familial incidence with only a small socio-economic class difference for more HA children in the low social classes. The course of the disorder is characterized by an initial expression of motor overactivity starting from the ages of 2 to 6. By the teenage years, gross motor activity appears to be more controlled but the child will be described as fidgety and having persistent attention and aggression problems. Learning problems, if present, will persist through into young adulthood. Fidgety, restless problems sometimes also continue into early adult life. There is, however, in recent group data no clear indication of a high incidence of psychopathology in adult life. The incidence of sociopathy is greater in this group than in comparison groups, but there is not the extreme excess of sociopathy that had been expected from earlier work (Hechtman, Weiss, Finkelstein, Werner, Benn, 1976; Borland, Hechtman, 1976).

The first step in evaluating long term effects of stimulants is extrapolation from the acute drug effects. Stimulants clearly provide effective, immediate reduction of overactivity and inattentiveness in HA children (Safer and Allen, 1976). Stimulants also improve the HA child's performance on attention and vigilence tasks (Sprague, Barnes, Werry, 1970; Sykes, Douglas, Morganstern, 1972; Anderson, Halcomb, Doyle, 1973) and in some cases even improve IQ performance scores (Connors, 1972). However, they do not appear to affect the retention of new information (Aman, Sprague, 1973; Connors, 1974; Rie, 1977; Gittelman-Klein, and Klein, 1976). Stimulants also do not appear to have even a short term (6 months or less) benefit for academic achievement in either the learning disabled child or in the HA child (Gittelman-Klein, 1976; Rie, et al., 1976).

The questions of long term efficacy therefore become: One, do immediate stimulant drug-induced decreases in overactivity and inattention persist. Two, do these gains create a condition permitting—over the long run—more years in school and better school achievement. And, three, does the decrease in this abnormality permit over the long run better social and life adjustment.

In evaluating long term risk, one has to ask if the well-documented short term side effects persist for reduction in appetite with a possible associated reduction in normal growth, cardiovascular changes in response to the medication, irritability and sleep disturbances. In evaluating the long term side effects of stimulants, there is also a question of whether or not continued use of a drug of abuse would increase a risk of drug abuse in later life. It is commonly asserted that the long term use of medication in these children creates a drug-reliant psychology with increased drug abuse in adult life. Such a problem would presumably be exacerbated by the abuse potential of stimulants. In this chapter we shall primarily attempt to evaluate the three benefits and four risks involved in the stimulant maintenance of therapy in HA children.

Long Term Efficacy

When stimulant therapy benefits the HA child by reducing motor activities and improving attention, the drug therapy will generally continue to be effective from childhood through adolescence. Sleater, VonNeumann, and Sprague (1974) used yearly placebo trials of one month for hyperactive children on stimulant therapy. They obtained monthly teacher ratings of class room behavior covering the stimulant and placebo treatment periods; the children and the teacher were "blind" to the placebo trial. Sleater, et al. found that 7 of 42 HA children needed an increase in dose over a one or two-year period to maintain efficacy of the medication. Interestingly, also, 11 of the 42 children did as well on placebo and presumably could be taken off the medication within the first two years. These results indicating little tolerance to the behavioral effects of the stimulants are also reported by Gross and Wilson (1974). The persistence of the stimulant effect is striking and indeed, Safer and Allen (1975a) have noted that the stimulant therapy reduces restlessness and inattentiveness even in early and mid-adolescence. Thus, there appears to be little tolerance to the therapeutic effect of stimulants in hyperactivity and there also appears to be no indication that stimulants fail to reduce HA symptoms as children get older. The symptoms, particularly motor overactivity, decrease with age; but whenever the symptoms are present in developmentally HA individuals, they appear to respond to stimulants. This is an important issue. It is the severity of the symptoms not the age which is crucial in planning the chemotherapy. Thus, there is a need for yearly trials off medication to determine whether or not the symptoms have persisted and are sufficiently severe to justify continued chemotherapy.

The likelihood that the continued improved school behavior resulting from stimulant therapy will translate into improved academic success is quite a different matter. When HA children on stimulants for two or more years are compared with age-matched non-HA children or HA non-medicated children, there is no indication that the stimulant maintenance has corrected their problems. Drug treated HA children continue to show lower WRAT scores in reading and arithmetic than do controls (Riddle and Rapaport, 1976; Ackerman, et al., 1977). Weiss and colleagues (1975) compared those hyperactive children treated with methylphenidate for three or more years with those treated with long term chlorpromazine or no long term medication. They also reported no significant difference in academic achievement between HA children treated with methylphenidate and those not treated with stimulants. At their five-year follow-up evaluation, the three medication groups showed no overall significant differences in any outcome measure including general cognitive test scores of the WISC, Bender-Gestalt, and Goodenough Draw-a-Man test. The number of children who never failed a grade showed a tendency to be less for the subjects treated with methylphenidate. Thus, 54% (13/24) of HA children maintained on long term stimulant therapy passed all grades compared to only 30% (6/20) of HA children not on long term medication. This result is in the predicted direction; it is, however, the only outcome measure out of eleven studied by Weiss and colleagues that shows even a suggestion of a difference in the direction favoring the treatment group. The result is not statistically significant.

Weiss and colleagues similarly showed no greater improvement in hyperactivity or in general adjustment in the stimulant-treated group than in the non-stimulant-treated group. Specifically, emotional adjustment, delinquency, mother-child relationship, and mother's impression of change showed no statistically significant difference between the three treatment groups over a five-year follow-up period.

Fortunately Weiss and colleagues did not leave their analysis at this rather confusing point. They also asked whether or not other variables interacted with chemotherapy to predict treatment outcome. As in much modern psychological research, this type of multivariate predictive analysis provides the most significant results. In this five-year follow-up, the family diagnosis rating was important for the outcome in the hyperactive group treated with stimulant therapy. This family diagnosis rating was based on a 5 point scale with five indicating the most desired score. Each of the following items were included: (1) Stability in the home—relating to the number of moves made by the family in the child's lifetime. (2) Marital relationship. (3) Psychiatric illness of parents. (4) Continuity and presence of mother or mother substitute. (5) Deviant child-rearing practices, e.g., overprotective, excessive punishment or extreme inconsistencies. (6) Level of anxiety present in the family interaction or general emotional climate of family.

The family diagnosis was not significantly related to the five-year outcome for the non-stimulant treated HA children. In contrast, for the children maintained on stimulant therapy for most of this five-year period, family diagnosis correlated significantly with good outcome for academic achievement ($r = 0.36$, $P < 0.05$), absence of delinquency ($r = 0.38$, $P < 0.05$), and emotional adjustment ($r = 0.48$, $P < 0.01$). This important finding suggests that stimulant therapy combined with good family environment will produce a measurably positive outcome. Perhaps the stimulant therapy assists in part by permitting the family factors to be effective.

Noted by Weiss, et al. (1975) but not measured as such was the fact that—during the five-year period—the teachers of the stimulant treated HA children reported these students were more cooperative and diligent when on drugs. When the HA children went off drugs, the teachers could tell the difference and they requested that the children go back on their medication. This and similar reports indicate that stimulant drugs when given during the school day and continued for years improve the HA children's classroom behavior (Safer and Allen, 1976). This is true even though baseline vs long term measures of achievement and emotional adaptation are not significantly benefitted by stimulant drug treatment.

Long Term Side Effects

In terms of the undesirable effects of stimulant therapy for two or more years the most controversial has been the issue of growth suppression. Safer, Allen, and Barr (1972) first reported a mild growth suppression resulting during the first three years of stimulant therapy in hyperactive children. The growth suppression occurred for dextroamphetamine and for high doses of methylphenidate. Our (Safer and Allen, 1973) evaluation of methylphenidate and dextroamphetamine in long term use has demonstrated that this growth suppression relates to the following factors: (See Tables 1 and 2)

1. Medication choice: Growth suppression is more prominent for destroamphetamine than for even large therapeutic doses of methylphenidate.

2. Dose of medication: Methylphenidate in daily doses of 20 milligrams or less produce minor, if any, alterations in the growth curve; larger doses produce increasing growth suppression.

3. Dose regime: HA children after being taken off medication show a remarkable growth rebound, a growth rate above their age expected level (Safer, Allen, and Barr, 1975). This rebound was particularly useful for those children on dextroamphetamine. The size of the rebound over the 3 month (summer) period off medication sufficed to nearly reverse the losses of the previous nine months on the medication.

4. Daily dose frequency: At least for dextroamphetamine tablets, a morning only dose produced less growth suppression than the same daily dose divided into two or three different times.

Despite controversy over the mild growth suppression effects of dextroamphetamine and higher does of methlphenidate therapy, the findings reported above have received independent confirmation (McNutt, Ballard, and Boileau, 1976; Knights and Viets, 1975; Greenhill, et al., 1977). For example, Weiss and colleagues (1975) in their five-year follow-up showed that out of 16 children on methylphenidate three or more years, 9 showed growth suppression, 5 showed expected growth, and 2 showed growth greater than expected (Sign test, $P \leq 0.04$). They also report that on termination of long term methylphenidate therapy 8 out of 11 (73%) cases showed accelerated growth rate similar to the summer off growth-rebound noted in our work. The rebound effect aside from validating the growth suppression appears to be clinically important. Given the reported relatively mild suppression and a strong rebound effect, there appears to be little, if any, residual growth suppression two or three years after terminating stimulant therapy. It is, indeed, reassuring that Gross (1976) and Hectman, et al., (1976) report no growth reduction for older adolescents who were given stimulant therapy as children. Furthermore, group data to date suggest that the growth effect does not persist after 3 years on stimulant treatment. In individual cases growth rate can be easily monitored to minimize any drug induced suppression.

It is interesting to speculate on the mechanisms by which stimulant therapy temporarily impedes growth. The growth suppression is probably realted to a central appetite suppression effect of the medication (Innes and Nickerson, 1970; Lucas and Sells, 1977). The conjecture is supported by our observations of decreased meal consumption at lunch for HA children on long term stimulant therapy (Safer and Allen, 1975b) and by the report of the persistence of appetite suppression at 12 weeks of methylphenidate therapy (Gittelman-Klein, Katz, Saraf, and Pollack, 1976). Other possible mechanisms for growth suppression could be the drug's direct effect on lipid metabolism (Pinter and Pattee, 1970; Santi and Fassina, 1964), and increase in metabolic rate (Inness and Nickerson, 1970), or a reduction of growth hormone—possibly as an indirect result of a suppression of slow wave sleep. Recent evaluations of growth hormone on hyperactive children have indicated that those on prolonged methylphenidate treatment show less growth hormone response to amphetamine stimulation (Aarskog, Fevang, Kløve, Støa, and Thorsen, 1977).

The cardiovascular effects of long term stimulants can be examined in terms of either the cardiovascular response to the medication or the changes in basal cardiac function off medication. Regarding the latter, ECGs on 23 HA children treated with methylphenidate for three or more years were all reported as normal (Weiss, et al., 1975). Resting heart rate was normal in this group. Safer and Allen (1975b) found that resting, off-medication heart rates and blood pressures were within normal limits for 48 HA children on methylphenidate therapy. Regarding the response to the stimulant dose, it has been well established that acute dose of methylphenidate cause minor elevations in blood pressure (Connors, 1972; Greenberg, Deem, and McMahon, 1972; Knights and Hinton, 1969; Rapaport, Quinn, Bradbard, Riddle, and Brooks, 1974). Acute doses of 20 milligrams of methylphenidate elevate heart rate about 10 - 15 beats per minute whereas therapeutic dose of dextroamphetamine have little or no effect on heart rate (Knight and Hinton, 1969; Arnold, Wender, McCloskey, and Snyder, 1972; Connors, Taylor, Meo, Kurtz, and Forner, 1972; Greenberg, Deem, and McMahon, 1972). The significant question, then, is whether or not tolerance develops to the heart rate increases in response to methylphenidate. In our studies we have consistently found tolerance to this effect developing after two to five months on medication. We measured heart rate 70 minutes after 20 milligrams of methylphenidate was administered orally. Comparing 36 HA children not previously on medication with 26 tested during the first year on medication revealed a significant decrease in the heart rate response over the first year of medication use. In fact, heart rate for children on medication therapy for more than five months showed no average change following methylphenidate. For children on methylphenidate for two to five months, heart rate increases were approximately half those found in children that had been previously receiving stimulant therapy. Weiss, et al., (1975) report that after long term methlyphenidate therapy in three children, the ECG at two hours after medication showed no change in heart rate. These findings conflict with those from a carefully controlled report by Ballard, Boileau, Sleater, Massey, and Sprague (1976). They found mild, consistent heart rate and blood pressure increases following methylphenidate without evidence for tolerance with long term methylphenidate therapy. They also reported a relation between dose and the magnitude of the increase. It should be noted that the increases they reported were on an average about 10 or fewer beats per minute greater than the placebo condition. The blood pressure increased only about 8% above placebo level. Ballard and colleagues also reported that blood pressure and heart rate changes during exercise were greater for the methylphenidate condition than placebo conditions.

At this point it remains unclear to what extent the heart rate and blood pressure increases in response to methylphenidate persist. As noted there are several negative studies regarding blood pressure increases even to initial challenge by methylphenidate. There are two studies which suggest there is tolerance in the heart rate increases after prolonged methylphenidate therapy. The best controlled study, however, shows a persistent heart rate increase following methylphenidate. Clearly the heart rate effects can be minimized by using the minimally effective doses. It is also reassuring that no ECG abnormalities have been reported in relation to long term methylphenidate therapy. Presumably further research will be conducted into the heart rate response on methylphenidate in the future.

Stimulant therapy is also associated with some difficulties in falling asleep and some mood changes. One study with 30 hyperactive children given a relatively large dose of about 50 milligrams of methylphenidate daily in two divided doses reported three major side effects persisting from four weeks to twelve weeks on medication. The three persisting side effects were: Appetite decrease, irritability with anger outbursts, and difficulty falling asleep (Gittelman-Klein, Katz, Saraf, and Pollack, 1976). The appetite decrease persistence was discussed above. The irritability and sleep problems are less common clinically and may reflect the relatively high dose in this study. Nonetheless, there is a suggestion that these problems may persist at the clinically effective dosage levels, particularly when divided doses are used.

There have been four reported polysomnogram studies of all night sleep in HA children. One study (Small, Hibi, and Feinberg, 1971) reported shorter sleep latency for HA children than for normal children, but another study (Haig, Schroeder, and Schroeder, 1974) reported longer sleep latency for HA children. Dextroamphetamine therapy is reported (Small, et al., 1971) to increase sleep latency and reduce the number of sleep cycles in HA children. Methylphenidate therapy is reported to either have no effect (Haig, et al., 1974) or to cause marginal increases in REM latency and decreases in Stage 4 sleep (Nahas and Krynicki , 1971). After at least 21 days of stimulant therapy, marginal increases in Stage 4 sleep have been reported at withdrawal of the medication for both methylphenidate and dextroamphetamine (Nahas and Krynicki, 1977; Safer and Allen, 1975b). Thus, in general, stimulant therapy has a relatively small effect on sleep—in some cases slightly increasing sleep latency and decreasing Stage 4 sleep. However, drug induced sleep disturbances can contribute to daytime irritability and create anger outbursts.

Finally, one of the questions most often asked is whether or not stimulant treatment of HA will lead to later adolescent drug abuse. In this regard, the recent preliminay report on a ten-year follow-up of HA children is reassuring. In this study of hyperactive children in their young adulthood, the drug abuse arrests were significantly less for the HA than for the comparison groups (Hechtman, Weiss, Finkelstein, Werner, and Benn, 1976). The drug abuse of hallucinogens was virtually non-existent in the HA population and significantly less than that in the control. When comparing "grown up" HA males with their non-HA brothers, there is evidence for more cigarette use by the HA group but not for more alcohol abuse (Borland and Hechtman, 1976). In general, then, stimulant and hallucinogen drug abuse rarely occur for the HA population.

Risk Benefit Appraisal

In summary, the risks of long term stimulant therapy appear to be minimal. There may be some mild growth suppression with apparent "rebound" recovery after terminating medicine. Transient cardiovascular changes commonly occur with methylphenidate, but their persistence is in doubt and electrocardiograph assessement did not indicate any abnormality after long term use of stimulant therapy. Sleep loss and irritability are probably only persistent with larger divided doses of medication and are certainly easy enough to monitor. All of these risks can be managed clinically and the side effects appear to be reversable on termination of medication.

The above discussion on risks has centered upon dextroam-phetamine and methylphenidate as these are the best studied for long term use. To date, it appears that pemoline, another available and approved stimulant for treating the HA child, may produce similar effects (Knights and Viets, 1975).

Although the risks of prolonged stimulant treatment of HA children appear to be minimal, the long term benefits also appear to be disappointing. There is only one clear long term benefit, namely, the persistence of the dramatic immediate behavioral improvement with the medication. Thus, for HA children as long as the medication is taken, it improves classroom behavior and attentiveness as much or more than the effective interventions of behavior modification (Gittelman-Klein, et al., 1977). Teachers and parents report general satisfaction with the stimulant therapy to the extent that withdrawing children still severely overactive meets with resistance during "blind" placebo trials (Sleater, et al., 1974). One would expect that such behavioral improvement would translate into fewer suspensions, fewer disciplinary acts—such as office visits—better conduct and achievement of grades, fewer grade retentions, better academic achievement, and better life adjustment. Three long term studies to date have failed to show any of these findings, but they have also only looked principally at the more global issues of academic achievement and life adjustment. They do not as carefully examine data on the behavior related measures of disciplinary acts or conduct grades. The one report on retentions (Weiss, et al., 1975) shows a non-significant change in favor of the stimulant medication on a very small sample of HA children which could be seen as suggestive of a small-effect long term benefit. Thus, the academics and emotional adjustment gains some expected from stimulants have not been found in either short or long term studies. But whenever reduction of the disturbing behavioral symptoms have been looked at, the stimulant therapy appears to be very effective. No other available treatment offers this long term benefit (Safer and Allen, 1976).

In summary then, stimulant therapy effectively and with reasonable safety treats the primary HA symptoms of inappropriate overactivity, restlessness, and inattention. It does not, however, provide "brain food" for these children nor does it appear to contribute significantly to emotional factors in life adjustment. Stimulant therapy may, however, permit other therapeutic factors, such as good family support, to more successfully operate to improve outcome. In this respect, in addition to being useful for practical management, stimulant therapy may also be important for establishing efficacy of other therapeutic approaches.

Pragmatic therapists will, therefore, continue to use stimulants for the relative benefits they offer, more aware of their long term treatment limitations, yet more comfortable that the long term risk studies to date have produced so few bothersome findings.

Table 1.

Changes in Percentile Growth in Height
(Av. 3-4 Year Period)

	N	Mean percentile change	S.D.
Dextroamphetamine (all doses)	29	−13.4	16.3
High dose Methylphenidate (> 20 mg/day)	10	−9.4	15.9
Low dose Methylphenidate (> 20 mg/day)	10	−1.0	18.2
HA Controls (refused medication)	14	1.3	12.4

Table 2.

Factors Affecting Growth Suppression in Height Percentile
Based on Step-Wise Multiple Regression

Dextroamphetamine Treatment
(n = 29)

Methylphenidate Treatment
(n = 20)

Fator	Order Entered	Regression Coef. 't'	Order Entered
Dose		− 3.4	1st
Initial Height	3rd		
		−12.5	2nd
Duration of Treatment (Over 2 years)	1st	−16.3	
	2nd		Regression Coef. 't'
Fequency of Medication (1×, 2×, 3× daily)		−1.14 (N.S.)	−0.78
		−3.94**	−0.25
		−2.74**	−2.45*
			−2.08*

*p <0.05
**p >0.01

REFERENCES

Aarskog, D., Feang, F., Kove, H., Stoa, K., and Thorsen, T. The effects of the stimulant drugs, dextroamphetamine and methylphenidate, on secretions of growth hormone in hyperactive children. *Jnl. of Pediatrics, 90(1)*:136–139, 1977.

Ackerman, P., Dukman, R., and Peters, J. Teenage status of hyperactive and non-hyperactive learning disabled boys. *Am. Jn. Orthopsychiat.* 47:576–577, 1977.

Aman, M. and Sprague, R. "Effect of methylphenidate and dextroamphetamine on learning and retention," in Sprague, R., Principal Investigator, Progress Report of Grant MH18909 from 1970-1973.

Anderson, R., Halcomb, C., and Doyle, R. The measurement of attentional deficits. *Except. Child*, 39:534–538, 1973.

Arnold, L., Wender, P., McCloskey, K., and Snyder, S. Levoamphetamine and dextroamphetamine: Comparative efficacy in the hyperkinetic syndrome. *Arch. Gen. Psychiat.* 27:816–822, 1972.

Ballard, J., Boileau, R., Sleetor, E., Massey, B., and Sprague, R. Cardiovascular responses of hyperactive children to methylphenidate. *Jnl. Amer. Med. Assoc.*, 236:2870–2874, 1976.

Borland, B. and Heckman, H. Hyperactive boys and their brothers, a 25-year follow-up study. *Arch. Gen. Psychiat.*, 33:669–675, 1976.

Connors, C. Psychopharmacology of psychopathology in children. In Quay, H. and Werry, J. (Eds.), *Psychopathological Disorders of Childhood.* Wiley and Co., New York, 1972.

Connors, C., Taylor, E., Meo, G., Kurty, M., and Fourner, M. Magnesium pemoline and dextroamphatamine: A controlled study in children with minimal brain dysfunction. *Psychopharmacologia* (Berlin), 26:321–336, 1972.

Connors, C. Drug and cognitive studies in disturbed children. *Psychopharm. Bull.* 10:60–61, 1974.

Gittelman-Klein, R. Preliminary report on the efficacy of methylphenidate and behavior modification in hyperkinetic children. Proceedings. *Psychopharmacol. Bull.* 13:2, 53–54, 1976.

Gittelman-Klein, R. and Klein, D. Methylphenidate effects in learning disabilities: Psychometric changes. *Arch. Gen. Psychiat.* 33:655–664, 1976.

Gittelman-Klein, R., Klein, D., Katz, S., Saraf, K., and Pollack, E. Comparative effects of methylphenidate and thioridazine in nyperkinetic children. *Arch. Gen. Psychiat.* 33:1217–1231, 1976.

Greenberg, L., Deem, M., and McMahon, S. Effects of dextroamphatamine, chlorpromazine and hydroxyzine on behavior and performance in hyperactive children. *Amer. Jnl. Psychiat.*, 129:532–539, 1972.

Greenhill, L., Puig-Antich, J., Sassin, J., and Sachar, E. Hormone and growth responses in hyperkinetic children on stimulant medication. *Psychopharm. Bull.* 13:33–36, 1977.

Gross, M. Growth of hyperkinetic children taking methylphenidate dextroamphetamine, or imipramine/desipramine. *Pediatrics*, 58:423–431, 1976.

Gross, M. and Wilson, W. *Minimal Brain Dysfunction*, Brunner/Mazel, New York, 1974.

Haig, J., Schroeder, C., and Schroeder, S. Effects of methylphenidate on hyperactive children's sleep. *Psychopharmacologia* (Berlin), 37:185–188, 1974.

Hechtman, L., Weiss, G., Finklestein, J., Werner, A., and Benn, R. Hyperactives as young adults: Preliminary report. *Can. Med. Assoc. Jnl.*, 625–630, 1976.

Innes, I. and Nickerson, M. "Drugs acting on post-ganglionic adrenergic nerve endings and structures ennervated by them." In Goodman, L. and Gilman, A. (Eds.) *The Pharmacological Basis of Therapeutics*, (4th Ed.) Macmillan, New York, 1970.

Knights, R. and Hinton, G. The effects of methylphenidate (Ritalin) on the motor skills and behavior of children with learning problems. *Jnl. Nerv. Ment. Dis., 148*:643, 1969.

Knights, R. and Viets, C. Effects of pemoline on hyperactive boys. *Pharm. Biochem. and Behav. 3*:1107–1114, 1975.

Krager, J. and Safer, D. Type and prevalence of medication used in the treatment of hyperactive children. *New Eng. Jnl. Med., 291*:1118–1120, 1974.

Lucas, B. and Sells, C. Nutrient intake and stimulant drugs in hyperactive children. *Jnl. Amer. Dietic. Assoc. 20*:373–377, 1977.

McNutt, B., Ballard, J., and Boileau, R. The effects of long-term stimulant medication on growth and body composition of hyperactive children. *Psychopharm. Bull. 12*:13–15, 1976.

Nahas, A. and Krynicki, V. Effect of methylphenidate on sleep stages and ultradian rhythms in hyperactive children. *Jnl. Nerv. Ment. Dis. 164*:65–69, 1977.

Pinter, E. and Pattee, C. Fat mobilizing action of amphetamine. In Costa, E. and Garatini, S. (Eds.) *Amphetamines and Related Compounds*. Raven Press, New York, 1970.

Rapoport, J., Quinn, P., Bradbard, G., Riddle, K., and Brooks, E. Imipramine and methylphenidate treatments of hyperactive boys. *Arch. Gen. Psychiat. 30*:789–793, 1974.

Riddle, K. and Rapoport, J. A 2-year follow-up of 72 hyperactive boys. *Jnl. Nerv. Ment. Dis. 162*(2):126–134, 1976.

Rie, H., Rie, E., Stewart, S., and Ambud, J. Effects of Ritalin on underachieving children. *Amer. Jnl. Orthopsychiat. 46*:313–322, 1976.

Rie, E. and Rie, H. Recall retention and Ritalin. *Jnl. Consult. & Clin. Psychol. 45*:967–972, 1977.

Safer, D. and Allen, R. Factors influencing the suppressant effects of stimulant drugs on the growth of hyperactive children. *Pediatrics, 5*:660–667, 1973.

Safer, D. and Allen, R. Stimulant drug treatment of hyperactive adolescents, *Dis. Nerv. Syst., 36*:8, 454–457, 1975A.

————"Side effects from long-term use of stimulants in children." In Gittelman-Klein, R. (Ed.) *Recent Advances in Child Psychopharmacology, Int. Jnl. Ment. Health, 4*:105–118, 1975B.

————*Hyperactive Children: Diagnosis and Management*, University Park Press, Baltimore, 1976.

Safer, D., Allen, R., and Barr, E. Depression of growth in hyperactive children on stimulant drugs. *New Eng. Jnl. Med. 287*:217–220, 1972.

Safer, D., Allen, R., and Barr, E. Growth rebound after termination of stimulant drugs. *Jnl. Pediat., 86*:113–116, 1975.

Santi, R. and Fassina, G. Dextroamphetamine and lipid mobilization in obesity. *Jnl. Pharm. Pharmacol., 16*:130–131, 1964.

Silverstone, J. and Stuckard, A. The anorexic effect of dextroamphetamine sulfate. *Brit. Jnl. Pharmacol., 33*:513, 1968.

Sleator, E., vonNeumann, A., and Sprague, R. Hyperactive children: A continuous long-term placebo-controlled follow-up, *Jnl. Amer. Med. Assoc.*, 229:316–317, 1974.

Small, A., Hibi, S., and Feinberg, I. Effects of dextroamphetamine sulfate on EEG sleep patterns of hyperactive children. *Arch. Gen. Psychiat.* 25:369–380, 1971.

Sprague, R., Barnes, K., and Werry, J. Methylphenidate and thioridazine: Learning, reaction time, activity, and classroom behavior in disturbed children. *Amer. Jnl. Orthopsychiat.* 40:615–628, 1970.

Sykes, D., Douglas, V., and Morgenstein, G. The effect of methylphenidate (Ritalin) on sustained attention in hyperactive children. *Psychopharmacologia* (Berlin), 25:262–274, 1972.

Weiss, G., Minde, K., Werry, J., Douglas, V., and Nemeth, E. Studies on the hyperactive child, VIII. Five-year follow-up. *Arch. Gen. Psychiat.*, 24:409–414, 1971.

———Kruger, E., Danielson, U., and Elman, M. Effect of long-term treatment of hyperactive children with methylphenidate. *Canad. Med. Assoc. Jnl.*, 112:159–165, 1975.

———Minde, K., Douglas, U., Werry, J., and Sykes, D. Comparison of the effects of chlorpromazine, dextroamphetamine, and methylphenidate on the behavior and intellectual functioning of hyperactive children. *Canad. Med. Assoc. Jnl.*, 104:20–25, 1971.

9

DRUG THERAPY—
CHILDREN'S RIGHTS

LOIS WEITHORN, M.S.

Children, including adolescents, constitute one of the most poorly
represented and underprotected classes of citizens in our society.
Adults, in their roles as parents, educators, mental health and health
care professionals, and representatives of the state, wield broad dis-
cretionary power in the determination of what happens to minors.
This situation might not present serious problems if those adults em-
powered to act on the child's behalf always did so "in the best interests" of the child. Unfortunately, the question of exactly what constitutes the "best interest" of each unique child in any particular situation is complex and defies standard or absolute definition. The processes by which what is "best" for a child is frequently determined
may be faulty and in need of revision (Goldstein, Freud, & Solnit,
1973; Rodham, 1973). It is becoming increasingly clear that those
adults charged with the care and protection of children sometimes do
not act in the child's "best interests."

The public has been made aware of some of the issues relating to
the mismanagement of institutionalized children and some of the

questionable child custody placements. However, there has been little discussion in the media of problems associated with the use of psychoactive medications with children. When such medication is prescribed for a child identified as having some behavioral, learning, or psychological problem, it is because someone believes that medication can change the child's behavior so that it will become more desirable or appropriate. Often the rationale for drug therapy is that it is the best intervention available for the child's needs. However, a distinction between the needs of the child and the needs of others in the child's environment, such as parents, teachers, classmates, or "society," is not always drawn. This raises a number of questions relating to the use of psychoactive drugs with children. Do those requesting, recommending, or prescribing psychotropic drugs for children always perform a careful and unbiased assessment of the child's needs? Do they independently evaluate their assumptions as to what may be "desirable" or "appropriate" behavior for a child in a specific situation or setting? Do they systematically consider and investigate other alternative and perhaps less intrusive or dangerous interventions? And, most important, do they always offer the consumers (the child and his or her parents) the opportunity to make a fully informed choice whether or not to participate in drug therapy?

Unfortunately, the answers to many of these questions are often negative. Some of those who recommend or prescribe psychotropic medication for children do not have the information, skills, or resources to carefully evaluate each child's needs. Some have rigid or simplistic notions as to what is "desirable" or "appropriate" behavior for children in certain settings. Many may be unaware of alternative interventions. Drug therapy may be chosen as the "best" treatment because it is one of the more convenient and effective remedies. Parents, as the indirect consumers of treatment, may not always be offered the opportunity to make or guide their children in making a fully informed decision about the use of medication (Ross, Chapter 5). The layperson's presumption as to the health care professional's total expertise and infallible good judgment is reinforced by the professional's inability or unwillingness to provide the consumer with comprehensive and detailed information about the recommended treatment (whether or not such information is requested). In most situations, it is the duty of mental health and health care professionals to provide a prospective patient or client with a full disclosure of information relevant to a particular treatment prior to considering consent to treatment morally or legally valid.[1] For example, it is probably rare

[1]The notion of fully informed consent for treatment has become a "legal" concept defined by the courts during the past two decades. Meisel, Roth, and Lidz (1977) suggest a model of informed consent and delineate the central components that consti-

that a parent will be told that "we" simply do not know "everything" about the "long-term" effects of prolonged use of stimulant drugs among school-age children diagnosed as "hyperactive." Children, as the direct consumers of the medication and as the individuals to whom any decision about treatment should have the most relevance, are not always consulted by their parents or the professional before the commencement of chemotherapy. In reality, it probably is not common practice for a professional to attempt to explain the pertinent details about the treatment to the child in a candid and comprehensible way. Furthermore, it probably is less common that a mental health or health care professional allows the child's preferences or concerns to influence his or her decision whether or not to recommend or prescribe a particular medication.

When attempts are made to manipulate the behavior of a child, certain questions must be asked: Does the child possess the minimal intellectual, social, and emotional capabilities necessary to render a "competent" decision or register an opinion about his or her treatment? If so, has he or she been made fully aware of the goals and possible effects of that treatment? Is the child given the opportunity to make a fully voluntary and informed choice about whether or not to undergo treatment? If the child is not competent to participate in decision making, it is important to ask whose interests are being served by the child's treatment. If the treatment is said to be in the child's bests interests, by whose standards are those interests judged? If the treatment is said to be in the best interests of others, because the child's behavior is judged to be dangerous or disruptive, is the intervention of choice the most conservative, least intrusive, and least restrictive possible?

Certain classes of individuals within society (e.g., institutionalized psychiatric patients, prisoners) have suffered the abuses of mental health and health care professionals. These individuals, because they live in coercive environments that deprive them of the information and resources to ask questions and influence their own "treatment," cannot always deal effectively with attempts by others to modify their behavior with "therapy" (*Aden V. Younger, Clonce V. Richardson; Knecht V. Gillman; Mackey V. Procunier;* Opton, 1974; Shapiro, 1974; *Souder V. McGuire;* Spece, 1972; *Winters V. Miller).* Minors, as a class of citizens also lacking power and resources and often unable to resist the pres-

tute a legally valid decision. They indicate that the patient must be in a position to act voluntarily; that he or she must be informed as to the "1) risks, discomforts, and side effects of proposed treatments; 2) the anticipated benefits of such treatments; 3) the available alternative treatments and their attendant risks, discomforts, and side effects; and 4) the likely consequences of a failure to be treated at all"; that the patient must be considered "competent" to make an informed decision about treatment; and that it be ascertained that the patient "understands" that of which he or she had been informed.

sures exerted by family, school, or the community, constitute a group openly vulnerable to abuse from any sector of adults in their environment. Children, like hospitalized psychiatric patients, prisoners, or other similar psychological minorities, are unable to protect themselves effectively against violations of their integrity and therefore need the assistance of others more capable to speak for their needs and rights.

Some suggest that many elements of existing social, legal, educational, and health care systems fail to meet both the "everyday" and special needs of children. The child advocacy movement is premised upon a belief that the needs and interests of many children are not served adequately by those individuals and institutions designated to provide for children. Child advocates emphasize that these systems often discriminate against children, denying them some of the most basic of human and civil rights, simply because they are children.

In the following pages, there is presented a review of the legal, psychological, social, and ethical issues raised by the administration of psychoactive medication to children. This presentation is designed to (a) examine the basic "rights of children" with respect to this type of medical treatment, (b) explore relevant issues and questions, and (c) survey the pertinent trends in legal thinking.

"HUMAN RIGHTS" VERSUS "LEGAL RIGHTS"

"Human rights" or "natural rights" encompass those prerogatives and that treatment due to an individual simply because he or she is a human being (Jorgensen & Lyons, 1972). These "rights" are not privileges that can be granted or withheld by others. "Legal rights" or "civil rights," in contrast, are guaranteed to citizens by the constitution or legislative codes of a state (Coughlin, 1973). Some natural rights have been encoded formally into law and therefore are protected by the state. Other natural rights are not so protected, although some may feel that they should be. Finally, the law may protect rights not considered to constitute vital human rights.

The distinction between "human rights" and "legal rights" is crucial to a discussion of the rights of children. As is noted in the following pages, there are important differences between human rights and legal rights.

THE HUMAN RIGHTS OF CHILDREN

Children, as human beings, are entitled to the same basic rights as are adults. However, the special needs of children deserve to be recognized because the physical, emotional, and intellectual development of children are such complex and delicate processes.

Many writers have enumerated the basic rights that are due to children (Foster & Freed, 1972; Fraser, 1973; Goldstein et al., 1973; Martin, 1975; Polier, 1975; Rodham, 1973; United Nations General Assembly, 1973; Wilkins, 1975). *A Bill of Rights for Children,* developed by Foster and Freed, provides a compilation of certain "moral" rights which include, among others, a right to parental love and affection; a right to be regarded as a person within the family, at home, and before the law; a right to be heard and listened to; and a right to seek and obtain medical care and treatment and counseling.

In any discussion of the human rights of children, particular attention must be given to how these rights are related to the uses of medication with children. The issue relevant to the uses of medication with exceptional children are similar to those relating to the use of any medical, psychological, or psychiatric treatment. The administration of medication, like any other intervention that alters physical and psychological processes and states, constitutes an invasion of an individual's autonomy. Whether or not that invasion is "moral" or "proper" may be determined by a variety of factors, the most obvious of which is the degree to which the patient or client affirmatively acquiesces in the treatment.

When raising issues concerned with the mental health and health care needs of children, four broad categories of rights seem particularly relevant: the right to treatment; the right to refuse treatment; the right to remain apprised of relevant assessment and treatment information; and the right to privacy. These rights are basic human prerogatives and should be protected for all individuals, regardless of age. Undoubtedly, there are instances when, because of exceptional circumstances, one or more of these rights may be abridged or violated. Yet, any abrogation of these rights should result from systematic procedures with inherent safeguards, so as to prevent casual or frequent abuse of individual rights.

Minors lack power and resources in society and so sometimes are unable to articulate their own needs. Therefore, a fifth right might appropriately be added to these four: Children should have a right to convenient access to an impartial and independent person or agency to serve as an advocate and spokesperson for them, their needs, and their interests. The presence of child advocates in the courtroom and psychiatric hospitals (Tauber & Houston, 1977) is a reality in some situations and settings.

THE LEGAL RIGHTS OF CHILDREN

The Honorable Lois G. Forer has referred to the "rights of children" as a "legal vacuum" (Forer, 1969). Whereas the adult citizens of the United States are entitled to enjoy those legal rights and safeguards guaranteed by the Constitution, minors sometimes are deprived of these guarantees.

For example, children are not permitted to vote, nor are they allowed to choose whether they would prefer to attend school or to hold a job (Rodham, 1973). With few exceptions, minors are not legally qualified to consent to their own medical, psychological, or psychiatric treatment[2] *(Brigham Young University Law Review,* 1976; *Maryland Law Review,* 1971; Wilkins, 1975). In most jurisdictions, minors are unable to petition for their own discharge after having been admitted as psychiatric in-patients by their parents[3] *(Bartley v.*

[2]There are some exceptions to the legal tradition that denies minors the right to consent to their own medical treatment. Wilkins (1975) reviews such exceptions which exempt certain categories of minors from the obligation to obtain parental consent prior to the commencement of treatment. "Emancipated minors" are those minors who, by virtue or their life circumstances, are determined to be "independent" from their parents (e.g., some married minors who are parents, some minors who live away from home and support themselves financially). "Mature minors" are those minors who are judged to be competent enough to make fully informed and legally binding decisions about treatment. Wilkins (1975) notes that the statutes of some states allow minors to consent to certain types of treatment (e.g., treatment for venereal disease, pregancy or birth control counseling, treatment for drug or alcohol abuse). Finally, Wilkins (1975) points out that very few states, although some, have enacted laws that provide all minors or older minors the right to consent to medical treatment.

[3]The statutes of most states allow parents to commit their child to a psychiatric institution (Ellis, 1974). "Involuntary" commitments are obtained by the "state" against a patient's will. "Voluntary" admissions supposedly are the products of patients' willfull decisions to enter the hospital. Parents, assumed to be the agents of their child, maintain the right to "voluntarily" admit their child to a psychiatric institution. That child's parents remain the only individuals who can legally petition for that child's discharge until the child reaches the age of majority. In a case challenging the Pennsylvania Mental Health and Retardation Act of 1966, five minors who had been "voluntarily" committed by their parents to Haverford State Hospital claimed that the State's statutes were unconstitutional *(Bartley v. Kremens).* In 1975, a three-judge District Court held that the 1966 statutes violated the Fourteenth Amendment's Due Process clause. In 1976, the Mental Health Procedures Act was revised to provide due process protections for children aged 14 and older. The case reached the Supreme Court on appeal in 1977. The majority opinion delivered by Justice Rehnquist held that the claims of the children were mooted by the facts that (1) the 1976 Act revised those provisions which related directly to the claims of the specific plaintiffs, e.g., minors between the ages of 14 and 18 and (2) most of the named members of the "class" of minors had reached the age of majority by the of the hearing of the case. Therefore, the "class" was said to be "frag-

Kremens,; Beyer & Wilson, 1976; Ellis, 1974; *J.L. v. Parham; Kremens v. Bartley).* It was not until the 1960s that the courts specified that juveniles accused of crimes should be afforded some of the basic due process protections provided adult defendants *(In re Gault; Kent v. U.S.).* Minors guilty of "status offenses"[4] often are remanded to a state or county detention center where little or no distinction is made by staff between them and juvenile delinquents guilty of serious crimes, such as rape, murder, or felonious assault. In April 1977, the Supreme Court of the United States denied minors in schools due process safeguards (e.g., a hearing) and legal recourse when their bodily integrity was threatened or assaulted by the use of corporal punishment *(Ingraham v. Wright).*

Ironically, the lack of appropriate or comprehensive legal protection for children is attributable primarily to their uniquely vulnerable and dependent status (Rodham, 1973). For example, Wilkins (1975) points out that the requirement of parental consent for medical treatment developed, in part, from an early concern that minors might enter into legal contracts without the full capacity to comprehend the terms and obligations of such agreements. The parental consent doctrine was an outgrowth of attempts to protect minors from incurring inappropriate legal obligations. This doctrine, however, has served to prevent many young people from seeking or receiving medical treatment without parental consent. The statutes of some states permit special categories of minors to receive medical treatment for certain "sensitive" problems, such as counseling for birth control and pregnancy, treatment of drug and alcohol abuse, or treatment of venereal disease. Yet, these statutes are far from comprehensive and frequently allow the attending physician to provide the minor's parents with the specific treatment information (Wilkins, 1975). This factor alone probably discourages many minors from engaging the services of a physician or counselor for certain problems.

---

mented." Justice Brennan, dissenting, stated that the changes in the Pennsylvania Law and the status of the plaintiffs were not sufficient rationales for the Court to deny its duty in failing to deliver an opinion on the relevant constitutional issues. The Court rejected the opportunity to present a decision which might have had major import for the way in which our Constitution is applied to juveniles. Most states still maintain statutes allowing parental discretion to be the major determinant of a minor's "voluntary" admission.

[4]"Status offenses" are those acts which are considered to be criminal only when the offender is a minor (i.e., truancy, running away from home, incorrigibility). Many status offenders, whose parents are unable or unwilling to care for them, are labeled "Persons in Need of Supervision" and are sometimes institutionalized with juvenile delinquents who have committed serious crimes. These individuals "have committed no crime . . ." stated Senator Birch Bayh, "they are merely unable to adjust to difficult family environments, unable to handle the pressures of schools that do not address their needs, unable to cope with the demands of today's youth culture" (1974).

In the case of *Kent v. U.S.*, Supreme Court Justice Fortas, recognizing the realities of the way in which the juvenile justice system traditionally has regarded and treated children, stated:

> There is evidence, in fact, that there may be grounds for concern that the child receives the worst of both worlds: that he gets neither the protection accorded to adults nor the solicitous care and regenerative treatment postulated for children. P. 556.

The following sections contain a discussion of each of the five categories of human rights relating to the use of psychotropic medication with children. The definitions of those rights are developed and the legislative and judicial trends that serve to protect or deny those rights are surveyed.

THE RIGHT TO TREATMENT

Principle 5 of the "United Nations Declaration of the Rights of the Child" reads as follows:

> The child who is physically, mentally or socially handicapped shall be given the special treatment, education and care required by his particular condition. (United Nations General Assembly, 1973. P. 5.).

Ideally, every human being should have the opportunity to develop his or her physical, emotional, and intellectual potentialities to the fullest extent possible. A human "right to treatment" assures to each individual access to ameliorative therapy whenever his or her healthy development is threatened or impeded by environmental or endogenous factors.

The Right to a Comprehensive and Relevant Professional Assessment

Prior to the commencement of any treatment regimen, whether psychotherapy, behavioral management, drug therapy, or even perceptual training and other remedial techniques, a thorough and relevant assessment of the problem should be performed by the appropriate professionals. Although this seems to be a necessary prerequisite to the process of recommending a course of treatment, some professionals may not have access to the most reliable and relevant assessment data and procedures.

Some authors point out that most physicians who prescribe psychoactive medication to children have not observed the target behavior directly (Stewart, 1976; Weithorn & Ross, 1976). Instead, they rely upon the reports of parents and teachers, observers whose impressions may be influenced by a variety of factors that mitigate against the reliability and validity of their reports.

Many of those who prescribe psychoactive medication for children have not had comprehensive training and experience with the evaluation and modification of a gamut of psychological, intellectual, or behavior problems of childhood. Sometimes, they have little more information about those medications they prescribe for "problem children" than what they receive from the pharmaceutical corporations (Brown & Bing, 1976). Grinspoon and Singer (1973) suggest that it is unlikely that all of the children receiving stimulant medications for the treatment of hyperactivity actually are suffering from hyperkinetic problems with central nervous system involvement. One can conclude that those who prescribe the drugs have been overdiagnosing "hyperactivity" and therefore overprescribing stimulant drugs for children.

A thorough assessment of a child's difficulties often is a lengthy and complex process involving the time of professionals representing several disciplines. The skills of a psychologist, a pediatrician, a neurologist, a social worker or family therapist, a psychiatrist, an educator, an optometrist, a speech and audiology specialist, or others may be utilized in connection with the evaluation of a particular problem. McCoy and Koocher (1976) suggest four areas important to any investigation of the problems of a child: psychological–psychiatric, total environmental, medical history, and neurological.

The Right to a Choice of Available Treatments

An important aspect of the right to treatment is the right to a choice of available treatments (Wells, 1973). Professionals representing many disciplines attest to the reality that often there may be several different "generally acceptable" approaches to the handling of the same problem. Definitions and explanations of a problem also may differ among professionals. The training, experience, and theoretical biases of each professional may lead him or her to advocate one approach in favor of the others. Mental health, medical, and educational professionals rarely can be certain that their preferred treatment approaches always are "best."

Although professionals may feel that one mode of treatment is more "effective," "efficient," or otherwise "better" than another, they do not retain the right to deprive patients and clients of the opportunity to make an educated decision as to that issue. The principle of fully informed and voluntary consent requires that patients or clients be systematically informed of the availability of alternative modes of therapy (Meisel, Roth, & Lidz, 1977).

Pharmacological therapy, as one of the alternative interventions available to treat certain psychological, learning, or behavioral problems, is not without concommitant risks. The short-term side effects of any medication may be unpleasant or detrimental to the general health or wellbeing of a child. For example, stimulant drugs are known to cause insomnia or anorexia in some children for whom they are prescribed. Whether the resultant lack of sleep or nutritional intake is sufficient to lead one to reject stimulant medication as a preferable alternative treatment depends upon the potential risks and benefits. The options inherent in that consideration process rightly belong to the client.

In addition to having short-term side effects, medication may lead to certain long-term difficulties, many of which are not known until several years after a particular drug has been used prevalently. For example, chlorpromazine, a major tranquilizer, has been known to produce symptoms similar to those of Parkinson's disease. Certainly, then, patients and clients have the right to be informed that, as yet, professionals are unable to postulate as to the long-term effects of many types of medication prescribed for children over prolonged periods.

All of this leads to another crucial question: When a child is the target of any intervention, who is the most appropriate person to make a decision regarding the choice of treatment? It might be assumed that most minors, because of their respective ages, are not competent to share in the decision-making process or autonomously to decide questions of relevance to themselves. On that basis, children often are regarded as incapable of deciding upon a course of medical, psychiatric, or psychological treatment and thus may not even be asked to express their feelings or opinions about treatment modality.

Of course, those children that are exceptionally young or seriously disturbed cannot play a relevant role in decision-making about their treatment. Most children, however, can play such a role. The assumption that anyone who is under the age of 21 years is incompetent to formulate meaningful views about what is to be done for or to him or her has been seriously challenged by some (Wilkins, 1975). For instance, Supreme Court Justice William O. Douglas, dissenting in the case of *Wisconsin v. Yoder*, vigorously criticized the Court's failure to solicit the views of two out of three minors, ages 14 and 15, in a matter that concerned them directly. The case involved three adolescents whose Amish parents had been found guilty of violating the compulsory education law of the state of Wisconsin. The parents had decided that public school attendance by their children past the eighth grade would violate their freedom to raise their children in the manner which they preferred, particularly with respect to religious beliefs and training. The Court held that the First and Fourteenth Amendment protections entitled the parents to withdraw their children from school. Justice Douglas argued, however, that the Court neglected to reach its decision based upon the religious preference or beliefs of the children, whose interests would be directly affected by the outcome of the case. The children had not been given an opportunity to express their opinions on the matter. Justice Douglas, citing literature in developmental psychology which included the writings of Piaget, Elkind, Kohlberg, Kay, Gessell, and Ilg, suggested that children of particular ages possess the requisite intellectual and moral judgment to reach decisions about matters concerning themselves. Furthermore, the Justice cited precedents supporting the legal rights of children to be "masters of their own destiny."

The inattention of the Supreme Court to the views of minors in the case of *Wisconsin v. Yoder* parallels the approach reflected in many state statutes which provide that minors cannot consent to their own medical, psychological, or psychiatric treatment *(Brigham Young University Law Review,* 1976; *Maryland Law Review,* 1971; Rodham, 1973; Wilkins, 1975). The assumption that minors are incompetent to consent to treatment because they are under the age of 21 is similar to the common assumption that individuals suffering from "mental illness" are incompetent to make an informed decision about their own treatment (Shapiro, 1974). Some individuals who are considered "mentally ill" may be so severely impaired in their functioning that their competency to make decisions about their own welfare must be questioned. However, in their discussion of issues of competency to consent to treatment, Roth, Meisel, and Lidz (1977) conclude that one alternative approach to the question of competency is to presume each individual competent to make an informed decision about treatment until the contrary is determined. This was the thinking underlying the decision in the case of *Winters v. Miller.* A federal court held that "a finding of 'mental illness' even by a judge or jury, and commitment to a hospital, does not raise even a presumption that the patient is 'incompetent' or unable to adequately manage his own affairs." This approach of not using "status" alone to determine competency also is relevant when considering the "status" of legal minority (Rodham, 1973; Wilkins, 1975).

Roth et al. (1977) have reviewed the basic categories of "tests" of competency to consent to treatment. One such test requires that in order to demonstrate competency, an individual only needs to show evidence of a choice. This test, the authors suggest, is that "most respectful of the autonomy of the patient." Another such test requires that the choice preferred by the patient be evaluated as "reasonable" by other qualified individuals as well. It is implied by the conditions of this test that it is appropriate to substitute the judgment of one individual whose opinion is considered to be more "reasonable" for that of the individual whose welfare is the focus of the decision-making, a concept which may not be valid. A third test determines competency based upon the degree to which the "reasons" for the individual's choice are deemed rational. Another test requires that an individual be able to understand the "risks, benefits, and alternatives to treatment (including no treatment)." As Roth et al. suggest, this test allows the patient the right to make what others may consider an "unwise" choice, which is one aspect of the right of self-determination. If one were to apply any of these tests to children, instead of relying on an arbitrary and unsubstantiated test of age, one might find a significant percentage of minors competent to make informed decisions about their own treatment. Wilkins (1975) suggests that many children may prefer to waive their decision-making rights so that their parents may resolve all treatment questions. This phenomenon parallels the willingness of many patients to have important decisions about their treatment made by their doctors. Where individuals choose to waive their rights, that should be their prerogative. However, the fact that many may choose not to exercise their right to make an informed decision should not serve to deprive others of the freedom to exercise that right.

Most children treated with psychotropic medication are not so young or so severely disturbed that they are utterly without skills as decision-makers within their environments. It is a complex process to determine the degree to which a child's social, emotional, intellectual, and verbal maturity renders him or her competent to make decisions. However, as Wilkins (1975) suggests, we do not have the authority to abridge the rights of all children to make decisions about their treatment simply because the process of determining competency may be inconvenient, inefficient, and time consuming.

Parents usually are consulted for legal consent to their children's treatment because minors are not legally qualified to provide such consent. That the parents retain this legal right to consent to their children's treatment assumes that the parents are those persons most competent to judge their children's best interests. The prevalence of physical and emotional child abuse and neglect testifies to the fact that parents may not always be persons who decide and act in ways consonant with a child's welfare. Most parents do not abuse their children, however. Nevertheless, a parent's level of tolerance and concommitant life stresses may be relevant to a decision to change a child's behavior. It is not difficult, for example, to envision a responsible and loving parent who agrees readily to the administration of some recommended medication to a child whose behavior seems to be "too much to handle." It is not always easy to evaluate those whose best interests are served by a particular intervention. Furthermore, it is difficult to assess the point at which it becomes ethical or moral to manipulate one person's behavior to serve the interests of others in that person's environment.

Mental health and health care professionals, when acting as "behavior modifiers," regularly must ask themselves whose agents they are. Are they acting in behalf of the direct consumer of their services (in this case, the child), or indirect consumers of their services (the parents), or society in general? Some professionals feel strongly about the importance of defining clearly their role *vis à vis* all of the involved parties, a policy that probably avoids a good deal of misunderstanding which may occur when a child is being treated at the request of some other interested party. Some specify that the individual who is to be the target of any intervention is their client, and therefore the party whose interests must take precedence. Other professionals feel that the interests of those who are paying the bills or who initially have sought the professional service must take precedence. Others put the needs of society in general first. Finally, certain professionals utilize a formula incorporating some varying combinations of these perspectives. Obviously, there is no one answer to this often touchy issue. It is incumbent upon professionals to evaluate carefully the human rights of children so that due consideration is given to ethical and moral handling of the problems of conflicting loyalties.

The Right to the Most Conservative (Least Intrusive or Least Restrictive) Alternative Treatment

It seems to be sound and ethical medical practice that mental health or health care professional should recommend to patients or clients that they begin with "the most conservative treatment" (Brown & Bing, 1976). The most conservative treatment may be defined as the intervention that entails the least risk or possible danger to a patient. Moreover, the most conservative treatment also may be the least "intrusive" alternative. Shapiro (1974) enumerates some of the criteria for intrusive of treatments for behavior control:

(i) the extent to which the effects of therapy upon mentation are reversible;

(ii)) the extent to which the resulting psychic state is "foreign" "abnormal" or "unnatural" for the person in question, rather than simply a restoration of his prior psychic state;
(iii) the rapidity with which the effects occur;
(iv) the scope of the change in the total "ecology" of the mind's functions;
(v) the extent to which one can resist acting in ways impelled by the psychic effect of therapy.
(vi) the duration of change.

Shapiro suggests that nonbiological therapies are less intrusive than biological interventions. In the former processes, such as those we call psychotherapy, patients have greater capacity to act as "free agents . . . free to reject it and free to leave with no more scar than in any other human transaction." The more "intrusive" an intervention, the more that treatment infringes upon the personal integrity and being of the patient. In this discussion of the human rights of children, the degree to which the individuality of each child is intruded upon constitutes an important consideration in the recommendation of particular treatments.

An additional criterion of conservativeness might be the "restrictiveness" of a particular treatment. For example, institutionalization, and its concommitant abridgements of personal freedoms, is one of the most restrictive alternatives currently employed to "treat" problem children. The isolation of a particular child in a special school or class that deprives him or her of some of the more vital aspects of an "integrated" environment also may be considered a "restrictive" treatment.

The Right to Have Treatment Carefully Monitored and Periodically Reassessed

The progress of a child's drug therapy often is not carefully monitored (Weithorn & Ross, 1975). Assessment is an aspect of mental health and health care services that should be repeated throughout the course of an individual's contact with the professional. It is not, as many assume, sufficient to assess a client's condition only once, prior to the commencement of treatment. Unless a careful assessment of a client's or patient's condition is performed at regular intervals during and after treatment, the professional has no mode to determine the extent to which the treatment intervention has helped, harmed, or otherwise affected the patient. The value of experimental controls (such as no treatment or placebo control periods) as integral aspects of such evaluations should not be overlooked.

The wide scope of individual differences in symptomatology, environmental circumstances and responses to chemical, psychological, or educational interventions necessitates thorough and continued monitoring of all "therapeutic" approaches. Children, unlike adults, continually are maturing and changing rapidly in many ways. The development progression of a child may facilitate drastic alterations of his or her behavior within a relatively brief period of time. This fact alone should mandate the need for frequent and thorough follow-up assesment of treatment effects.

Legal Protections of the Right to Treatment

Judicial or case law

In the field of mental health law, there have been a number of landmark cases leading to a broad acceptance of the concept of a constitutionally protected "right to treatment" for adults who are inpatients in psychiatric institutions. These precedents have influenced later decisions supporting such a right for juveniles who are detained by the state in treatment centers or penal institutions. Some of these decisions have included specific recommendations relating to the standards within these institutions and have focused upon many of the concepts delineated in previous sections of this chapter as well.

Judge David Bazelon, presiding over the federal Circuit Court of Appeals for the District of Columbia, held that hospitalized psychiatric patients have a legal right to treatment (*Rouse v. Cameron*). The violation of this right, he stated, was not justifyable by "lack of staff or facilities." In 1969, in the case of *Covington v. Harris,* Judge Bazelon reaffirmed this right to treatment. He reasoned, as he had in the case of *Rouse v. Cameron,* that because the "principle justification for involuntary hospitalization . . ." and its concommitant loss of liberty ". . . is the prospect of treatment. . . A failure to provide treatment would present 'serious constitutional questions.' " Further, the judge specified that the "principle of the least restrictive alternative" is applicable not only to the decision whether or not to commit an individual involuntarily, but also to "alternate dispositions within a mental hospital."

Perhaps the case that has had the greatest impact on legal thinking about a constitutional right to treatment for hospitalized psychiatric patients is that of *Wyatt v. Stickney.* Judge Frank Johnson, in this landmark Alabama decision, specified the "Minimum Constitutional Standards for the Adequate Treatment of the Mentally Ill." He found the conditions at Bryce Hospital, Searcy Hospital, and Partlow State School and Hospital unconstitutional in that they failed to provide "(1) a humane psychological and physical environment, (2) qualified staff in numbers sufficient to administer adequate treatment and (3) individualized treatment plans." The Judge ordered that the institutions raise their standards of treatment in accordance with the criteria specified in the Minimum Standards. In addition to ordering that adequate staff and facilities be available to provide all hospitalized patients with individualized treatment regimens, the Judge held that these regimens must involve the "least restrictive conditions" necessary for treatment.

The case law with respect to the right to treatment for children includes decisions guaranteeing "adequate treatment" to "Persons in Need of Supervision" (*Maratella v. Kelley*) and inmates of a state correctional facility for boys (*Nelsen v. Heyne*). In the later case, treatment was ordered to meet "minimum acceptable standards" and to be "individualized."

In August 1974, a United States District Court in Texas, citing the precedent of *Wyatt v. Stickney*, held that involuntarily incarcerated juveniles had a constitutional right to treatment (*Morales v. Turman*). The Court further specified the minimal professional standards to be maintained in the delivery of treatment services (see Appendix to this chapter). The Judge also stressed that psychotropic medication frequently was used inappropriately, and in place of psychotherapy in certain juvenile institutions, and he held that children have a right to be free of such "indiscriminate, unsupervised, unnecessary, or excessive . . . psychotropic medication."

The constitutional right to treatment, as upheld by the courts, relates only to those individuals detained in institutional facilities. The judicial reasoning holds that an individual who is deprived of his or her liberties for the purpose of receiving rehabilitative treatment must have access to adequate professional services to justify the constitutionality of such detention. It has already been noted that there may be a natural right of all children to receive needed treatment services. However, the courts have not yet dealt with issues of a constitutional right to treatment for those children not under institutional care.

There have been precedents, however, establishing a "right to education" which, in many respects, serve the needs of exceptional children in a manner analogous to a right to treatment. In 1971, a three-judge District Court in Pennsylvania held that all children in the State of Pennsylvania, including "exceptional children," should have access to a "free public program of education and learning" (*P.A.R.C. v. the State of Pennsylvania*). The Court specified that training commensurate with each child's capacities should be available preferably within a "regular" public school class. If such placement is not available, a special class within a regular school was specified as a second alternative, which is preferable to all other alternative placements.

One year later, the District Court for the District of Columbia also upheld a constitutional right to education for exceptional children (*Mills v. Board of Education*). It was determined that no child could be excluded from the District of Columbia public schools "regardless of the degree of the child's mental, physical or emotional disability or impairment." A child who has been denied a publicly supported education is entitled to "a right to receive a free educational assessment and to be placed in a publicly-supported educational program suited to his needs." Many children judged to be "slow" or "troublesome" or otherwise different from the majority of children in school have been denied access to a free public education in a regular school. Many have resided in custodial institutions for lack of more suitable alternatives (Herr, 1972). These precedents in case law have led to a reexamination of the need for legal protections for the human rights of children who need special care and attention.

Statutory Law or Legislative Codes

The statutes of several states have guaranteed hospitalized individuals a "right to treatment" (McGarry & Kaplan, 1975). The State of Pennsylvania, for example, recently has enacted statutes that protect patients according to the standards set forth by Judge Johnson in *Wyatt v. Stickney* (Mental Health Procedures, 1976).

In 1975, the Ninety-fourth Congress of the United States passed the Education for All Handicapped Children Act (Education for All Handicapped Children Act, 1975). This law mandates that all handicapped children, including children diagnosed as having a "learning disability," be provided a special education "in the least restrictive" environment, as well as extensive evaluation and individualized program services. Provisions were specified to allow the states to obtain federal funds to help finance these programs.

THE RIGHT TO REFUSE TREATMENT

The right to refuse treatment is, of course, an integral aspect of the doctrine of fully informed consent. If no treatment can commence without the informed consent of the subject, then the subject is guaranteed the right to refuse a recommended treatment.

How encompassing should be the right to refuse treatment? If an individual's behavior infringes upon the rights of others because it is dangerous or seriously disruptive, should the right to refuse treatment be abrogated and coercive therapeutic interventions instituted? Do others retain the prerogative to compel a person to undergo treatment if that person's behavior is judged to be self-destructive?

According to Kittrie's "Therapeutic Bill of Rights" (1971), only those individuals whose behavior is determined to be posing a "clear and present danger" to themselves or others should be compelled to undergo treatment. In those cases, he suggests that the treatment recommendation be "the least required" to protect society or that individual, as there exists a basic human right "to remain free of excessive forms of human modification." This concept is similar to that of the most conservative, least intrusive, or least restrictive alternative treatment. Kittrie elaborates upon these points by stating that all persons should have the right to petition enforced treatment with the aid of appropriate advocates or counsel.

Many children who take medication do so voluntarily, whereas others, who are not dangerous to themselves or others, are "required," by physical force, social pressure, or mandate from an authority figure, to participate in psychotropic drug therapy. Some of those children are medicated because their caretakers do not wish to deal with their normal energies and needs *(Morales v. Turman)*. Some are medicated because drugs provide the simplist and most expedient alternative for the adults in the child's environment. Although many children who take psychoactive medication have been directed to do so because they manifest some problem which is expected to respond favorably to that therapy, there probably are many instances where other, less intrusive, more conservative, or less dangerous alternatives are available. A school child who manifests behavior that is disruptive to other classmates and the teacher needs to be treated in order not to infringe upon the rights of others. It is only appropriate, however, and in accordance with the right to a choice of available treatments, that all of the less intrusive and more conservative options be explored prior to the coercion of any medication regimen. Even where an individual's behavior endangers or is harmful to others, that individual retains a basic right to refuse any specific mode of treatment until all less radical alternatives have been tried.

Some children's behavior, although not dangerous or otherwise harmful, is merely "different." That is, it may be disruptive to some because it is "odd" or a bit harder to deal with than the behavior of other children. Kittrie (1971) suggests that all persons maintain a natural "right to be different." The failure of a person's behavior to meet socially prescribed standards of acceptability does not necessarily indicate that that person should be forced to undergo treatment to modify the objectionable behavior. It is possible that the tolerance for deviance of others is low, and that should be the target for modification rather than the so-called "deviant" behavior.

In discussing the right to refuse treatment, an important aspect of another fundamental human right must be considered: the right to self-determination. Unless their behavior is dangerous to others, individuals should, to the greatest degree that their capabilities and functioning allow, be permitted the right to determine their destinies. Many children have the ability to formulate and express views about matters that concern their welfare. There are no data to indicate that decisions about treatment which are made by minors are less consonant with their own best interests than those decisions made by adults. Therefore, there does not seem to be any defensible rationale to deny minors the right to self-determination when treatment decisions are involved. Obviously, some minors will be judged incompetent to make informed decisions about treatment because they are nonverbal, immature, or seriously disturbed. Other children readily waive their prerogatives so that their parents may make all such decisions. Others, however, will choose to exercise fully their right to accept or reject treatment alternatives. There are some cases in which minors should have the right to choose to endure their own symptomatology rather than undergo what they may consider less preferable treatment alternatives.

Judicial or Case Law

The courts, in cases involving both adults *(O'Connor v. Donaldson, Whitree v. State, Wyatt v. Stickney)* and children *(Bartley v. Kremens; J.L. v. Parham)* have supported the rights of individuals to resist the restrictive confinement of treatment imposed upon them as involuntary or voluntary commitment to institutions. The courts also have protected the rights of adult prisoners *(Knecht v. Gillman; Mackey v. Procunier; Souder v. McGuire)* and mental patients *(Aden v. Younger; Wyatt v. Stickney)* to refuse certain "intrusive" therapies, such as electroconvulsive shock therapy (ECT) or any of several pharmacological interventions. Juveniles committed to institutions, however, have not fared as well in the courts. For example, the case of *Morales v. Turman*, the Court ruled that juveniles have a right to "freedom from indiscriminate, unsupervised, unnecessary, or excessive medication, particularly psychotropic medication." Obviously, this protection against abusive and improper usage of psychotropic medication is an important right for juveniles. However, the Court neglected to provide juveniles with the right to make their own decisions as to when medication is indiscriminate, unnecessary, or excessive. The Court failed to specify that the children should have a right to refuse psychotropic medication unless their behavior is seriously problematic or self-destructive.

In the case of *Price v. Sheppard,* the parent of a minor who had been involuntarily committed brought an action against the medical director of the hospital for violation of the minor's civil rights because she had not been asked to consent prior to electroshock treatments being given to her son. The Court found that if the ECT "served legitimate purpose rather than deterrence or reprimand," and if the patient had failed to respond to other forms of treatment, then such involuntary treatment was constitutionally acceptable. However, the question of the right to refuse treatment does not relate simply to the "appropriateness" of a particular treatment. Instead, the right is a guarantee that individuals maintain the prerogative to decide for themselves whether or not they wish to undergo a given treatment, regardless of whether or not that treatment is regarded as "appropriate" by someone else.

In the case of *Nelson v. Heyne,* the intramuscular injection of tranquilizers to juveniles at a medium security institution for boys was held to be unconstitutional in that such "treatment" violated the Eighth Amendment protection against cruel and unusual punishment. However, the holding was based on the facts that the tranquilizer injections were administered by personnel not legally authorized to prescribe such injections, because they were dangerous to the children's health, and because they were intended as "punishment" rather than treatment. However, the Court did concede that such medications could be prescribed by the appropriate personnel for treatment purposes. Thus, most unfortunately, this holding does not provide protection for the right of juveniles to refuse treatment.

These cases concerning minors differ in important ways from those involving adults. In cases involving juveniles, the courts have ruled against certain "intrusive" involuntary treatments because those treatments obviously were not being recommended for "therapeutic" purposes. Instead, they were being improperly utilized as "punishments" and, therefore, were struck down as "cruel and unusual punishments" in violation of the Eighth Amendment of the Constitution.

An examination of the landmark judicial precedents involving adults indicates that in addition to reliance on the constitutional prohibition against "cruel and unusual punishment," the courts have afforded protection to "a right to privacy of mind" *(Aden v. Younger).* In *Aden v. Younger,* the Court held that the First, Third, Fourth, Fifth,

Ninth, and Fourteenth Amendments of the Constitution, in combination, protect a right to privacy of the mind and, therefore, a right to refuse treatment in state institutions. The plaintiffs protested the "intrusive" and possibly "hazardous" treatments of psychosurgery and ECT. The Court defended the Fourteenth Amendment protection against the performance of medical procedures on "unwilling patients" and affirmed the necessity of obtaining "informed consent" from patients prior to the commencement of treatment. Such "informed consent," stated the Court, includes the revelation of "all possible risks and possible side effects." In the case of *Scott v. Plante*, a person who had been committed to a state institution by reason of insanity and the commission of a crime claimed that he was forced to take drugs and other treatments against his will. In its opinion, the Court referred to a First Amendment guarantee of a right to bodily privacy and a Fourteenth Amendment right either to be consulted for "informed consent" or to have due process protections prior to commencement of medication treatment. In the case of *Souder v. McGuire*, where an inmate at a state hospital for the criminally insane alleged that medication had been administered to him against his will, the Court protected his Eighth and Fourteenth Amendment rights against such involuntary treatment.

Thus, with respect to adults, there appears to be a judicial trend toward recognition of a Constitutional right to refuse treatment based upon the need for "informed consent" and a right to "privacy of the mind." However, the courts have not concluded that such a right is inherent in the Constitutional protections due to minors. Instead, children are protected from "cruel and unusual punishment,"[5] as are adults, but not from the "impermissible tinkering with mental processes" which occurs when a drug is administered without consent (*Mackey v. Procunier*).

Statutory Law or Legislative Codes

Obviously, the fact that most states prevent minors from providing legally valid consent to their own treatment means that those minors also are prevented from withholding such consent (Wilkins, 1975). Perhaps the most significant impediment to the recognition of a right

---

[5]It should be noted, however, that a recent Supreme Court decision has denied children protection against certain types of punishment. In the case of *Ingraham v. Wright*, the Court held that corporal punishment in the schools, administered without prior notice or a hearing, does not constitute "cruel and unusual punishment." Thus, the Supreme Court seems not to consider that children are deserving of Constitutional protections identical to those afforded to adults.

of a minor to refuse treatment is the statutory law of most states under which minors are not considered competent to make informed decisions about their own medical treatment. The statutes of some states do provide that fully informed consent must be obtained before the commencement of most treatment will be considered valid (McGarry & Kaplan, 1975). However, those statutes generally afford protection to adults with respect to consent to their own treatment and the treatment of their children, but not the right of children to consent to their own treatment.

Unfortunately, the right to refuse treatment and the right to self-determination and mind privacy, although basic human rights, are not guaranteed to minors by the judicial precedents or statutory codes of most jurisdictions in the United States. Perhaps the most needed legislation in this area is a federal statute that affords competent minors the right to give or refuse consent to their own medical, psychological, and psychiatric treatment. This recognition that children are persons with basic rights and, as such, entitled to influence what happens to them should be an important step in the granting of full Constitutional protections to children with regard to the use of medication. Children in institutions, in schools, and at home are instructed to take medication for a variety of reasons, but it is unlikely that many of them has been given the opportunity to determine whether or not he or she feels that this is the most suitable alternative treatment.

THE RIGHT TO REMAIN APPRISED OF RELEVANT ASSESSMENT AND TREATMENT INFORMATION

Observance of the doctrine of informed consent guarantees that clients and patients will be provided with a minimal education as to the findings and recommendations of their attending professional. However, the right to be informed as to assessment findings and treatment indications is basic enough to be discussed independently as a human right.

When a child is the subject of an assessment, that child has a right to be informed as to the professional's findings and impressions in a manner commensurate with the child's ability to understand the relevant issues. The right of parents to be informed as to assessment findings is somewhat different. Material obtained from clients, whether children or adults, usually is gathered under conditions in which the client is assured that all disclosures and other information will be maintained "in confidence," and not revealed to a third party.

Professionals who make this promise to clients who are minors must be careful not to violate that ethical standard when communicating with the client's parents. Parents, however, as the individuals who usually seek the services of a professional for their child, do have some rights, as well. Practically, because the parents are the only ones who can consent to the child's treatment, they must be provided with enough relevant information to enable them to make fully informed and legally valid decisions about treatment. Furthermore, they are engaging the services of the professional because they too expect to be provided with information about their child's situation. And, finally, the interests of many parents are in harmony with the best interests of their children. Therefore, providing them with pertinent information ordinarily will be in keeping with the most appropriate needs of the child. It may be desirable to enlist the parents' assistance in the execution of a treatment regimen, or to engage them in some mode of family or parent counseling. Thus, it often is in the best interests of everyone, the child, the parents, and the professional, to apprise parents of relevant assessment information.

However, under such circumstances, the professional should bear in mind his or her responsibility to protect the child's right to privacy. By following certain guidelines a professional may avoid certain potential conflicts of interest in this area. For example, one can make certain, from the outset, that the child's parents are aware of the standard of "confidentiality" and that they agree to respect this principle. Morever, the professional can obtain the child's permission before revealing any sensitive information to parents. It is possible that if a child wishes to withhold information from a parent, the child has good reason for doing so. In fact, the child's wish to deny certain types of information to a parent may serve to alert the professional about certain aspects of the parent–child relationship.

The right to be apprised of relevant assessment information means that an individual is entitled to be provided with more than a mere diagnostic label, which, in itself, may be meaningless or subject to misinterpretation. The information obtained by the professional should be transmitted to the client in a manner that is understandable, and that is responsive to those questions which stimulated the request for professional assistance.

The right to be apprised of relevant treatment and assessment information implies that a client has a right to review those official records maintained in connection with his or her care. Although professionals certainly have rights of their own with respect to the privacy of the personal notes and comments relating to their clients, they also must be cautious about what they commit to a client's formal records. Although the records maintained in file cabinets, hospital or clinic re-

cord rooms, and hospital computer systems theoretically are confidential, the potential for invasions of privacy with respect to that data is
substantial. Patients and clients should be entitled to inspect all records maintained in connection with their treatment. One important
reason for this right of inspection is to afford such individuals an opportunity to challenge and have removed any information they believe to be incorrect or subject to misuse by persons with inappropriate access to those records (Kaiser, 1975). Mental health professionals sometimes maintain an air of mystery about a case when they discuss it with the client involved, often withholding information that
may be part of the permanent case record. The appropriateness of
such an approach is questionable. Although there may be some information that should not be revealed to clients, it seems probable
that many professionals often are too quick to conclude that certain
communications may be "harmful" to the client or may impede
treatment. If impressions are too speculative to reveal to clients then
they should not be placed in permanent classified records.

In the cases of children, a difficult, if not unanswerable, question
is whether children *and* their parents should have access to files. Legally, of course, the parents of a child under treatment retain whatever
rights may exist to gain access to their child's files. However, the
child is denied such access unless it is provided by his or her parents
(Brant, Garinger, & Brant, 1976). Furthermore, children do not have
the legal right to deny their parents access to their medical,
psychological, or psychiatric records until they reach the age of
majority (Brant et al., 1976). In order that the confidences of minors
not be violated when their parents seek access to treatment records,
professionals must consider new techniques of record keeping. In
fact, more careful and precise modes of record keeping certainly
would be an improvement on the often sloppy compilations of notes,
student impressions, and other nonimperative data permanently
stored in client case files. It is important that a child be given the right
to see what is in his or her file. A sense of control and mastery over
one's environment is a significant aspect of positive therapeutic
growth. Therefore, an individual, particularly a child, who wishes to
obtain information that may assist him or her to better understand
and cope with his or her environment should not be denied that opportunity. To deny a curious or suspicious child access to records may
create in that child a feeling that there is secrecy and, possibly, deceit
involved. Of course, professionals should be present when children
examine their own records so that, where necessary, concepts may be
explained and misconceptions corrected. It also seems appropriate
that parents not be permitted "carte blanche" access to all of their
child's medical, psychological, and psychiatric records. It is difficult to

determine when access to a child's records by parents actually is in the child's best interests. However, access to records by those parents acting as their child's true agents should not be denied simply because other parents may abuse the privilege. While there is no simple resolution for this problem, the issues warrant further examination.

Legally, parents retain the right of access to their children's school records. This right was guaranteed in the federal legislation known as "the Buckley Amendment" or "Protection of the rights and privacy of parents and students." This statute refers to educational records, but its central concept of access to records may serve as a model for legislation permitting clients access to medical, psychological, and psychiatric records. However, the issue of whether it is the child, the parents, or both who are to be allowed access must be resolved so as to best serve the interests of the child.

The statutes of some states, such as Massachusetts (Brant et al., 1976), permit access by patients to their own medical records. Federal legislation providing individuals with a right to access is likely to follow soon, as such legislation would be consistent with the trend established by the "Buckley Amendment" and other similar enactments (Kaiser, 1975).

THE RIGHT TO PRIVACY

In the discussion of the right to refuse treatment, above, the concept of "the right to privacy of mind" was introduced. This concept refers to a basic human right to protect one's private thoughts and feelings from intrusive and unwanted tampering by others. In this section of the chapter, the "right to privacy" refers to a basic human right to deny to certain other individuals access to information about one's thoughts, feelings, or affairs. In part, the "Buckley Amendment," and other legislation guaranteeing persons access fo their own files, protects the right to privacy, as it provides individuals with the opportunity to examine, to challenge, and to have removed any information on file that he or she feels should not be maintained in a public record.

When a child is seen by a professional for assessment and treatment services, detailed and often "sensitive" records are maintained. In addition, much information may be communicated to the professional by the child and by his or her parents, teachers, or others. Most mental health and health care professionals are bound by the ethical standards of their professions which mandate that information transmitted to a professional about a client must remain "in confidence." "Confidential" material should be released to other interested parties only at the express request or with the written consent of the client. Professional ethics often specify that waiver of the protections afforded by the doctrine of "confidentiality" is a privilege that belongs only to the client and not to the professional.

In the foregoing section, it is suggested that professionals reevaluate those of their attitudes which casually allow them to breach the confidence of children who are their clients by providing parents with information. A careful explanation to parents of the concept of "confidentiality," and the obtaining of the child's consent prior to the release of information were recommended as procedures that might permit the professional greater comfort and flexibility when dealing with the issue of "privacy" with respect to clients who were minors.

A child for whom psychotropic medication is prescribed may be forced to waive the right to some aspect of privacy in the interests of his or her treatment. In that regard, although teachers are not always made aware of the drug regimens prescribed for their students, it seems that such knowledge may, in some instances, facilitate optimum care for the child (Weithorn & Ross, 1975). For example, the teacher may be one of the primary sources of information concerning the apparent effects of or changes resulting from such therapy. Alternatively, a special education program may be implemented for the child. In such event, it might be crucial that the educators be aware of concurrent treatment regimens (such as drug therapy) so as to permit the most careful evaluation of the relative effects of the educational program. All clients should be made aware that the communication of "confidential" information to a third party may, in some instances, be an important aspect of assessment or treatment. This is one of the commitant "risks" which clients should weigh when deciding whether one mode of treatment is preferable to another.

In the landmark case of *Whalen v. Roe,* the Supreme Court of the United States failed to protect a child's right to privacy with respect to the dissemination of information about his or her treatment with psychotropic drugs. The Court, in February, 1977, held that the provisions of the New York State Controlled Substances Act[7] were not unconstitutional. The Act requires physicians prescribing certain specified drugs to file copies of the prescriptions with the State of New York. The relevant information then is maintained in a central computerized file. The plaintiff, a minor, claimed that the maintenance of such medical treatment information represented an unlawful invasion of the constitutional right to privacy. Those "Schedule II"

[6]20 U.S. Service Code, Section 1232g.
[7]44 N.Y.S. Public Health Law Section, Article 33.

drugs which require the registration of duplicate prescriptions in the State of New York include Ritalin and other stimulant medications sometimes prescribed for "hyperactivity." In one of the lower court hearings in this case, doctors testified that the New York State law "entrenches upon the confidentiality of the patient–doctor relationship" *(Roe v. Ingraham)*. The New York State law requires classification of the so-called "dangerous" and "potentially harmful" Schedule II drugs so that the State may monitor the use and abuse of those medications. The Supreme Court, in upholding the right of the State to monitor the affairs of its citizens with respect to such matters, determined that the monitoring program was not impermissible as an unconstitutional invasion of the right of privacy.

The impact of the decision in *Whalen v. Roe* on new statutory law and judicial decisions is as yet unknown. However, the finding that the "police power" of the State takes precedence over the rights of the individual represents a significant reduction in the protection which the law affords to the civil liberties of the individual.

As mentioned above, "confidentiality" is an ethical concept relating to professional standards. "Privileged communication" refers to that information which, when transmitted by a client to a professional, is protected by the law as confidential. For example, those communications between a lawyer and his or her client are considered privileged by the courts, and, therefore, cannot be subpeonaed as evidence in any case. Some states protect the privacy of the professional–client relationship by providing the clients and patients of psychologists and psychiatrists with a similar privilege (Shah, 1969). The right to waive the privilege belongs to the client, not to the professional. Thus, although, in some jurisdictions the confidentiality of the professional realtionship is protected from intrusion by the courts, in other jurisdictions professionals have been required to testify as to "confidential" information at the risk of being held in contempt of court (Shoben, 1950).

The "Buckley Amendment" and the "Education for All Handicapped Children Act" provide for the maintenance of confidentiality with respect to all record keeping relating to students. Moreover, the statutory provisions in the mental health laws of some states, particularly those developed on the basis of the decision in *Wyatt v. Stickney*, similarly guarantees the rights of clients to determine who may have access to their records.

Although the right of a client or patient to privacy is protected by the law in some instances, it is not uniformly protected. Therefore, professionals should educate themselves as to those exceptional instances where the privacy of their client or patient may be violated. Informing clients and patients of these exceptions is an essential aspect of ethical professional behavior. Clients and patients should have the right to decide whether the attendant "risks" to the maintenance of their privacy are acceptable to them. A fully informed decision to permit the use of psychotropic medication necessitates an understanding on the part of the client or patient of the likelihood of such information about such treatment being disclosed to others, either in the best interests of the client or patient or in the observance of particular legal requirements.

THE RIGHT OF ACCESS TO AN IMPARTIAL AND INDEPENDENT ADVOCACY AGENT OR AGENCY

As mentioned above, children may require the aid of an independent spokesperson or advocate because they often are unable to articulate fully their needs and interests. Advocates may be of many types. For example, in some states, legal counsel is available to minors in many situations where their interests are ruled by the courts (e.g., in cases of child abuse and neglect, in cases involving custody decisions, and in delinquency hearings). As a result of the *Wyatt v. Stickney* decision in Alabama, Bryce Hospital now maintains an advocacy program staffed by five full-time professionals with backgrounds in psychology, social work, and special education (Tauber & Houston, 1977). That staff investigates all complaints relating to patient care and treatment according to the standards set forth in the *Wyatt* decision. This type of program may serve appropriately as a model for all psychiatric hospitals and schools, as well as for correctional or detention facilities, particularly because individuals who are detained in insitutions rarely have the resources to seek outside assistance.

In some areas, community-based and/or private advocacy agencies have been created to meet the above described need. These agencies, comprised of concerned professionals and other members of the community, attempt to look out for the needs of children requiring special care. In that regard, they have pressed for legislation to protect children who are abused or neglected; they have worked to bring about changes in the disposition of and treatment imposed upon children found guilty of "status offenses"; they have lobbied for the "right to education" and the "right to treatment"; and they have fought against the abuse of children by institutions and professionals. An aspect of this "professional abuse" is the "overdrugging" of children (Walker, 1974). Such "overdrugging" might be related to improper diagnostic procedures, failure to examine alternative treatments, or simply a professional preference for modifying the behavior of a child instead of attempting to modify other aspects of the child's environment.

The activities of advocacy agencies are crucial to the well being of children in a society which only partially attends to their needs. Government financing of such agencies undoubtedly would be an important step forward in the struggle to protect the legal rights of children in the United States.

SUMMARY

For some children, treatment with psychotropic medication may indeed be the most appropriate way of helping them to cope with some physiologically based disorder or with environmental demands. However, certain questions must be asked prior to the election of the drug therapy alternative as a part of a treatment regimen.

Issues of "control" and "management" of "difficult" children often lead parents, teachers, or other involved adults to seek or accept medication for those children. The realities of certain situations, such as the classroom, often require that disruptive behavior be modified. In those cases, it is important to evaluate the pros and cons of all options. For example, Grinspoon and Singer (1973) state that:

> Behavior modification techniques, while they are no panacea and possess their own significant potential for abuse, do have this virtue: their proper application requires on the part of those who employ them a sensitivity to the needs, talents, and preferences of the individual child. Rather than simply making a child more manageable, as drugs often do, such techniques may bring out his best qualities. Moreover, these techniques allow the child to discover his impulses and to make use of his own powers of self-control in dealing with them. They do not just abolish temporarily the more disturbing impulses, thereby rendering control unnecessary. Behaviors learned through the use of such techniques potentially can be generalized to many situations beyond the specific situation in which the behaviors were originally conditioned . . . in contrast, drug-facilitated learning is not only not generalized to a broad spectrum of situations, but evidence suggests it is actually forgotten quite readily. . . P. 549.

The points raised by Grinspoon and Singer (1973) are crucial to the considerations of treatment of behavior, learning and psychological problems in children. Learning how to interact appropriately with one's environment is a life-long process. The learning which takes place in childhood is vital in that it serves as a foundation for that process. One of the negative "side effects" of psychotropic medication is that, in many instances, children are deprived of the opportunity to learn how to regulate their own behavior without the assistance of chemical intervention.

It is true that types of difficulties or impairments experienced by some children may not be treatable except with medication. Yet, the use of medication may have long-term impact on a child's sense of mastery of his or her world. As indicated by the court in the case of *Morales v. Turman*, the use of psychoactive medication for some children is contraindicated, as "it only reinforces their feelings that life's problems may be solved by ingestion of chemical substances."

Some of the abuse of children who pass through (or fail to pass through) mental health or health care systems may be traced to the failings of professionals (Polier, 1975). The Honorable David L. Bazelon, in his essay "The Perils of Wizardry" (1974) offers some relevant cautions to professionals dealing with psychiatric problems. He notes that professionals rarely acknowledge the limits of their expertise. This failure to be frank with clients often results in the neglect of some of the needs of the client or patient. He further states that psychiatrists and other mental health professionals fail to acknowledge the social impact of their strategies and interventions. Many of the problems manifested by children currently treated by medication may, in fact, be caused by social ills: poor child-rearing practices, family conflict, poverty and malnutrition, poor schooling, etc. Under such circumstances, modification of the behavior of the child fails to address the central social issues. Judge Bazelon states that:

> The treatment of pneumonia surely cannot be equated with shaping and changing the brain and behavior in the treatment of mental illness. Ignoring social causes actually makes no sense in either case. Recurrent pneumonia in malnourished children is not cured by repeated penicillin injections. Nor will tranquilizers still the fevers of rage and despair nurtured by poverty and discrimination. P. 1320.

The Judge eloquently states that the "biological binge", while holding the promise of the "relief of overwhelming distress," is accompanied by a "peril": the peril of "relieving society of the responsibility for caring."

APPENDIX

Minimal Professional Standards to be Maintained in the Delivery of Treatment Services to Juveniles Involuntarily Incarcerated by the State. (Reprinted from sections of *Morales v. Turman*, 383 F. Supp. 53, 1974.)

Assessment and placement.

On the basis of the evidence given by expert witnesses with respect to the assessment and placement of juveniles, it is concluded that a juvenile's constitutional right to treatment requires the maintenance of the following minimal professional standards:

(1) Every child committed to a state agency by the juvenile court must have the benefit of an individual assessment, to serve as the basis for his treatment plan. The plan should include, *inter alia*, a family history, a developmental history, a physical examination, psychological testing, a psychiatric interview, community evaluation, and a language and education analysis evaluation.

(2) Social work staff involved in the assessment must be trained at the Master's degree level in social welfare or closely related fields.

(3) Social work staff must not have caseloads exceeding fifteen cases per week.

(4) Psychologists with Master's degree and properly trained in testing procedures are adequate, but only if a Doctoral-level psychologist is available to supervise their work. A psychiatrist, however, must be available for interviews.

(5) For adequate classification, there must be daily contact between caseworker and juvenile, so as to evaluate the juvenile's amenability to guidance and counseling.

(6) The Wechsler individualized intelligence quotient test, rather than the group Lorge–Thorndike IQ test, must be utilized.

(7) The Leiter and Weschler tests, which are standardized for Blacks and Mexican Americans and are calculated to better alleviate the discrimination factor, must be utilized.

(8) Adequate psychological testing should take approximately fifteen hours and require the services of one psychologist for every three boys classified per week.

Academic education

On the basis of the evidence produced by expert witnesses with respect to academic education testing, it is concluded that a juvenile's right to treatment requires the maintenance of the following minimal professional standards:

(1) the Weschler IQ Test, rather than the Lorge–Thorndike IQ Test, must be used for testing generally.

(2) Neither the Lorge–Thorndike IQ Test nor the Gray–Votow–Rogers Achievement Test, which is inappropriate for testing Mexican Americans and Blacks on many subjects, should be used for testing for dyslexia.

Using as a foundation the evidence of expert witnesses, it is concluded that, for the purpose of detecting mental retardation in juveniles and providing them with the proper special education, the juvenile's right to treatment requires the maintenance of the following minimal professional standards:

(1) Normal IQ and achievement tests (both verbal and nonverbal) must be utilized with special emphasis on tests which are appropriate for the student's background.

(2) Examiners who are familiar with the background of the student and of his culture and language must be a part of the staff.

(3) Information must be obtained about the student's family background and emotional status, as well as observations relating to the student's behavior.

Again postulated upon the testimony of expert witnesses, it is the conclusion of this court that, as to special education teachers, a juvenile's right to treatment requires the maintenance of the following minimal professional standards:

(1) Special education teachers, certified by the state as qualified to each either emotionally disturbed, mentally retarded, or minimally brain-damaged children, must be utilized to treat children in these categories.

(2) In-service training by an outside consultant must be provided for special education teachers at least once a week. (Such consultants are available from the Texas Education Agency.)

(3) A minimal teacher–student ratio for TYC students in the categories above specified is one special education teacher for each eight of such students, plus supporting personnel (such as educational diagnosticians and the like).

As to other supporting personnel, this court adopts the opinion of expert witnesses that a juvenile's right to treatment requires the maintenance of the following minimal professional standards:

(1) One educational diagnostician is essential for each 150–200 TYC students.

(2) Assessment by language pathologists, sometimes referred to as speech therapists, is an essential complement to any other professional assessments, and such an assessment is necessary to diagnose the underlying learning difficulty that may be initially identified by a psychologist or teacher.

Medical and psychiatric care

The court concludes that juveniles under the authority of the Texas Youth Council have a constitutional and statutory right to medical and psychiatric care that has been grossly violated and are entitled to care that conforms to the following minimally acceptable professional standards:

(1) Adequate infirmary facilities, properly utilized.

(2) Access to medical staff without delay or interference.

(3) A psychiatrist staff consisting of individuals certified by a Board of Psychiatry and Neurology as qualified in the field of child psychiatry, sufficient in number to assure treatment of individual children who require individual therapy; effective training and supervision of other treatment staff; and coordination of treatment programs.

(4) A psychological staff, to consist of psychologists holding either Master's degrees or Doctorates in psychology and experienced in work with adolescents, sufficient in number to meet the needs of the children.

(5) Provision of either individual or group psychotherapy for every child for whom it is indicated.

(6) Sufficient psychiatric nursing assistance.

(7) Sufficient medical staff and nursing staff to provide effective preventive and curative care for the health of all juveniles.

(8) Freedom from indiscriminate, unsupervised, unnecessary, or excessive medication, particularly psychotropic medication.

REFERENCES

Aden v. Younger, 129 Cal. Rptr. 535 (1976).

Bartley v. Kremens, 402 F. Supp. 1039 (1975).

Bayh, B. Juveniles and the Law: An Introduction. *American Criminal Law Review,* 1974, *12,* 1–7.

Bazelon, D. The Perils of Wizardry. *American Journal of Psychiatry,* 1974, *131,* 1317–1322.

Beyer, H.A., & Wilson, J.P. The Reluctant Volunteer: A Child's Right to Resist Commitment. In Koocher, G. P. (Ed.), *Children's Rights and the Mental Health Professions.* New York: John Wiley and Sons, 1976. Pp. 133–148.

Brant, J., Garinger, G., & Brant, R.T. So You Want to See Our Files on You? In Koocher, G.P. (Ed.), *Children's Rights and the Mental Health Professions.* New York: John Wiley and Sons, 1976. Pp. 123–130.

Brigham Young University Law Review. Minor's Right to Privacy Versus Parental Right of Control—Access to Contraceptives Absent Parental Consent. 1976, 296–317.

Brown, J.L., & Bing, S.R. Drugging Children: Child Abuse by Professionals. In Koocher, G.P. (Ed.), *Children's Rights and the Mental Health Professions.* New York: John Wiley and Sons, 1976. Pp. 219–228.

Clonce v. Richardson, 379 F. Supp. 338 (1974).

Coughlin, B.J. The Rights of Children. In Wilkerson, A.E. (Ed.), *The Rights of Children, Emergent Concepts in Law and Society.* Philadelphia: Temple University Press, 1973. Pp. 7–23.

Covington v. Harris, 419 F. 2d 617 (1969)

Education for All Handicapped Children Act of 1975. Public Law 94–142. Ninety-fourth Congress of the United States. November 29, 1975.

Ellis, J.W. Volunteering Children: Parental Commitment of Minors to Mental Institutions. *California Law Review,* 1974, *62,* 840–916.

Forer, L.G. Rights of Children: The Legal Vacuum. *American Bar Association Journal,* 1969, *55,* 1151–1156.

Foster, H.H., Jr., & Freed, D.J. A Bill of Rights for Children. *Family Law Quarterly*, 1972, *6*, 343–375.

Fraser, B.G. The Pediatric Bill of Rights. *South Texas Law Journal*, 1975, *16*, 24-5–308.

Goldstein, J., Freud, A., & Solnit, A.J. *Beyond the Best Interests of the Child*. New York: The Free Press, 1973.

Grinspoon, L., & Singer, S.B. Amphetamines in the Treatment of Hyperkinetic Children. *Harvard Educational Review*, 1973, *43*, 515–555.

Herr, S. Toward Equal Rights for the Unequal: The Handicapped Child's Right to Education. *National Legal Aid and Defender Association Briefcase*, 1972, *31*, 292–297.

In re Gault, 387 U.S. 1 (1967).

Ingraham v. Wright, 430 U.S. 651 (1977).

J.L. v. Parham, 412 F. Supp. 112 (1976).

Jorgensen, G.T., & Lyons, D.D. Human Rights and Involuntary Civil Commitment. *Professional Psychology*, 1972, *3*, 143–150.

Kaiser, B.L. Patients' Rights of Access to their Own Medical Records: The Need for New Law. *Buffalo Law Review*, 1975, *24*, 317–330.

Kent v. U.S., 383 U.S. 541 (1966).

Kittrie, N.H. *The Right to Be Different*. Baltimore: Johns Hopkins University Press, 1971.

Knecht v. Gillman, 488 F. 2d 1136 (1973).

Kremens v. Bartley, 431 U.S. 119 (1977).

Mackey v. Procunier, 477 F. 2d. 877 (1973).

Maratella v. Kelley, 349 F. Supp. 575 (1972).

Martin, R. Ethical and Legal Implications of Behavior Modification in the Classroom. *Ethical and Legal Factors in the Practice of School Psychology*. Pennsylvania Department of Education and Department of School Psychology, College of Education, Temple University, 1975. Pp. 53–66.

Maryland Law Review. Counseling the Counselors: Legal Implications of Counseling Minors without Parental Consent. 1971, *31*, 332–354.

McCoy, R., & Koocher, G.P. Needed: A Public Policy for Psychotropic Drug Use with Children. In Koocher, G.P. (Ed.), *Children's Rights and the Mental Health Professions*. New York: John Wiley and Sons, 1976. Pp. 237–244.

McGarry, A.L., & Kaplan, H.A. Overview: Current Trends in Mental Health Law. In Allen, R.C., Ferster, E.Z., & Rubin, J.G., *Readings in Law and Psychiatry*. Baltimore: Johns Hopkins University Press, 1975. Pp. 34-4–353.

Meisel, A., Roth, L.H., & Lidz, C.W. Toward a Model of the Legal Doctrine of Informed Consent. *American Journal of Psychiatry*, 1977, *134*, 285–289.

Mental Health Procedures. Act No. 143. 5 Pa. Leg. Serv. 345 (1976).

Mills v. Board of Education, 348 F. Supp. 866 (1972).

Morales v. Turman, 383 F. Supp. 53 (1974).

Nelson v. Heyne, 491 F. 2d 352 (1974), 355 F. Supp. 451 (1973).

O'Connor v. Donaldson, 95 S.Ct. Rptr. 2486 (1975).

Opton, E.M., Jr. Psychiatric Violence Against Prisoners: When Therapy is Punishment *Mississippi Law Journal*, 1974, *45*, 605–644.

Pennsylvania Association for Retarded Children (P.A.R.C.) v. Commonwealth of Pennsylvania, 334 F. Supp. 1257 (1971).

Polier, J.W. Professional Abuse of Children: Responsibility for the Delivery of Services. *American Journal of Orthopsychiatry*, 1975, *45*, 357–362.

Price v. Sheppard, 239 N.W. Rptr. 905 (1976).

Rodham, H. Children Under the Law. *Harvard Educational Review*, 1973, *43*, 487–514.

Roe v. Ingraham, F. Supp. 931 (1975).

Ross, R. Drug therapy for Hyperactivity: Existing Practices in Physican-School Communication. In Cohen, M.J. (Ed) *Drugs and the Special Child.* N.Y.: Gardner Press, 1978.

Roth, L.H., Meisel, A., & Lidz, C.W. Tests of Competency to Consent to Treatment. *American Journal of Psychiatry*, 1977, *134*, 279–284.

Rouse v. Cameron, 373 F. 2d 451 (1966).

Scott v. Plante, 532 F. 2d 939 (1976).

Shah, S.A. Privileged Communications, Confidentiality and Privacy: Privileged Communications. *Professional Psychology*, 1969, *1*, 57–69.

Shapiro, M.H. Legislating the Control of Behavior Control: Autonomy and the Coercive Use of Organic Therapies. *Southern California Law Review*, 1974, *47*, 237–356.

Shoben, E.J., Jr. Psychologists and Legality: A Case Report. *American Psychologist*, 1950, *5*, 496–498.

Souder v. McGuire, 423 F. Supp. 830 (1976).

Spece, R.J. Conditioning and Other Technologies used to 'Treat?' 'Rehabilitate?' 'Demolish?' Prisoners and Mental Patients. *Southern California Law Review*. 1972, *45*, 616–684.

Stewart, M.A. Treating Problem Children with Drugs: Ethical Issues. In Koocher, G.P. (Ed.), *Children's Rights and the Mental Health Professions.* New York: John Wiley and Sons, 1976. Pp. 229–236.

Tauber, D., & Houston, J. The Advocacy Program. *Hospital and Community Psychiatry*, 1977, *28*, 360–361.

United Nations General Assembly. United Nations Declaration of the Rights of Children. In Wilkerson, A.E. (Ed.), *The Rights of Children, Emergent Concepts in Law and Society.* Philadelphia: Temple University Press, 1973. Pp. 3–6.

Walker, S. Drugging the American Child: We're too cavalier about Hyperactivity. *Psychology Today*, 1974, *8*, 43–48.

Weithorn, C.J. & Ross, R. Who Monitors Medication? *Journal of Learning Disabilities*, 1975, *8*, 458–461.

Weithorn, C.J., & Ross, R. "Stimulant Drugs for Hyperactivity: Some Additional Disturbing Questions." *American Journal of Orthopsychiatry*. 1976, *46*, 168–173.

Wells, W.W. Drug Control of School Children: The Children's Right to Choose. *Southern California Law Review*, 1973, *46*, 585–616.

Whalen v. Roe, 429 U.S. 589 (1977).

Whitree v. State, 290 N.Y.S. 2d 486 (1968).

Wilkins, L.P. Children's Rights: Removing the Parental Consent Barrier to Medical Treatment of Minors. *Arizona State Law Journal*, 1975, 31–92.

Winters v. Miller, 446 F. 2d 65 (1971).

Wisconsin v. Yoder, 406 U.S. 205, 32 L.Ed. 2d 15 (1972).

Wyatt v. Stickney, 334 F. Supp. 373 (1972).

APPENDIX

Report of the Conference
on the Use of
Stimulant Drugs in the Treatment of
Behaviorally Disturbed Young
School Children

INTRODUCTION

On January 11–12, 1971, the Office of Child Development and the Office of the Assistant Secretary for Health and Scientific Affairs, Department of Health, Education, and Welfare, called a conference to discuss the use of stimulant medications in the treatment of elementary school-age children with certain behavioral disturbances. In convening the conference, the Office of Child Development was aware of public concern about the increasing use of stimulant medications (such as dextroamphetamine and methylphenidate) in treating so-called hyperkinetic behavior disorders. Were these drugs—so widely misused or abused by adolescents and adults—truly safe for children? Were they properly prescribed, or were they used for youngsters who, in fact need other types of treatment? Is emphasis on medications for behavior disorders misleading? Might this approach tempt many to oversimplify a complex problem, leading to neglect of remedial social, educational or

Sponsored by the Office of Child Development and the Office of the Assistant Secretary for Health and Scientific Affairs, Department of Health, Education, and Welfare, Washington, D.C., January 11–12, 1971.

239

psychological efforts on the part of professionals, parents, schools and public agencies?

In order to clarify the conditions in which these medications are beneficial or harmful to children, to assess the status of current knowledge, and to determine the best auspices for administering these drugs to children, a panel of 15 specialists was invited to meet in Washington. The panelists were from the fields of education, psychology, special education, pediatrics, adult and child psychiatry, psychoanalysis, basic and clinical pharmacology, internal medicine, drug abuse and social work. The panel's task was to review the evidence of research and experience and to prepare an advisory report for professionals and the public.

This report briefly outlines the general nature of behavioral disorders in children and then focuses on those disorders that are being treated with stimulant medications. It discusses appropriate treatment and the concerns voiced by the public and media. Finally, the report examines the role of the pharmaceutical industry, professionals, and the news media in publicizing stimulant drugs for children and outlines the glaring gaps in needed research, training and facilities.

BEHAVIOR DISORDERS OF CHILDHOOD

A wide range of conditions and disabilities can interfere with a child's learning at home and in school, his socialization with peers, and his capacity to reach his maximum development. Social deprivations and stress at home or school may retard optimal development. Mental retardation, the more rarely occurring childhood autism and psychosis, and other such disabilities may cause serious problems. Some difficulties arise because of clearly definable medical conditions such as blindness, deafness or obvious brain dysfunction. Some are associated with specific reading or perceptual defects, and others with severe personality or emotional disturbance.

Such dysfunctions are known to require careful evaluation, thoughtfully planned treatment employing a variety of methods on the child's behalf, and conscientious monitoring of remedial treatments. Individualized evaluation and treatment is important for any childhood behavior disorder. There are appropriate occasions for use of medications such as tranquilizers and antidepressants in some children with these disorders. For over three decades, stimulant medications have been selectively used for children under medical supervision. We now focus upon issues related to the current use of these drugs.

"HYPERKINETIC DISORDERS"

The type of disturbance which has evoked misunderstanding and concern has many names. The two most familiar—neither entirely satisfactory—are "minimal brain dysfunction" and, more commonly, "hyperkinetic behavioral disturbance." There is no known single cause or simple answer for such problems. The major symptoms are an increase of purposeless physical activity and a significantly impaired span of focused attention. The inability to control physical motion and attention may generate other consequences, such as disturbed mood and behavior within the home, at play with peers, and in the schoolroom.

In its clear-cut form, the overt hyperactivity is not simply a matter of degree but of quality. The physical activity appears driven—as if there were an "inner tornado"—so that the activity is beyond the child's control, as compared to other children. The child is distracted, racing from one idea and interest to another, but unable to focus attention.

Incidence of Hyperkinetic Disorders

This syndrome is found in children of all socioeconomic groups and in countries throughout the world. A conservative estimate would be that moderate and severe disorders are found in about 3 out of 100 elementary school children—an estimate that would vary somewhat in different communities. More males than females are affected, as is true in a number of childhood ailments. Children so afflicted are generally of normal or superior intelligence. A significant number so diagnosed have special learning or reading disabilities, in addition to the major symptoms. A near majority are reported to have had behavioral problems since infancy. There is a smaller group of more severely afflicted children upon whom most studies have focused; they may show increased clumsiness and a variety of physical symptoms. Thus, some of the children show hyperactivity and reduced attention which ranges in degree from mild to severe, with or without associated physical signs or special learning impairments; some have complex behavioral and personality problems, as well as special learning and reading difficulties, along with the major hyperkinetic symptoms.

Causes of Hyperkinetic Disorders

We know little about definitive causes. The disorder has been ascribed to biological, psychological, social or environmental factors, or a combination of these. There is speculation that the core set of symptoms—those affecting control of attention and motor activity—may have their origin in events taking place before the child is born, or during the birth process, or they may be related to some infection or injury in early life. The neurological and psychological control of attention is an important but incompletely researched topic, as are the nutritional, perinatal and developmental factors. Thus, in many instances, it is not yet possible even to speculate as to original causes.

The Course of Hyperkinetic Disorders

Usually, the excessive activity and attentional disturbances are less apparent after puberty. Specialists citing experience and some fragmentary research data believe that treatment enables many to lead productive lives as adults, while severely afflicted children who remain untreated may be significantly at risk for adult disorders. Extensive research is still required on these points. Because the ages of 5 to 12 are crucial to the child's development and self-image, treatments which permit the child to be more accessible to environmental resources are warranted and useful.

Diagnosis of Hyperkinetic Disorders

In diagnosing hyperkinetic behavioral disturbance, it is important to note that similar behavioral symptoms may be due to other illnesses or to relatively simple causes. Essentially healthy children may have difficulty maintaining attention and motor control because of a period of stress in school or at home. It is important to recognize the child whose inattention and restlessness may be caused by hunger, poor teaching, overcrowded classrooms, or lack of understanding by teachers or parents. Frustrated adults reacting to a child who does not meet their standards can exaggerate the significance of occasional inattention or restlessness. Above all, the normal ebullience of childhood should not be confused with the very special problems of the child with hyperkinetic behavioral disorders.

The diagnosis is clearly best made by a skilled observer. There unfortunately is no single diagnostic test. Accordingly, the specialist must comprehensively evaluate the child and assess the significance of a variety of symptoms. He considers causal and contributory factors—both permanent and temporary—such as environmental stress. He distinguishes special dysfunctions such as certain epilepsies, schizophrenia, depression or anxiety, mental retardation or perceptual deficiencies. The less severe and dramatic forms of hyperkinetic disorders also require careful evaluation. Adequate diagnosis may require the use not only of medical, but of special psychological, educational and social resources.

TREATMENT PROGRAMS

The fact that these dysfunctions range from mild to severe and have ill-understood causes and outcomes should not obscure the necessity for skilled and special interventions. The majority of the better known diseases—from cancer and diabetes to hypertension—similarly have unknown or multiple causes and consequences. Their early manifestations are often not readily recognizable. Yet useful treatment programs have been developed to alleviate these conditions. Uncertainty as to cause has not prevented tests of the effectiveness of available treatments, while the search for clearer definitions and more effective kinds of therapy continues. The same principles should clearly apply to the hyperkinetic behavior disorders.

Several approaches now appear to be helpful. Special classes and teachers can be directed to specific learning disabilities and thus restore the confidence of the child who experiences chronic failure. Modification of behavior by systematic rewarding of desired actions has been reported to be useful in some children. Elimination of disturbing influences in the family or classroom through counseling may often tip the balance, and a happier child may show improved control and function.

There will be children for whom such efforts are not sufficient. Their history and their examination reveal symptoms of such a driven nature that skilled clinicians undertake a trial of medical treatment. Medicine does not "cure" the condition, but the child may become more accessible to educational and counseling efforts. Over the short term and at a critical age, this can provide the help needed for the child's development.

Stimulant medications are beneficial in only about one-half to two-thirds of the cases in which trials of the drugs are warranted. The stimulant drugs are considered to be the first and least complicated of the medicines to be tried. Other medications—the so-called tranquilizers and anti-depressants—are generally reserved for a smaller group of patients. Without specialized medical therapy, the consequences for these children of their failure to manage— even in an optimal environment—are clearly very severe. In such cases, the aim is not to "solve problems with drugs," but to put the severely handicapped child in a position to interact with his environment to the extent that his condition permits.

Response to stimulant medication cannot be predicted in advance. Fortunately, the issue can be resolved quickly. When stimulants are given in adequate doses, a favorable response—when it occurs—is fairly rapidly obtained and is unmistakably the consequence of the drug. Thus, if an adequate test of pharmacotherapy (a few days or weeks) produces only doubtful benefits or none at all, treatment can be promptly terminated. The physician will, of course, adjust dosage carefully to assure an adequate therapeutic trial. It would be tragic to deprive a child of a potentially beneficial treatment by inattention to dose. Thus, it is clear that not all affected children require medication and that of those who do, not all respond.

When the medication is effective, the child can modulate and organize his activities in the direction he wishes. The stimulant does not slow down or suppress the hyperkinetic child in the exercise of his initiative. Nor does it "pep" him up, make him feel high, overstimulated, or out of touch with his environment. Much has been made of the "paradoxical sedative" effect of stimulants in such children. The term is inappropriate. Although their exact mechanism of action is not known, stimulants do not provide a chemical straitjacket. They do not act as a sedative. Rather, they appear to mobilize and to increase the child's abilities to focus on meaningful stimuli and to organize his bodily movements more purposefully.

The hoped-for secondary consequences are better peer relationships, improved self-image, and pleasure in acquiring competencies. Any coexisting dysfunctions—such as special perceptual and learning handicaps—must not be left unattended, simply because pharmacotherapy is available and sometimes helpful. Similarly, personality and psychological problems, social and family problems, may require continued attention.

During drug treatment, the dosage may require shifting to minimize unwanted effects, of which the major ones are loss of appetite and insomnia. Drug treatment should not and need not be indefinite, and usually is stopped after the age of 11 or 12. Frequently, following a sustained improvement over several months or a year or so, drugs may be discontinued, as during a vacation period. Drug-free intervals can be prolonged as observers assess the child's condition.

The decision to use drug treatment thus depends on the commitment to diagnose and to monitor the response to treatment in the best traditions of medical practice. When there is informed parental consent, parents, teachers and professionals can collaborate in organizing and monitoring treatment programs.

CONCERNS RAISED BY THE PUBLIC AND THE NEWS MEDIA

We will now turn to various concerns about hazards and abuses when stimulant medications are used for children. For example, concern has been expressed that the medical use of stimulants could create drug dependence in later years or induce toxicity. This subject touches on the rights of the child to needed treatment, as well as risks to both the child and the public, and requires continued intensive scrutiny.

1. *Does the medication produce toxicity?*

One should not confuse the effects of intravenous stimulants and the high dosages used by drug abusers with the effects or the risks of the low dosages used in medical therapy. In the dosage used for children, the questions of acute or chronic toxicity noted in the stimulant abuser are simply not a critical issue. Unwanted mental or physical effects do rarely appear in children; cessation of therapy or adjustment of dosage quite readily solves the problem.

2. *Is there a risk of drug dependency in later years?*

Thirty years of clinical experience and several scientific studies have failed to reveal an association between the medical use of stimulants in the pre-adolescent child and later drug abuse. Physicians who care for children treated with stimulants have noted that the children do not experience the pleasurable, subjective effects that would encourage misuse. They observe that most often the child is willing to stop the therapy, which he views as "medicine." Thus, the young child's experience of drug effects under medical management does not seem to induce misuse. The medical supervision may "train" him in the appropriate use of medicines. When adults are given stimulants—or even opiates—for time-limited periods under appropriate supervision and for justifiable reasons, there is relatively little misuse. Similarly, in treating epilepsy, barbiturates have been given from infancy to adulthood without creating problems of dependency or abuse.

It is not ordinarily the drug which constitutes abuse but the way in which a drug and its effects are used and exploited by an individual. There are indeed adolescents who, in varying degrees and for varying periods of time, either misuse or dangerously abuse stimulants. They experiment with the effects of excessive dosages to create excitement, to avoid sleep, to defy constraints, and to combat fatigue and gloom. It should be noted that these drugs are not commonly prescribed to children after the age of 11 or 12, when the actual risks of such experimentation or misuse might possibly become more significant.

Alter monitoring of drug use at any age is a part of sensible medical practice. With such precaution and with the available evidence, we find minimal cause for concern that treatment will induce dangerous drug misuse. To the contrary, there are very good reasons to expect that help, rather than harm, will be the result of appropriate treatment.

3. *Are there safeguards against misuse?*

There are some sensible steps, in addition to medical control, that guard against possible misuse. The child should not be given sole responsibility for taking the medication. He usually need not bring the drug to school. The precautions that surround the medicine cabinet—whether antibiotics, aspirins, sedatives, or other medications are present—should be applied. Many such medicines, when misused, can be more dangerous to health and life than even the stimulant drugs. No child in the family should have access to medications not prescribed for him. These are general precautions comprising a part of the child's education in the "etiquette of the medicine cabinet."

4. *Do stimulants for children create a risk for others?*

The panel agrees that stimulant drug abuse is seriously undesirable and not infrequently dangerous, although views vary on the scope of the problem and the number of actual casualties. Experts also agree that far more stimulants are prescribed for adults than are medically needed and far more are manufactured than prescribed. Overprescription of any medication is deplored, whether or not it is liable to abuse. The question is whether the availability of stimulants for a very few of the childhood behavior disorders threatens the public health.

The prescribed dosage for an individual child constitutes an insufficient quantity to supply the confirmed abuser of stimulants with the amounts he requires. It is also true that illicitly manufactured stimulants are quite readily available and abused in this country. We must weigh the advantages of having appropriate medication available against the dangers of withholding treatment from a child who can clearly benefit from it. We doubt that prescriptions for the children who benefit from stimulants will require the manufacture of excessive and dangerously divertible supplies. With sensible precautions, there is at present no evidence justifying sensational alarm, either about the safety of the individual child who can benefit from therapy or about the safety of the general public.

5. *Does medication handicap the child emotionally?*

It is sometimes suggested that treated children may not be able to learn normal responses and master adjustments to the stresses of everyday life. These fears are understandable but are not confirmed by specialists who have experience with the conditions and the situations in which medications are properly used. For the correctly diagnosed child, these medications—if they work at all—facilitate the development of the ability to focus attention and to make judgments in directing behavior. Such children can acquire the capacity to tolerate and master stress. The medications, in these circumstances, help "set the stage" for satisfactory psychological development.

The hyperkinetic behavioral disturbance is a form of disorganization that creates great stress in the afflicted child. The use of therapeutic stimulants for this disturbance should not be equated with the misuse of medication aimed at allowing a normal child or adult to avoid or escape the ordinary stresses of life.

6. *What are the rights of the parents?*

Under no circumstances should any attempt be made to coerce parents to accept any particular treatment. As with any illness, the child's confidence must be respected. The consent of the patient and his parents or guardian must be obtained for treatment. It is proper for school personnel to inform parents of a child's behavior problems, but members of the school staff should not directly diagnose the hyperkinetic disturbance or prescribe treatment. The school should initiate contact with a physician only with the parents' consent. When the parents do give their approval, cooperation by teachers, social workers, special education and medical personnel can provide valuable help in treating the child's problem.

STIGMATIZING THE MEDICINES AND CHILDREN, AND THE ROLE OF PUBLIC EDUCATION

A child who benefits from stimulants or other psychotropic medications should not be stigmatized; his situation is no different from that of the child who benefits from eyeglasses. It is unjust to stigmatize a child in later life, when competing in various situations (applying for college, employment or organization memberships), by labeling him early in life as "stupid," an "emotional cripple," a "drug-taker," or by any other kind of unjustified and unfortunate stereotype.

Nor should the medicine be stigmatized. Where bad practices prevail—and a number of complaints have been called to our attention—these practices should be squarely dealt with. This is not only a responsibility of physicians and educators, but also of the news media. Yet indignation must be tempered with perspective and scrupulous respect for the facts. An informed and understanding public can foster the growth and development of children, and these public attitudes may lead to the development of more refined and better delivered health services. Either bad practices or exaggerated alarm can threaten the availability of medical resources for those who critically need it. This has happened before in the history of valuable medicines, and it can take years to repair the damage.

THE PROMOTION OF DRUGS BY INDUSTRY AND THE MEDIA

Pharmaceutical companies producing stimulants or new medications which may become useful for hyperkinetic disorders have a serious obligation to the public. These medicines should be promoted ethically and only through medical channels. Manufacturers should not seek endorsement of their products by school personnel. In the current climate, society can best be served if industry refrains from any implicit urging that nonspecialists deal with disorders and medications with which they are unfamiliar. Professionals and the news media can play useful roles by not pressing for treatments in advance of their practical availability.

THE DELIVERY OF SPECIAL HEALTH CARE: A DILEMMA

Our society has not as yet found complete solutions to the problem of the delivery of special health care. When available treatments cannot be confidently and appropriately delivered by physicians, they are perhaps best withheld until such treatments can be provided—especially with milder dysfunctions. This is not to say that severely afflicted hyperkinetic children should not or cannot receive available medical treatment. But until systems of continuing professional education and ready access to consultants are financed and perfected, some judgment about the pace at which unfamiliar treatments can be widely fostered is required. Finally, we must recognize that it is not only the scarcity of trained personnel, but factors such as poverty and inadequate educational facilities which prevent accessibility to individualized treatment.

THE NEED FOR SKILLS AND KNOWLEDGE

In preparing this report, the Committee was repeatedly struck by our lack of information in many crucial areas. The facts are that children constitute well over half our population but receive a disproportionately low share of skilled research attention. We have noted the difficulties in arriving at accurate methods of diagnosis and the importance of launching careful longitudinal and follow-up studies. The investigation of causal factors lags. Such factors as perinatal injury, environmental stress or the development of the neurological and psychological controls of attention require study. Variations in different socioeconomic and ethnic groups must be considered in order to arrive at better definitions of behavior properly regarded as pathological. All such research efforts would have aided us in assessing the numbers of affected children and in recommending designs for more effective treatment programs.

Clinical pharmacologists have repeatedly found that drugs may act differently in children than in adults. To use medicines of all kinds effectively in children, more specialists must be trained in drug investigation—pharmacologists who can develop basic knowledge about the action of drugs in the developing organism. There is the obvious need for better and more precisely targeted drugs for the whole range of severe childhood behavior disorders. This requires intense research and training efforts. Such efforts provide the means for developing, testing and delivering better treatment programs. There is a similar need for research in the techniques of special education and also a need to make these techniques available to children who can benefit. It would appear to be a sound Federal investment to conduct such research and training.

In summary, there is a place for stimulant medications in the treatment of the hyperkinetic behavioral disturbance, but these medications are not the only form of effective treatment. We recommend a code of ethical practices in the promotion of medicines, and candor, meticulous care and restraint on the part of the media, professionals and the public. Expanded programs of continuing education for those concerned with the health care of the young, and also sustained research into their problems, are urgently needed.

Our society is facing a crisis in its competence and willingness to develop and deliver authentic knowledge about complex problems. Without such knowledge, the public cannot be protected against half-truths and sensationalism, nor can the public advance its concern for the health of children.

PARTICIPANTS IN THE PANEL

Dr. Daniel X. Freedman, Chairman
Professor and Chairman, Department of Psychiatry, University of Chicago

Dr. T. Berry Brazelton
Practicing Pediatrician and Research Associate and Lecturer in Cognitive Studies, Harvard University

Dr. James Comer
Associate Professor of Psychiatry, Yale Study Center, and Associate Dean, Yale Medical School

Dr. William Cruickshank
Director, Institute for the Study of Mental Retardation, University of Michigan

Dr. E. Perry Crump
Professor of Pediatrics, Meharry Medical College, Nashville, Tennessee

Dr. Barbara Fish
Professor of Child Psychiatry, New York University School of Medicine ʻ

Dr. George H. Garrison
Clinical Professor of Pediatrics, University of Oklahoma

Dr. Frank Hewett
Associate Professor in Special Education and Psychiatry, University of California

Dr. Leo E. Hollister
Clinical Pharmacologist and Medical Investigator, Veterans Administration Hospital, Palo Alto, California

Dr. Conan Kornetsky
Research Professor, Division of Psychiatry and Department of Pharmacology, Boston University School of Medicine

Dr. Edward T. Ladd
Professor of Education, Emory University, Atlanta, Georgia

Dr. Robert J. Levine
Associate Professor of Medicine and Pharmacology, Yale University School of Medicine

Dr. Patricia Morisey
Associate Professor, School of Social Service, Fordham University

Dr. Irving Schulman
Professor and Head of the Department of Pediatrics, University of Illinois College of Medicine

Dr. Martin H. Smith
Practicing Pediatrician in Gainesville, Georgia, and Past Chairman of the Georgia Chapter, American Academy of Pediatrics

SUBJECT INDEX

Achievement Tests, 11
Actometer, 10, 19
Aden v. Younger, 207, 221–223
Aggressivity, 4, 8, 70, 91, 159, 165–168, 190
American Academy of Cerebral Palsy, 54
American Academy of Ophthalmology, 54
American Academy of Ophthalmology & Otolaryngology, 54
American Academy of Pediatrics, 54
American Psychiatric Association, 56, 136
Amphetamines, 2, 11, 12, 13, 14, 41, 51, 67, 89, 115, 131, 161, 195
Anoxia, 6, 132
Antidepressants, 37, 41, 75, 120
Anxiety, 35, 40, 48, 51, 52, 55, 87, 114, 118, 120, 125, 139, 168, 193, 242
Association for Retarded Children, 123
Association for Children with Learning Disabilities, 123
Atarax, (see Hydroxyzine)
Ataxia, 39, 41

Ballistograph, 10, 19
Baltimore County, Maryland, 107
Barbituric acid derivatives, 43, 44
Bartley v. Kremens, 208–209, 221
Behavior Modification, 2, 24, 70, 72, 135, 198, 231, 242
Bender-Gestalt Test, 192
Benzedrine, 2, 12, 48, 49, 67, 88
Brain Damage, 8, 11, 47, 132, 138
Brigham Young University Law Review, 208, 213
Bryce Hospital, 218, 230
Buckley Amendment, 227, 229

Caffeine, 12, 49
California Education Code 6871, 65–66

Canadian Association for Retarded Children, 54
Canadian Mental Health Association, 56
Celontin, 43, 44
Cerebral dysfunction, 3, 5
Cerebral Palsy, 132, 158
Chlordiazepoxide, 11, 40
Chlorpromazine, 11, 38, 192
CIBA, 3
Circuit Court of Appeals for the District of Columbia, 217
Clonce v. Richardson, 204
CNS (Central Nervous System) 7, 12, 42, 43, 47, 51, 69, 72, 73, 85, 86, 87, 88, 89, 100, 131, 133, 135, 137, 139, 169, 180, 211
Codeine, 41
Committee on Government Operations, 88
Connecticut Juvenile Court-New Haven, 163
Conners' Teachers' Rating Scale, 93, 107, 109, 147
Continuous Performance Test, 89
Counseling Service of Addison County, Inc., 141
Covington v. Harris, 217
Cylert (see Pemoline)

Deanol, 11
Demerol, 41
Depression, 4, 40, 41, 168
Dexedrine, 12, 41, 49, 50, 63, 64, 67, 68, 69, 74, 117
Dextroamphetamine, 9, 41, 49, 50, 51, 64, 68, 69, 74, 99, 152, 166, 168, 170, 194, 195, 197–199, 239
Diasepam, 40
Dilantin (see also Hydantoin derivatives), 53, 120
Diparthria, 6

Diphenylhydantoin, 170
Dyslexia, 47, 54
Dyscalcula, 47
Dysgraphia, 47
Dysrhythmia, 6, 71, 72

Education for All Handicapped Children Act, 1975, 219, 229
Electrocardiogram (ECG), 195, 196, 197
Electroconvulsive Therapy (ECT), 41
Electroencephalogram (EEG), 6, 100, 117, 125, 133, 134, 138, 169
Emma Pendleton Bradley Home, 9, 13, 14, 131
Encephalitis, 87
Enuresis, 37, 38, 45, 162
Epilepsy, 42, 132, 148, 163, 169, 242

Finger Twitch Test, 164
Frostig Test of Developmental Perception, 9

Georgetown University, 161
Gilles de la Tourette syndrome, 45
Goodenough Draw-a-Man Test, 192
Gray Reading Test, 11
Gray-Votow-Rogers Achievement Test, 234
Group for the Advancement of Psychiatry, 100

Haldol (see Haloperidol)
Haloperidol, 3, 40, 45
Haverford State Hospital, 208
Heroin, 41
Herring-Binet Test, 10
HEW News, 64
Hydantoin derivatives, 43, 44
Hydroxyzine, 40
Hyperactivity, 2–8, 10, 12–16, 18, 20, 23–26, 36, 43, 46–49, 51–53, 60, 64, 70, 73, 76, 86, 87, 89, 90–92, 94–96, 99, 100, 102, 103, 105–107, 112, 116, 119, 125, 129–136, 138, 140, 141, 155–172, 174–177, 179, 190, 192, 211, 229, 241
Hyperexcitability, 3
Hyperflexia, 6
Hyperkinetic, 3, 7, 12, 18, 47, 64, 66, 76, 164
Hyperkinetic Impulse Syndrome (Disorder) 3, 4, 6, 11, 70, 71, 132, 160, 239–242, 246

Hypoglycemia, 56–57, 137
Hypokinesis, 39

Imipramine, 40, 45, 53, 169–171
Impulsivity, 8, 47, 86, 129, 136, 137, 155, 157, 162, 164, 166, 168
Ingraham v. Wright, 209, 223
Iowa Hospital Schools, 101
Intelligence Quotient (IQ), 10, 18, 137, 155, 157–159, 171, 178, 191, 133

J.L. v. Parkam, 209, 221
Johns Hopkins Hospital, 155
Juvenile deliquency, 8, 10, 25, 157, 161–164

Kent v. U.S., 209, 120
Knecht v. Gillman, 205, 221
Kremens v. Bartley, 209

Learning disabilities, 15, 46, 47, 49, 54, 55, 56, 57, 58, 59, 60, 112, 131, 137, 141, 219
Leiter International Performance Test, 233
Librium (see Chlordiazepoxide)
Lithium Carbonate, 41, 53
Lorge-Thornkike Intelligence Test, 233

Mackey v. Procunier, 205, 221, 223
Maratella v. Kelley, 218
Maryland Law Review, 208, 213
MBD (Minimal brain damage; minimal brain dysfunction), 3, 7, 33, 46–48, 56, 57, 60, 61, 112, 114, 118, 120, 122–125, 129–131, 133, 138, 141, 142, 147, 148, 151, 155–157, 160–162, 165–171, 177, 179, 180
Mebaral (see Barbituric acid derivatives)
Megavitamin Therapy, 55, 56, 112, 114
Mellaril (see also Thioridazine), 38, 119
Mental Health Procedures Act, 209
Mental Retardation, 8, 9, 19, 163, 240, 242
Methamphetamine, 170
Methylphenidate, 3, 9, 11, 12, 15, 25, 50, 51, 69, 74, 88, 89, 93, 95, 99, 165, 168, 170, 192, 194–199, 239
Mills v. Board of Education, 219
Milonton, 43, 44
Miltown (see also Meprobamate), 40

Minnesota Multiphasic Personality Inventory (MMPI), 176
Mongolism, 138
Montreal Children's Hospital, 158
Morales v. Turman, 218, 220, 221, 232, 233
Morphine, 41
Mysantoin (see Hydantoin derivatives)
Mysolin (see also Barbituric acid derivatives), 53

National Institute of Mental Health, 24
Nelson v. Heyne, 218, 222
Neurolepsis, 37
New York City, 101, 106
New York State Controlled Substances Act, 228

O'Connor v. Donaldson, 221
Optometric Therapy, 53, 54
Organic behavior syndrome, 3, 4, 71
Organic brain dysfunction, 4
Organic factors, 3, 6, 7, 69, 70, 71, 76, 131, 134
Orthomolecular medicine (OM), 24, 55
Oxazolidine derivatives, 43, 44–45

Paired Associative Learning Test, 9
Paradione (see Oxazolidine derivatives)
P.A.R.C. v. the State of Pennsylvania, 218, 219
Parkinson's disease, 39, 118, 212
Partlow State School & Hospital, 218
Patterning, 53, 54
Peers, 4, 8, 34, 114, 121, 136, 157, 159, 163, 179, 240
Pemoline, 51, 170, 198
Pennsylvania Mental Health & Retardation Act of 1966, 208
Phenothiazine, 38, 39, 53, 118, 169
Phenobarbital (see also Barbituric acid derivatives), 43
Porteus Maze Test, 9
Price v. Sheppard, 222
Primidone, 53
Psychogenic factors, 3, 6, 69, 70, 71, 72, 76, 134, 139
Psychostimulant drugs, 36, 37, 46, 49, 50, 51, 52, 53
Public Health Service Committee, 136–137

Queens, New York, 102

Rational Basis Test, 66
Report on the Conference on Stimulant Drugs, 87, 95, 100, 101, 106, 239–248
Reserpine, 11, 34, 39
Ritalin (see also Methylphenidate), 3, 12, 15, 16, 51, 63, 64, 67, 69, 74, 93, 115, 117, 118, 121, 122, 125, 166, 229
Roe v. Ingraham, 229
Rouse v. Cameron, 217

School phobia, 8, 40
Schizophrenia, 9, 35, 38, 55, 56, 138, 146, 167, 169, 176, 180, 242
Scott v. Plante, 223
Searcy Hospital, 218
Seizures, 9, 42, 43, 138
Sensory-Integrative Therapy, 53–55
Serpasil (see Reserpine)
Sounder v. McGuire, 205, 221, 223
South End Family Project, 134
Southern California Law Review, 65
Speech pathology, 24
Stanford-Binet Intelligence Test, 10, 13
Stelazine (see also Trifluroperazine), 38, 39
Stimulant Drugs, 12, 13, 24, 25, 51, 52, 63, 64, 65, 67, 68, 69, 71, 72, 73, 74, 82, 85, 86, 87, 89, 93, 98, 100, 107, 112, 115, 116, 118, 120, 131, 162, 164, 165, 189–191, 193, 195, 197, 211, 212, 229, 239, 243–245
Succinimide derivatives (see Celontin, Milonton, & Zarontin)

Texas Youth Council, 234
Thioridazine, 38, 45
Thorazine (see also Chlorpromazine), 11, 8, 35, 38, 119, 125
Tofranil (see Imipramine)
Tranquilizers, 12, 34, 35, 37, 39, 40, 41, 49, 52, 53, 63, 75, 90, 112, 114, 116, 120, 125, 232, 240, 243
Tremor, 6, 39, 41, 75, 145
Tridone, (see Oxazolidine derivatives)
Trifluroperazine, 38

United Cerebral Palsy of Texas, 54
United Nations Declaration of the Rights of the child, 210

United Nations General Assembly,
      207, 210
United States Constitution,
      First Amendment, 222, 223
      Third Amendment, 222, 223
      Fourth Amendment 222, 223
      Eighth Amendment, 222
      Ninth Amendment 222, 223
      Fourteenth Amendment 213, 222,
      223
United States Supreme Court, 208–210,
      228, 229
University of Vermont College of Med-
      icine, 148

Valium (see Diasepam)
Vermont, 130, 141, 160

Vistaril (see Hydroxyzine)

Whalen v. Roe, 228, 229
Whitree v. State, 221
Winters v. Miller, 205, 213
WISC (Weschsler Intelligence Scale
      for Children), 9, 10, 68, 159, 171,
      192, 233
Wisconsin, 213
Wisconsin v. Yoder, 212, 213
World Health Organization, 136
WRAT (Wide Range Achievement
      Test), 11, 68, 192
Wyatt v. Stickney, 217–219, 221, 229,
      230

Zarontin, 43, 44

AUTHOR INDEX

Aarskog D., 195
Abrams, A.L., 47
Ackerman, P.T., 87, 192
Adams, J., 11
Aichorn, A., 164
Allen, R., 12, 74, 107, 135, 165,
    190–195, 197, 198
Aman, M., 191
Amatruda, C., 132
Anderson, C.M., 135,161
Anderson, R., 191
Arnold, L.E., 168, 195
Arthur, B., 20
Ayres, A.J., 54, 55

Bach-y-Rita, G., 167
Badham, J., 9
Bailer, I., 107
Bakwin, R.M., 125
Balla, D., 163
Ballard, J., 194, 196
Barcai, A., 5, 164, 166
Bard, H., 7
Bardon, L., 9
Barnes, K., 191
Barr, E., 194
Beck, L., 165
Beecher, H., 17
Bell, A., 9
Bell, R.Q., 138
Bender, L., 2, 89
Benn, R., 190, 197
Bergersen, B., 12
Bernstein, A., 90
Beverly, B.I., 131
Beyer, H.A., 209
Bibace, R.M., 164
Bierman, J., 129
Bing, S.R., 211, 215
Birch, H.G., 133, 134, 165
Black, D., 9
Blackburn, R., 166,166
Blair, C.L., 169–171

Blair, H., 9
Blau, A., 131
Blumberg, E., 9
Boileau, R., 194, 196
Boldrey, E., 6, 8, 9, 10, 19
Bond, E.D., 131
Borland, B.L., 156
Borland, R., 190, 197
Bowen, M., 2, 14, 89
Bower, K.,7
Bowman, P., 9
Boydstun, J., 14
Bradbard, G., 195
Bradbury, W., 125
Bradley, C., 2, 9, 13, 14, 49, 88, 89,
    131, 135
Brant, J., 226, 227
Brant, R.T., 226
Bronner, A.F., 162, 164
Brooke, E., 136, 195
Brooks, E., 195
Brown, J.L., 211, 215
Burks, H.F., 132, 135
Burr, C.W., 131
Bussaratid, S., 174

Campbell, M., 129
Canter, A., 11
Cantwell, D., 25, 87, 100, 101, 172, 173,
    176
Capella, B., 170
Carlson, P.V., 54
Carney, R., 176
Carroll, H., 10
Chess, S., 3, 6, 8, 9, 11, 129, 133, 134
Childers, A.T., 133, 162
Christenson, D.E., 107
Cleckley, H., 166
Clements, S., 27, 47, 87, 132, 133–134,
    136–137
Climent, C.E., 167
Cloninger C.R., 153, 173
Cloward, R.A., 163

Cohen, A., 151, 160, 163, 178
Cohen, B., 25
Cohen, D., 91
Cohen, L., 87, 131
Cole, J., 17, 18, 19
Comly, H., 4, 5, 8
Conners, C. K., 5, 9, 10, 11, 12, 57, 89,
    92, 93, 107, 135, 142, 162, 191,
    195
Connor, A., 129
Conrad, P., 90
Conrad, W.G., 68
Cott, A., 56
Cottington, F., 2, 89
Coughlin, B.J., 206
Coyette, C.H., 57
Craig, A.G., 129–130
Cromwell, R., 9, 10, 11, 18, 19
Cruickshank, W., 4
Cutler, M., 2

Davis, J., 17, 21
Deem, M., 195
Delacato, C., 53–54
DeLong, A., 10, 13
Denhoff, E., 4, 6, 8, 87, 129, 131,
    131–132, 135, 164
Detre, T.P., 156
Dieruf, W., 129–130
Dinitz, S., 171
Dixon, J., 165
Doman, R., 53–54
Douglas, J., 9, 24, 25
Douglas, U.I., 132, 134
Douglas, V., 4, 8, 89, 158, 159, 191
Doyle, R., 191
Drillien, C.M., 178
Dubey, D., 7, 24
Durkin, H., 162
Dworkin, E.S., 68
Dykman, R., 14, 87

Ebaugh, F., 87, 131
Eccles, A., 2, 9
Effron, A., 2
Eisenberg, J., 3, 6, 8, 11
Eisenberg, L., 5, 87, 89, 133, 135, 136,
    162
Ellis, J.W., 209
Epstein, L., 90
Erickson, M.T., 176
Ervin, F.R., 167
Escoll, P., 156

Fassina, G., 195
Febang, F., 195
Feinberg, I., 197
Feingold, B.F., 57, 91
Finkelstein, J., 190, 197
Fish, B., 5, 9, 87, 89
Forer, L.G., 208
Foster, H.H.Jr., 207
Foster, T.W., 171
Fourner, M., 195
Fowler, G., 11, 12, 15
Frank, T., 162
Freed, D.J., 207
Freed, H., 17
Freedman, A., 2
Freeman, R., 9, 12, 17, 88
French, F., 129
Freud, A., 203
Friedin, M.R., 172
Frisk, M., 171
Froelich, R.E., 89
Frosch, J., 166

Garinger, G., 226
Gendron, R.M., 130, 147, 148
Gentile, J.R., 170
Gesell, A., 132
Giles, M.K., 112
Gittleman-Klein, R., 7, 23, 191, 195,
    196, 198
Glaser, G.H., 135
Goldberg, A., 7
Goldman, A., 7
Goldman, H., 171
Goldstein, J., 203, 207
Green, E., 2, 13
Green, M., 176
Greenberg, L., 90, 195
Greenhill, L., 194
Greenspan, S.I., 169
Greenspoon, N.K., 54
Grinspoon, L., 90, 94, 211, 231
Gross, M.B., 135, 165, 192, 194
Gunnarson, S., 171
Guze, S.B., 153, 173

Haig, J., 197
Halcomb, C., 191
Hallgren, B., 171
Hammar, S.L., 165
Harold, W., 9
Hartocollis, P., 166
Hayden, B., 11

Healy, W., 162, 164
Heaton-Ward, W., 17
Hechtman, L., 197
Heckel, R.V., 89
Heckman, H.K., 156, 190
Heims, L.W., 162
Henis, J., 163
Herr, S., 219
Herring, V., 10
Hertzig, M.D., 165
Hibi, S., 197
Hill, D., 161
Hinton, G., 5, 8, 9, 20, 195
Hoffer, A., 55, 56
Hohman, L.B., 131
Holden, R.H., 131–132
Hollingworth, L., 10
Horn, J.M., 176
Hortling, H., 171
Houston, J., 208, 230
Huessy, H., 25, 130, 135, 141, 147, 148,
    151, 160, 169–171, 178, 179
Hurwitz, I., 164

Ingram, T.T.S., 132
Innes, I., 195

Jeans, R.F., 168
Johnson, E., 131
Johnson, N., 156, 157
Jones, D. B., 162
Jorgensen, G.T., 206
Juliano, D.B., 170

Kahn, E., 89, 131
Kaiser, B.L., 226, 227
Kaplan, H.A., 219, 224
Karduck, W.A., 174
Kato, J., 9
Katz, S., 23, 24, 195, 196
Kaufman, I., 162
Karpman, B., 166
Keith, R., 7
Keough, B., 10
Kephart, N., 132
Kittrie, N.M., 220
Klein, D., 7, 23, 167, 191
Klove, H., 195
Knights, R., 5, 8, 9, 20, 194, 195, 198
Knobel, M., 3, 6, 8, 11, 69, 70, 135
Knoblock, H., 132, 178
Koocher, G.P., 211
Koral, J., 156

Korey, S., 161
Kraft, I., 5, 11, 18
Krager, J.M., 107, 189
Krippner, S., 24
Krug, E., 12
Krynicki, V., 197
Kupfer, D.J., 156
Kupietz, S., 107
Kurty, M., 195

Ladd, E., 90, 94–95
Lambert, N.M., 26
Laties, V., 89
Laufer, M., 4, 6, 8, 87, 129, 131,
    131–132, 135, 162, 164
Lebovici, S., 136
Lehtinen, L., 87, 132
Lennard, H., 90
Lesser, L., 3, 5
Levy, S., 131, 132
Lewis, D.O., 183
Lidz, C.W., 204, 205, 212, 213
Lilienfield, A.M., 129, 132
Lin, T.Y., 136
Lindner, L.A., 171
Lion, J.R., 167
Lipman, R., 90
Little, J., 2
Lockner, A., 162
Lubechenco, L., 7
Lucas, B., 195
Lurie, L.A., 131
Lyons, D.D., 206
Lytton, G.J., 135

MacKay, M., 155
Magoun, H.W., 87
Maletzky, B.M., 163
Malone, C.A., 134
Mandell, M., 57
Mann, H.B., 169
Marcus, I., 5
Marshall, C., 148
Martin, J., 4, 8, 134
Martin, R., 207
Marwitt, S.J., 135
Masini, A., 11
Mason, E., 131
Massey, B., 196
Meisel, A., 204, 205, 212, 213
Mellsop, B., 154
Mendelson, N., 159
Mendelson, W., 157, 171, 178

Menkes, J., 6, 8, 154, 155
Menkes, M., 6, 8, 154, 155, 177, 179
Meo, G., 195
Mercer, C., 7
Metoyer, M., 25, 160, 178
Middlekamp, J., 131
Miles, R.S., 131
Miller, R., 10
Miller, W., 163
Millichap, J., 6, 8, 9, 10, 11, 12, 15, 19, 120
Minde, K., 89, 132, 133, 158–160, 177, 179
Minkoff, K., 168
Mizeile, J.D., 162
Molling, P.A., 162
Moltich, M., 2, 9, 10
Morgenstern, G., 191
Morris, H., 156, 171
Morrison, J.R., 168, 172–177
Munro, B., 24
Murray, C.A., 164
Murray, J.N., 67
Myers, G., 6
McCloskey, K., 195
McConnell, T., 9, 10, 11, 18, 19
McCord, J., 168
McCord, W., 166
McCoy, R., 211
McGarry, A.L., 219, 224
McGinty, A., 10
McIntosh, P., 78–79
McKinney, J.K., 173
McMahon, S., 195
McNutt, B., 194

Nahas, A., 197
Needleman, H., 91
Nemeth, E., 158
Neustadt, J., 20
Nickerson, M., 195
Novotny, M., 147

Oettinger, L., 165, 178
Ohlin, L.E., 163
Olds, S., 73–74
Opton, E.M., Jr., 205
Osmond, H., 55, 56
Ounsted, C., 131

Paine, R., 6, 86
Parker, J., 165
Pasamanick, B., 129, 132, 178
Paul, J., 4

Palkes, H., 10
Pattee, C., 195
Pauling, L., 55
Pavlov, I., 87
Payson, H., 20
Pearson, G., 133
Penderson, F.A., 138
Perault, P., 147
Peters, J., 14, 87, 133–134
Philpott, W.H., 57
Pincus, J.H., 135
Pinter, E., 195
Pitts, F.N., 129–130
Pless, I., 6
Plymate, H.B., 135, 162
Polier, J.W., 207, 232
Pollack, E., 195, 196
Prechtl, H.F.R., 130
Preis, K., 163

Quay, H., 166
Quinn, P., 7, 195
Quitkin, F., 167

Rabkin, L.Y., 166
Ransom, D., 90
Rapaport, J., 7, 161, 192, 195
Redl, F., 164
Reeves, P., 9
Rexford, E.N., 133
Rice, D., 20
Richardson, S., 24
Riddle, K.D., 161, 192, 195
Rie, H.E., 69, 191
Riester, A., 168
Robins, L.M., 153
Robinson, E., 5, 89
Rodham, H., 203, 207, 208, 209, 213
Rogers, M.E., 129, 132
Ross, R., 7, 25, 92, 101, 204, 211, 216, 228
Roth, L.H., 204, 205, 212, 213
Rothschild, G., 5
Rothschild, M., 89, 92
Rowbotham, B.M., 164
Rowe, J., 6, 8, 154, 155
Rumage, N., 5
Rutter, M., 136, 174
Ryter, Z., 162

Sadoun, R., 136
Safer, D., 12, 74, 107, 135, 165, 174, 189–195, 197, 198
Sandaval, J., 26

Santi, R., 195
Saraf, K., 23, 195, 196
Satterfield, B.T., 87, 100, 101
Satterfield, I., 25
Satterfield, J.M., 87, 88, 89, 100, 101
Schroeder, C., 197
Schroeder, S., 197
Schulhofer, E., 5
Schwartz, L., 5, 89
Seels, C., 195
Shaffer, D., 133
Shah, S.A., 229
Shai, A., 68
Shanock, S., 163
Shapiro, M.H., 205, 213, 215
Sharpe, L., 89, 135
Shelly, E.M., 168
Sherman, M., 131
Shoben, E.J., Jr., 229
Silbergeld, E., 7
Silver, L., 47, 53, 54, 174
Simonian, K., 129
Simpson, D., 23
Singer, S., 90, 94, 211, 231
Sinton, D., 14
Sleator, E., 93–94, 101, 107, 191, 196, 198
Sly, W.S., 174
Small, A., 197
Smith, L.H., 131
Smith, R.S., 129
Smythies, J., 55
Sneznevskij, A.V., 134
Snell, L., 163
Snyder, S., 195
Solnit, A.J., 203
Solomons, G., 92, 93, 95, 101, 111, 116, 122–123, 163
Southwick, D.A., 57
Spece, R.J., 205
Sprague, R., 12, 25, 88, 93, 94, 101, 107, 191, 196
Stemmer, C.J., 130
Stenner, A.J., 135
Stevens, D., 14
Stewart, M.A., 10, 67, 73–74, 129–130, 132, 133, 134, 135, 157, 162, 172, 173, 174, 175, 176, 177, 211
Still, G.F., 131
Stoa, K., 195
Stone, E., 162
Straumanis, J., 11
Strauss, A., 2, 46, 87, 132
Strobl, D., 168

Sullivan, J., 2, 10
Swander, D., 5
Sykes, D., 89, 132, 191

Tauber, D., 208, 230
Taylor, E., 195
Taylor, R., 165
Tenhunem, T., 171
Thach, B.T., 172
Thomas, A., 133
Thorsen, T., 195
Thuma, B., 132
Thurston, D., 131
Tobiesson, J.E., 68
Townsend, M., 25, 160, 178

Uhlenhuth, E., 20

Van Amerongen, S.T., 133
Viets, C., 194, 198
Von Hilsheimer, G., 57
Von Neumann, A., 191

Wagenheim, L., 131
Waldrop, M.F., 138
Walker, G., 9, 24
Walker, S., 230
Warren, R.J., 174
Webb, G., 132
Wegelius, E., 171
Weisenberg, A., 168
Weiss, B., 89
Weiss, G., 4, 8, 89, 132, 134, 158, 159, 165, 190, 192–198
Weithorn, C., 7, 25, 92, 101, 211, 216, 228
Wells, W.W., 211
Wender, P.H., 133, 135, 195
Werner, A., 190, 197
Werner, E., 129, 133
Werner, H., 46, 132
Werry, J., 3, 4, 6, 8, 10, 11, 12, 25, 88, 101, 107, 130, 132, 134, 135, 158, 191
Westman, J., 20
Wetter, J., 10
Wexler, R., 156
Widholm, O., 171
Wikler, A., 165
Wilkins, L.P., 207–209, 212–214, 223
Wilson, J.P., 209
Wilson, W., 5, 135, 165, 192
Windmiller, M., 26

Wineman, D.T., 163
Winsberg, B.G., 107
Woerner, P.I., 173
Wolff, P.H., 163, 164
Wolfgram, E.D., 173
Worland, J., 24
Wortis, S.B., 166

Young, A., 9

Zachman, R., 162
Zaro, M., 24
Zilback, J., 162
Zrull, J., 11, 20
Zubek, J., 9